28-55

NEWCASTLE COLLEGE LIBRARY

00151165

SANDYFORD ROAD
LIBRARY

Newca

To be re

− 3 MAR 2014

NEWCASTLE
COLLEGE
LIBRARY

ERENCE BOOK
ONLY

D1348589

THE BOOK OF
GREAT
Soups
SANDWICHES
AND
Breads

# THE BOOK OF GREAT
# GREAT
# Soups
# Sandwiches
# and
# Breads

## Terence Janericco

A CBI Book
Published by Van Nostrand Reinhold Company

A CBI Book
(CBI is an imprint of Van Nostrand Reinhold
Company Inc.)

Copyright © 1984 by Terence Janericco

Library of Congress Catalog Card Number 83-23418
ISBN 0-442-24387-1

All rights reserved. No part of this work covered
by the copyright hereon may be reproduced or
used in any form or by any means—graphic,
electronic, or mechanical, including photocopy-
ing, recording, taping, or information storage
and retrieval systems—without written permis-
sion of the publisher.

Printed in the United States of America

Published by Van Nostrand Reinhold Company Inc.
135 West 50th Street
New York, New York 10020

Van Nostrand Reinhold Company Limited
Molly Millars Lane
Wokingham, Berkshire RG11 2PY, England

Van Nostrand Reinhold
480 La Trobe Street
Melbourne, Victoria 3000, Australia

Macmillan of Canada
Division of Gage Publishing Limited
164 Commander Boulevard
Agincourt, Ontario M1S 3C7, Canada

16  15  14  13  12  11  10  9  8  7  6  5  4  3  2  1

**Library of Congress Cataloging in Publication Data**

Janericco, Terence.
  The book of great soups, sandwiches, and breads.

  "A CBI book."
  Includes index.
  1. Soups. 2. Sandwiches. 3. Bread. I. Title.
TX757.J36 1984   641.8   83-23418
ISBN 0-442-24387-1

NEWCASTLE UPON TYNE
COLLEGE OF ARTS AND TECHNOLOGY
LIBRARY

| Class | Acc. |
|---|---|
| 641.813<br>+<br>641.84 | 00151165<br>85/1435 |

To
Joseph Matzkin
Friend, Student, and Lawyer
Without his help, I would never have
been able to write not only this book,
but also those that preceded it.

# Contents

# 4
# Basic Recipes and Procedures

# Preface

A number of years ago, I had the good fortune to work for a restaurant that specialized in soups and sandwiches. Duck Soup, in Cambridge, Massachusetts, had been started by a good friend, Alice MacSorley, as a single-chef operation. After a while, she realized that even the most ardent cook needs some free time. We agreed that I would work one day a week as long as I could select my own menus. I had just begun to teach cooking, and students were not breaking down my door. The prospect of a steady income, no matter how small, and the freedom to cook a varied menu were too tempting to turn down.

I worked at Duck Soup for two and a half years, and during that time I did not repeat a soup recipe. I made soups from every continent, if not every country in the world. I prepared expensive soups, inexpensive soups, hot soups, cold soups, sophisticated soups, and peasant soups. I made soups of cheese, vegetables, fish, meat, and fruits. During this period, my classes became more successful and if I found a soup I could not prepare at the restaurant, I would make it in a class. Bouillabaisse, for example, is an expensive soup, very expensive when all of the fish are included. The top price at Duck Soup was too low to break even, much less make a profit, but I could afford to prepare it in my classes.

Naturally, not all the soups were raving successes. A Japanese soup, the name of which I have forgotten, consisted of a few beautifully cut vegetables floating in a delicate, subtle broth. It was a perfect beginning for a full meal, but as a meal in itself for a clientele of voracious college students, it definitely lacked substance.

Although I have always loved sandwiches, I have never been in a position to prepare a great variety of them professionally. The offerings at Duck Soup were limited and we found that the customers preferred it that way. However, in researching a book on sandwiches for professional chefs, I discovered many wonderful sandwich ideas. And my own appetite has given me cause to experiment and create over the years.

Breads comprise the final portion of this book, but last is certainly not the least herein. Soup and bread are almost inseparable, and a sandwich without bread is impossible. It is regrettable that so many areas do not have decent breads available. Either local bakeries do not exist, or they quickly develop the techniques of large commercial bakers. All too often, the bread is soft, pulpy, and tasteless. In recent years, however, an increased interest in health, nutrition, and fine eating has given rise to bakeries that are making serious efforts to produce quality breads. Unfortunately, these breads are often priced so that many people cannot afford them on a regular basis.

Good bread is easy and inexpensive to make. It freezes beautifully and for the most part, you need not do much to it. Generally, most of the time is required to let the bread rise. Once you learn how easy it is to prepare bread yourself and experience its superior quality, you will be hard put to return to commercial breads.

# 1
# Soups

Soup is probably one of the earliest foods. Certainly it closely followed the invention of the pot. Every country has soup in its culinary repertoire. Soups can range from ultrasophisticated double consommés to a few vegetables simmered in water.

Soups are a cook's best friend when guests arrive unexpectedly. You can quickly prepare a soup with only a few ingredients. Few soups are as quick and heartwarming as onion soup in one of its many preparations. Most homes have potatoes, onions, and milk to prepare a hot potato soup or cold Vichyssoise. Puréeing a selection of vegetables can produce a hot, filling winter soup, or a cold, refreshing summer soup.

If your budget is tight, you can make wonderfully delicious, filling meals readily; if you can afford it, you can prepare one of the more expensive soups. This chapter contains a recipe for fish soup that literally costs pennies a serving and another enlarged version that costs dollars per serving. Most of the soups fall somewhere between these extremes.

## EQUIPMENT

No special equipment is required to make soup. Most kitchens already have what is needed.

### Knives

For any kitchen work, good knives are a must. It always amazes me when people who have beautifully appointed homes stint on buying and maintaining good knives. Good knives are no longer inexpensive. A full set can be a major investment. But when the investment is weighed against the cost of possible injuries, poorly prepared food, and the extra effort required to prepare food, all because knives are dull or poorly designed, the cost becomes reasonable. A good knife makes cutting, chopping, and slicing easy and comfortable. If you are not capable of sharpening your knives, have them sharpened periodically. Learn how to maintain an edge on your knives. I prefer knives made of an alloy of stainless steel with a high amount of carbon steel. They are sturdy enough to hold an edge for a reasonable time and can be honed to keenness with a steel. I hone the edges regularly as I use them, and once a year I have them sharpened professionally.

## Kettles

Ideally, you should have a large stockpot for making stocks and several smaller pots for making different quantities of soup. A stockpot should hold at least twelve quarts, but it can be much larger if you wish to make a large quantity. Have on hand pots that hold two, six, eight, and ten quarts for making different amounts of soup.

The best pots are made of tin- or steel-lined copper. Unfortunately, they are extremely expensive. Stainless steel pots are suitable if they have well-weighted bottoms, but if the bottom is thin, they tend to burn heavy soups. Large aluminum pots are used commercially, but if an acid such as wine or tomato is cooked in them for any length of time, the stock tastes metallic. Calphalon is a coated aluminum that is expensive but still more reasonable than copper. It provides superb heat conduction and a surface that is impervious to acidic substances. Enamel-coated steel pots can be very reasonably priced and quite suitable for soups. However, care must be taken that the enamel does not chip and get into the food.

Stockpots are usually taller than they are wide. The bottom of the pot should fit the burner evenly: on a gas stove, the flame should spread to the outer edges of the pot; on an electric stove, the coils should reach the outer edges of the pot.

Flameproof casseroles can be used for making soups if another container is not suitable. If you are making a heavy soup, the casserole should be round rather than oval to provide even heat on the bottom.

## Food Mill, Processor, or Blender

All of these utensils are helpful in making soups and generally can be used interchangeably. However, food mills strain as well as purée the ingredients; hard, fibrous materials are thus easily discarded. Both the blender and the processor chop these materials into small pieces, and they remain in the soup unless you strain it.

I recommend a 2-quart food mill with interchangeable blades as the most useful size. Food mills with permanent blades cannot produce different textures.

## Sieves and Cheesecloth

Depending on the desired result, it may be necessary to strain the soup more finely than a food mill can. The velvety smooth finish of certain soups is achieved by forcing the soup through a very fine sieve (called a Chinoise or china cap) to make sure that any hard parts of the food are removed and only the essence of flavor and body remain.

Stocks and consommés often have a final straining through several thicknesses of very fine cheesecloth to remove tiny particles. The cheesecloth should be of the finest weave. Paint stores often have the best quality (painters use it to strain paint). Rinse the cheesecloth in hot water before using it to remove any store dust as well as the sizing. Those lucky enough to have old linen sheets will find them excellent for straining stock. Paper coffee filters used to line a sieve will filter out the impurities in a consommé perfectly.

## STORING AND FREEZING

Most soups can be made at least several days ahead without any loss of quality. In fact, the added time often allows the flavors to meld. Certain cream soups can be made ahead to the point at which the liaison of egg yolks and cream is to be added, and then stored for a day or two. Most soups freeze well. However, soups with cheese or cream are best if made and served, or refrigerated for a day or so, but not frozen. If you wish to freeze a soup that requires cream, wait until it has been defrosted before adding the cream.

When freezing soups, consider how much you will want at one time. Trying to chip two servings of consommé from a gallon block is not only frustrating, but likely to affect the flavor. I have found that the water of the soup seems to settle around the edges and the flavor concentrates in the center of the frozen block. Unless you know that you will need larger quantities, freeze the soup in 1-pint to 1-quart containers. In addition to being convenient to use, they freeze and thaw more quickly.

# STOCKS

The basis of a superb soup is a quality stock. I have never tasted a canned stock or broth, bouillon cube or powder, that compares with a carefully made stock. They are either too salty, or they taste rather stale and lack flavor. Fortunately, it does not take long to prepare stock, and while it is cooking you can be doing other things. Fish stock is ready in twenty to thirty minutes; chicken stock can be prepared in less than an hour. Beef and veal stock do take longer, but most of the time is required for simmering, without any effort on your part. I usually make large quantities of meat stock once or twice a year, and store it in the freezer. I make chicken stock monthly because I use it more often. What I cannot use in a few days I freeze until needed. I usually make fish stock as needed.

The virtues of homemade stock do not necessarily rule out the use of canned stocks, bouillon cubes, or powders. For a clear soup such as a consommé, you must make the stock yourself; if you are making a hearty soup with a number of ingredients, a prepared stock can be used. The other ingredients will improve its flavor. Be very careful about adding any additional salt.

The ingredients for stock are essentially free. The careful cook saves bones, carrot ends, celery leaves, onion bases, parsley stems, and the like. When enough ingredients are collected, make a stock. If you do not have room to store your collected ingredients, there is no need to be discouraged. When it comes time to make stock, the ingredients are still available at little cost. The bones for meat stock are often available from butchers at no charge, and in supermarkets they are sold for a small amount. Bones with meat attached, such as shin bones, will cost more. Fish bones generally are free at the fishmonger, although some shops charge a few cents to clean the gills and cut up the carcasses. Chicken bones can be saved and kept in the freezer until you accumulate enough. Stores that sell chicken parts often sell carcasses for a small amount. Supermarkets have backs and necks for pennies per pound. Vegetables suitable for stock can be purchased for less than premium (many markets have an area where they sell vegetables no longer at their prime that are suitable for soup making). There is, however, a difference between a slightly tired carrot and one that is over the hill.

## Cooking Stock

It is necessary to simmer a stock very slowly. If you boil it rapidly, it will be murky and unattractive. Slow, gentle simmering extracts the flavors from the ingredients, leaving a clear, well-flavored stock.

Always start the stock with cold water and bring it to a simmer very slowly. The cold water draws out the flavors from the ingredients; hot liquid seals the flavors inside the ingredients.

If possible, ladle the stock from the bones and other ingredients so that the small particles stay in the pot. If you must pour off the liquid, strain it through several thicknesses of cheesecloth.

## Clarifying Stock

It is necessary to clarify stock to remove the impurities. No amount of straining removes them completely.

With 3 quarts of cold stock, combine 2 egg whites and 2 egg shells. Bring the mixture to a boil slowly, stirring often. When it just reaches the boil and foams up, lower the heat and simmer about 10 minutes. Carefully remove the crust of scum on the surface and ladle the stock through several thicknesses of cheesecloth that has been wrung out in warm water. Do not press on the ingredients in the cheesecloth. The stock should be crystal clear. If there are any globules of fat on the surface, brush a sheet of paper toweling over the surface.

Another way to strain stock is to ladle it through a sieve lined with a coffee filter, after cooking it with the egg white mixture.

Stock has to be clarified only if it is going to be used for consommé or aspic. Most soups can be made with stock that is slightly unclear.

## Beef Stock

4 pounds beef bones, cut into 1- to 2-inch sections
2 pounds veal bones, cut into 1- to 2-inch sections
1 large carrot, chopped
1 large onion, chopped
beef or veal trimmings
raw or cooked chicken carcass
5 quarts cold water

1 tablespoon salt, if desired
6 peppercorns
3 celery stalks, chopped
5 parsley sprigs
2 tomatoes, chopped
2 leeks, chopped
1 onion, chopped
1 carrot, chopped
1 garlic clove, chopped
1 cup cold water

Preheat oven to 475°F.

Spread the bones in a roasting pan. Scatter the large carrot and onion on top and roast for 45 minutes to 1 hour, or until ingredients are well browned, but not burned, turning occasionally.

Transfer the bones and vegetables to a 12-quart kettle. Discard the fat in the roasting pan. Add 2 cups water to the pan and put over direct heat. Cook, stirring up the browned bits, until the pan is deglazed. Pour over the bones along with any meat trimmings or carcasses. Add 5 quarts of cold water, salt, and peppercorns. Bring slowly to a boil and simmer 5 minutes. Skim any scum from the surface. Add the celery, parsley, tomatoes, leeks, onion, carrot, and garlic.

Simmer for about 30 minutes, continuing to remove any scum that appears on the surface. Simmer very slowly for 4 to 5 hours, without stirring. At the end of the cooking time, gently ladle out as much stock as you can. Add 1 cup cold water to settle the small particles and ladle out as much additional stock as possible. Discard the dregs in the kettle.

Strain the stock through very fine cheesecloth or a paper coffee filter in a sieve. Chill thoroughly, uncovered. When cold, remove the fat from the surface and discard.

*Yield: about 3 quarts*

*Note:* If veal bones or chicken carcasses are not available, substitute more beef bones, especially shin bones. If beef and veal trimmings are not readily available, use about 1 pound of beef and/or veal stew meat.

## Chicken Stock

3 pounds chicken wings,
  backs, necks, or carcasses
1 veal knuckle, optional
5 quarts cold water
2 small carrots, sliced
2 onions, sliced
2 leeks, sliced
1 celery stalk, chopped

1 clove, stuck in a small
  onion
faggot of bay leaf, parsley,
  celery, 2 sprigs tarragon
  (see Index)
1 tablespoon salt
12 white peppercorns

In a large kettle, combine the chicken pieces, veal knuckle, and water. Bring slowly to a boil and simmer gently, removing any scum that appears. When the scum has stopped rising, add the carrots, onions, leeks, celery, clove-studded onion, faggot, salt, and peppercorns. Simmer gently for 2 hours.

Strain off the stock, discarding the solid ingredients.

Chill completely and remove the fat.

*Yield: 3 to 4 quarts*

*Note:* A simpler stock can be made by simmering 1 pound chicken parts, 1 chopped carrot, 1 chopped onion, 1 chopped celery stalk, 1 bay leaf, and a pinch of thyme for about 45 minutes.

## Fish Stock

3 pounds white fish bones
  and heads
2 celery stalks, chopped
2 cups chopped onions
2 garlic cloves, crushed
3 sprigs parsley

1/2 teaspoon dried thyme
2 bay leaves
12 peppercorns
2 cups dry white wine
3 quarts cold water

In a stockpot, combine the bones and heads, celery, onion, garlic, parsley, thyme, bay leaves, peppercorns, wine, and cold water. Bring slowly to a boil and simmer, uncovered, for 20 minutes, removing any scum that comes to the surface.

Strain through a cheesecloth or a paper coffee filter in a sieve. Can be stored for 3 or 4 days in the refrigerator or frozen. There is no fat to remove.

*Yield: about 3 quarts*

## Vegetable Stock

2 tablespoons olive oil
1 onion, minced
3 parsnips, chopped
3 carrots, chopped
3 turnips, quartered
2 celery stalks, chopped

salt and pepper
2 parsley sprigs
1/4 teaspoon thyme
1 bay leaf
pinch of cayenne
3 quarts water

In a 6-to-8-quart kettle, heat the oil. Stir in the onion and cook until soft, but not brown.

Add the parsnips, carrots, turnips, celery, salt and pepper to taste, parsley, thyme, bay leaf, cayenne, and water. Cover and simmer 1 hour. Strain.

*Yield: about 3 quarts*

*Note:* This recipe calls for the white purple top turnip, not the yellow turnip, also called a rutabaga or Swede.

Vegetable stock may be substituted for beef, chicken, or fish stock in many of the following recipes.

## CONSOMMÉ

Consommé is a double-strength stock that is served piping hot, usually in bouillon cups. If served in open soup plates, it tends to cool too quickly. Consommé should be almost boiling when put into the soup cups or tureen.

Consommés are titled by the garnish served with them. Looking through older cookbooks, such as those of Escoffier or Ranhoffer, you will find dozens of recipes for consommé that, for the most part, indicate what has been floated in them. Occasionally, consommés are lightly thickened with tapioca to give them more body.

The garnishes in this section call for a particular consommé. However, the garnishes can often be used with another consommé. Exceptions do exist and a careful review will indicate them. For example, Consommé Aurore calls for a julienne of chicken, which would be suitable with a beef consommé but probably not with fish. However, strips of fish could be substituted. Make your own decisions and mix the garnishes to suit your needs and the available ingredients.

No matter what garnish you use, from a few slivers of vegetables to small veal quenelles, the broth is the important ingredient. It must be full-flavored and absolutely fat-free.

## Consommé

3 quarts chilled beef stock, strained
1-1/2 pounds lean beef, chopped
1 carrot, chopped
2 leeks, chopped
2 celery stalks, chopped
3 chicken backs, skinned
2 egg whites and their shells

Remove any fat from the stock and discard.

In a large kettle, combine the chilled stock, beef, carrot, leeks, celery, chicken backs, egg whites, and their crumbled shells. Over medium heat, bring the mixture to a boil, stirring often. When it boils, stop stirring immediately. Cover and simmer over very low heat for 1 hour. Remove from heat and let stand for 10 minutes.

Carefully skim off any scum on the surface and discard. Strain the consommé through several thicknesses of cheesecloth or a paper coffee filter in a sieve. The consommé must be crystal clear. Occasionally, it may be necessary to repeat the process using just the egg whites. If there are any fat globules, brush a paper towel over the surface to remove them.

Can be refrigerated for 4 days or frozen for up to 1 year.

*Yield: about 3 quarts*

## Consommé Balzac

1-1/2 quarts beef consommé
1/2 cup diced raw shrimp
1/2 cup turnip balls, cooked
1/2 cup fresh peas, cooked

In a kettle, bring the consommé to a boil. Add the shrimp, turnip balls, and peas. Turn off the heat and let the consommé cook the shrimp. Serve immediately.

*Yield: 6 servings*

## Consommé Brancas

2 tablespoons shredded
  lettuce
2 tablespoons shredded
  sorrel
1 teaspoon butter
1 cup stock

2 tablespoons vermicelli
2 tablespoons julienned
  mushrooms
1 teaspoon butter
1-1/2 quarts consommé
1 tablespoon minced chervil

In a small skillet, sauté the lettuce and sorrel in 1 teaspoon butter until softened. Drain and set aside.

Heat the stock to boiling and simmer the vermicelli until al dente. Drain and set aside.

Sauté the mushrooms in the remaining butter until tender. Drain and set aside.

When ready to serve, heat the consommé to boiling and add the garnishes. Finish with a sprinkling of chervil.

*Yield: 6 servings*

*Note:* Use the butter sparingly to avoid creating a film of oil on top of the finished soup.

## Consommé Froid au Canteloupe (Cold Consommé with Melon)

1-1/2 quarts beef consommé
2 tablespoons lemon juice
salt and pepper
2 carrots, julienne

2 celery stalks, julienne
2 cups cantaloupe balls
6 mint sprigs

Combine the consommé with the lemon juice and correct the seasoning with salt and pepper.

Blanch the carrots and celery in boiling, salted water to cover until tender crisp. Drain. Divide the vegetables among 6 consommé cups and top with cantaloupe balls. Pour the consommé into each cup and chill until set, about 4 hours.

Serve cold, garnished with the mint sprigs.

*Yield: 6 servings*

## Consommé Brunoise

1/2 cup 1/4-inch diced
  carrots
1/2 cup 1/4-inch diced turnip
1/2 cup 1/4-inch diced leeks

1/2 cup 1/4-inch diced celery
1 tablespoon butter
1-1/2 quarts beef consommé

In a medium-size skillet, sweat the carrots, turnip, leeks, and celery in the butter until soft, but not brown.

When ready to serve, bring the consommé to a boil and add the vegetables.

*Yield: 6 servings*

## Consommé Carmen or Consommé à la Basquaise

1 tomato, peeled, seeded,
  and 1/4-inch diced
1 red pepper, cut in fine
  julienne

1 tablespoon cooked rice
1-1/2 quarts hot beef
  consommé

To serve, combine the tomato, pepper, rice, and consommé.

*Yield: 6 servings*

*Note:* For à la Basquaise, substitute chicken consommé.

## Consommé aux Cheveux d'Ange

1-1/2 quarts beef consommé

3 ounces capellini pasta

Bring consommé to a boil. Break pasta into 2-inch lengths and cook in consommé until just al dente.

*Yield: 6 servings*

## Consommé Olga

1/2 cup julienned celery root
1/2 cup julienned leeks
1/2 cup julienned carrots
2 teaspoons butter

1/4 cup julienned cornichons
1-1/2 quarts beef consommé
2 tablespoons port,
  approximately

In a saucepan, combine the celery root, leeks, and carrots with the butter. Stew over low heat until just tender.

Add to the consommé with the cornichons and bring to a boil. Add just enough port to give a hint of flavor.

*Yield: 6 servings*

*Note:* The vegetables must be in the thinnest possible strips. Cornichons are sour pickles, available in gourmet shops.

## Consommé San Quentin

| | |
|---|---|
| 2 hard-cooked eggs, sieved | 1 raw egg yolk |
| salt and pepper | 1/2 cup seasoned flour |
| pinch of nutmeg | butter |
| 1/2 teaspoon melted butter | 1-1/2 quarts beef consommé |

In a small bowl, combine the hard-cooked egg, salt and pepper to taste, and nutmeg. Stir in the melted butter and enough egg yolk to make a mixture you can shape. Roll into 1/2-inch balls.

Roll the balls in the flour and sauté in butter until lightly browned, shaking the pan constantly. Drain on paper toweling.

Bring the consommé to a boil and add the egg balls.

*Yield: 6 servings*

*Note:* Seasoned flour is flour mixed with salt and pepper, *not* with an infinite variety of herbs and spices.

## Consommé de Volaille (Chicken Consommé)

| | |
|---|---|
| 3 quarts cold chicken stock | 2 leeks, chopped |
| 1-1/2 pounds chicken backs, skinned | 2 celery stalks, chopped |
| 1 carrot, chopped | 2 egg whites and their shells |

Remove any fat from the chicken stock. Put into a kettle with the chicken backs, carrot, leeks, celery, egg whites, and the crumbled shells. Cook over medium heat, stirring often, until the mixture just reaches a boil. Stop stirring, cover halfway, and simmer for 1 hour. Remove from heat and let stand 10 minutes.

Skim off any matter floating on the surface and discard. Line a strainer with several thicknesses of fine cheesecloth or a paper coffee filter. Strain the consommé, discarding the solids.

Can be refrigerated for 4 days or frozen for up to 1 year.
*Yield: about 3 quarts*

## Consommé Aurore

1/2 cup tomato purée
1/2 cup fine julienne of
    chicken

1-1/2 quarts chicken
    consommé

In a kettle, combine the tomato purée and chicken with the consommé. Heat until very hot. The chicken should be just cooked.
*Yield: 6 servings*

## Consommé Diablotins

6 1/4-inch-thick slices French
    bread
2 teaspoons butter
1/2 cup grated Gruyère
    cheese

1-1/2 quarts chicken
    consommé

Preheat the broiler.

Spread the bread with butter and sprinkle with cheese. Arrange on a baking sheet and broil until golden.

When ready to serve, heat the consommé and float the diablotins on the surface.
*Yield: 6 servings*
*Note:* The diablotins can be made several weeks ahead and frozen.

## Consommé Eugenie

1-1/2 quarts chicken
  consommé
1/3 cup thinly sliced carrots
1/3 cup thinly sliced celery
1/3 cup thinly sliced
  mushrooms

1 tomato, peeled, seeded,
  and chopped
1-1/2 teaspoons minced
  parsley
1-1/2 teaspoons minced
  chervil

In a saucepan, simmer the consommé, carrots, and celery for 10 minutes or until the vegetables are tender crisp. Add the mushrooms and tomatoes and simmer 1 minute. Add the parsley and chervil and serve.

*Yield: 6 servings*


## Consommé Mimosa

1 hard-cooked egg
2 tablespoons minced
  parsley

1-1/2 quarts chicken
  consommé

Separate the yolk and white of the egg and sieve them separately. In a small bowl, mix the white, yolk, and parsley.

Heat the consommé and serve sprinkled with the mimosa garnish.

*Yield: 6 servings*

*Note:* It is necessary to sieve the white and yolk separately to obtain two distinct colors. If the whole egg is sieved, the color will be pale yellow, instead of white and bright yellow.


## Consommé Printanier

1-1/2 quarts chicken
  consommé
1/4 cup julienne carrot
1/4 cup julienne turnip
1-1/2 tablespoons diced green
  beans

1-1/2 tablespoons tiny peas
1-1/2 tablespoons asparagus
  tips
1 cup shredded sorrel leaves
1 cup shredded Boston
  lettuce leaves

Bring the consommé to a boil and simmer the carrot and turnip for 2 minutes. Add the beans and peas and simmer 1 minute. Add the asparagus, sorrel, and lettuce and simmer 2 minutes. Serve immediately.

*Yield: 6 servings*

## Consommé Profiteroles

| | |
|---|---|
| 36 cream puffs, 1/2-inch diameter (see following recipe) | 1-1/2 quarts hot chicken consommé |

Float the puffs in the consommé and serve.

*Yield: 6 servings*

*Note:* The cream puffs should be unsweetened and, for this recipe, unfilled. For other recipes, fill them with chicken or cheese fillings.

### Profiteroles for Soup

| | |
|---|---|
| 1/2 cup water | 1/2 cup flour |
| 1/4 cup butter | 2 eggs |
| pinch of salt | |

Preheat oven to 400°F.

In a small saucepan, combine the water, butter, and salt. Bring to a full rolling boil and add the flour, all at once. Stir briskly until the mixture forms a ball and begins to film the bottom of the pan. Remove from the heat and let cool for 5 minutes.

Beat in the eggs, one at a time, until fully incorporated. With two teaspoons, or a pastry bag fitted with a 1/4-inch plain tip, pipe 1/4-inch balls on a lightly buttered baking sheet. Bake for 20 minutes, or until puffed and golden. The puffs should be dry and crisp. If necessary, bake them a few minutes longer.

Can be frozen for 4 to 6 months.

*Yield: about 50 tiny puffs*

## Consommé Rejane

1-1/2 quarts chicken
    consommé
1/2 cup julienne of leeks

1/4 cup julienne of potato
1 cup julienne of raw
    chicken

In a kettle, combine the consommé, leeks, and potato and simmer 2 minutes. Add the chicken and return to simmer. The ingredients should be just cooked. If necessary, simmer 1 or 2 minutes longer.
*Yield: 6 servings*

## Clam and Chicken Consommé

1-1/2 quarts chicken
    consommé
1 apple, quartered
salt and pepper
1-1/2 cups clam broth

pinch of cinnamon
6 to 12 tablespoons
    unsweetened whipped
    cream
freshly grated nutmeg

In a 3-quart kettle, simmer the consommé, apples, and salt and pepper to taste for 30 minutes. Strain through a sieve.

Combine the consommé and clam broth. Season with cinnamon and reheat.

Serve hot, garnished with dollops of cream sprinkled with nutmeg.
*Yield: 6 servings*

## Consommé au Primeurs

6 cups chicken consommé
1/2 cup julienne of carrots
1/2 cup green peas
1/2 cup shredded spinach
    leaves
1/4 cup thinly sliced
    scallions

2 tablespoons minced
    parsley
salt and pepper
pinch of summer savory

In a kettle, heat the consommé to boiling. Add the carrots and peas and simmer 5 minutes.

Add the spinach, scallions, and parsley and simmer 2 minutes. Correct the seasoning with salt, pepper, and savory.

*Yield: 6 servings*

# CREAM SOUPS

Velvety smooth cream soups are the perfect beginning for an elegant dinner party; they are also suitable for a light luncheon, accompanied by a bread or salad. Although they may seem time-consuming to prepare, they can be made several days ahead and can also be frozen successfully. The base for *veloutés* can be prepared in quantity and frozen for several months.

Although most of these recipes do not call for it, many cream soups can be enhanced by the judicious addition of a fine-quality fortified wine, such as sherry, port, or Madeira. Care must be taken, however, not to add too much. Add the wine a tablespoon at a time until you just sense the flavor at the back of the throat. If you can actually taste the wine, you have added too much. Select only a wine that you would drink by itself.

There are three major bases for cream soups: bisques (including purées), veloutés, and creams.

## Bisques

Bisques are made by cooking minced vegetables with shellfish (and their shells) and rice to thicken, until the vegetables are tender. The bisque is then strained and enriched with cream. Occasionally the bisque is thickened with fish velouté or sautéed bread crumbs, rather than rice. The shells alone of many shellfish have enough flavor to make a bisque. Therefore, it is possible to prepare an elegant soup using normally discarded lobster and shrimp shells.

Purées are similar to bisques, but the soup is usually made with a vegetable base and the puréed vegetable becomes the thickening agent, rather than rice.

## Veloutés

These soups have a cream sauce base, flavored with chicken or fish stock, that is combined with a vegetable purée. It is possible to make almost any flavor of vegetable cream soup using this method. The soups are finished with a liaison of egg yolk and cream to bind and enrich the soup.

## Creams

These soups are made with a full-flavored stock, which is thickened and enriched with egg yolk and cream or by reducing the stock and cream to a delicate coating consistency. They taste deceptively light on the palate but beware of the calories.

## Temperature

Bisques, veloutés, and cream soups should be served hot but not boiling. If the soups have been enriched and bound with egg yolk, a temperature above 180°F will cause them to curdle. Moreover, because their consistency is heavier than consommé, they can easily burn the mouth. Ideally, these soups should be between 140° and 150° when served.

## Garnishes

No matter which cream soup you prepare, you should garnish it with some of the principal ingredient—slices of lobster meat for Bisque d'Homard (lobster bisque), perfectly cooked asparagus tips for Velouté Argenteuil (cream of asparagus soup), or poached mussels for Billi Bi (cream of mussel soup).

The choice of a cream soup base will depend on your mood and on the other ingredients in the meal. You might want the full quality of a velouté for one menu and the apparent lightness of a cream for another. After you have tried some of the following soups, it will be simple to choose the cream soup that suits a particular occasion.

## Bisque d'Homard (Lobster Bisque)

3 lobster carcasses
2 tablespoons olive oil
2 tablespoons butter
1 cup chopped onion
1/4 cup thinly sliced shallots
3/4 cup chopped carrot
1 cup chopped celery
1 bay leaf
1 teaspoon minced garlic
1/2 teaspoon dried thyme
12 peppercorns
1 dried hot red pepper
1/3 cup flour
6 tablespoons cognac
2 cups dry white wine
3 cups chopped ripe
    tomatoes (see note)
4 cups water
4 parsley sprigs
1/2 cup rice
1-1/2 cups heavy cream
1 to 2 cooked lobster tails,
    sliced
salt and pepper

Chop the lobster carcasses into 1- to 2-inch pieces and set aside.

In a 6-quart kettle, heat the oil and butter. Add the onion, shallots, carrot, celery, bay leaf, garlic, thyme, and peppercorns and cook, stirring, until the vegetables are wilted.

Add the lobster carcasses and red pepper. Sprinkle with flour and stir to coat pieces evenly. Add 4 tablespoons cognac, wine, tomatoes, water, and parsley and bring to a boil. Add the rice, cover, and simmer 20 minutes.

Force the mixture through the finest blade of a food mill (not a processor). Press on ingredients to extract as much liquid as possible. Discard the solids.

If the mixture seems coarse, force it through a fine sieve. If you do not have a fine sieve, you can purée it in batches in a processor or force it through several thicknesses of cheesecloth (a paper coffee filter will not work).

In a clean pot, reheat the bisque. Add the cream and correct the seasoning with salt and pepper. Bring almost to a boil and add the remaining cognac. Serve garnished with slices of lobster meat.

*Yield: 8 to 10 servings*

*Note:* If good fresh tomatoes are not available, substitute a similar quantity of drained canned tomatoes.

If you cannot purchase lobster carcasses separately, use 2 1-1/2-pound lobsters for the carcasses. Remove the claws and tails from the lobster bodies. Chop the bodies. Add all of the lobster to the kettle and simmer 5 minutes after adding the rice. Remove the claws and tails. Let cool, remove the meat, and return the shells to the simmering soup. Slice the tail and claw meat to use as a garnish for the finished soup.

For those who are willing to work to obtain the smoothest possible texture, place portions of the soup in a sieve lined with a cotton or linen sheet. Twist the ends of the cloth to force the soup through and into a pot.

## Bisque de Crevettes I (Shrimp Bisque I)

Substitute 1 pound shrimp for the lobster carcasses. Once the shrimp are cooked, remove the meat from the shells, saving 12 shrimp for garnish. Return the remainder to the soup. You can prepare the bisque using just the shells from 2 pounds of shrimp. Use reserved shrimp to garnish the bisque.

## Bisque de Crabe

Substitute 3 pounds cleaned, chopped crab for the lobster carcasses. Use some of the crab meat as a garnish.

## Bisque de Crevettes II (Shrimp Bisque II)

2 tablespoons butter
1/2 carrot, minced
1/2 onion, minced
2 parsley sprigs
1/2 bay leaf
pinch of thyme
1 cup dry white wine
24 medium shrimp, about 20 to 30 to the pound

2 quarts fish velouté (see Index)
milk, if required
3 tablespoons cream
2 tablespoons butter
2 tablespoons cognac or Madeira

In a 3-quart saucepan, melt 2 tablespoons butter. Sweat the carrot, onion, parsley, bay leaf, and thyme until the vegetables are tender. Add the wine and shrimp and bring just to a boil. Remove the shrimp from the liquid and cool.

Shell and devein the shrimp. Purée the shells and 16 shrimp in a processor or blender and return to the vegetable mixture. Add the velouté and simmer 20 minutes.

Strain through a very fine sieve. If too thick, thin with milk to desired consistency. Strain through several thicknesses of cheese-cloth (not a paper coffee filter).

Just before serving, reheat and add the cream, remaining butter, and wine. Garnish with reserved shrimp.

*Yield: 6 to 8 servings*

---

## Crème d'Aubergines (Cream of Eggplant Soup)

1-1/2 cups diced onion
1-1/2 cups diced celery
1 large eggplant, peeled and
   diced
1-1/2 cups diced potatoes
1/2 teaspoon curry powder

1/4 teaspoon thyme
1/4 teaspoon basil
3 tablespoons butter
4 cups chicken stock
2 cups heavy cream

In a 3-quart casserole, sauté the onion, celery, eggplant, potatoes, curry, thyme, and basil in the butter until softened, about 15 minutes. Stir in the stock and cook, uncovered, for 45 minutes until all the ingredients are very soft.

Purée in a processor or force through the fine blade of a food mill. Stir in the cream and reheat gently.

Can be frozen.

*Yield: 6 to 8 servings*

*Note:* Sauté a few cubes of eggplant in butter to serve as a garnish.

## Purée de Potiron (Cream of Pumpkin Soup)

1-1/2 pounds pumpkin, cut up
1/2 cup sliced potatoes
5 cups salted water
4 cups heavy cream
2/3 cup butter
2 tablespoons butter
1/4 cup chopped sorrel, optional

1/4 cup chopped spinach
1/4 cup chopped leeks
1/4 cup cooked rice
2 tablespoons cooked peas
1 tablespoon minced parsley
salt and pepper

In a 3-quart casserole, simmer the pumpkin and potatoes in the water until tender. Purée the vegetables in a food mill, reserving the cooking liquid.

In a clean casserole, combine the purée, cooking liquid, cream, and 2/3 cup butter; heat.

In a large skillet, melt the remaining butter and sweat the sorrel, spinach, and leeks until tender. Add to the soup with the rice, peas, and parsley. Correct the seasoning with salt and pepper.

Can be frozen.

*Yield: 8 servings*

## Purée de Germiny (Cream of Sorrel and Potato Soup)

1 cup chopped onion
1 tablespoon butter
1-1/2 pounds potatoes, cut in 2-inch cubes

5 cups chicken stock
1 pound sorrel, shredded
1 cup heavy cream
salt and pepper

In a 2-quart saucepan, sauté the onion in the butter until wilted. Add the potatoes, chicken stock, and 4 cups sorrel. Cook for 20 minutes.

Purée the soup in a food mill or processor. Return to the pan. Add the cream, salt, and pepper and reheat almost to boiling. Stir in the remaining sorrel.

Serve hot or cold. Can be frozen.

*Yield: 6 servings*

## Purée de Saint-Germain (Cream of Fresh Pea Soup)

3 cups chicken stock
1-1/2 pounds peas, shelled
1 onion, minced
1 carrot, minced
2 Boston lettuce leaves,
  shredded

2 tablespoons minced mint
1 teaspoon sugar
4 tablespoons butter
1/2 cup heavy cream

In a 3-quart casserole, simmer the stock, peas, onion, carrot, lettuce, mint, and sugar until the vegetables are tender. Purée in a processor and return to the casserole. Add the butter and cream. Reheat slowly. For a smoother texture, strain through a fine sieve before adding the butter and cream.

Serve hot or cold. Can be frozen.

*Yield: 4 to 6 servings*

*Note:* The flavor can be enhanced by adding a small amount of dry sherry.

## Cream of Squash Soup

2-1/2 pounds Hubbard
  squash, peeled
1 cup milk
1 cup heavy cream
1 cup chicken stock
2 tablespoons honey
1 tablespoon cognac

1/2 teaspoon grated orange
  rind
1/2 teaspoon salt
1/4 teaspoon ground ginger
1/4 teaspoon ground mace
1/4 teaspoon ground nutmeg
salt and pepper

Cut squash into 1-inch cubes. Cook in boiling, salted water until tender. Drain, purée in a processor, and put into a 3-quart casserole.

Stir in the milk, cream, stock, honey, cognac, orange rind, salt, ginger, mace, and nutmeg. Heat until hot. Correct the seasoning with salt and pepper.

Serve hot or cold. Can be frozen.

*Yield: 6 servings*

## Velouté de Poisson (Velouté Base for Fish Soups)

6 tablespoons butter
3/4 cup flour

8 cups fish stock (see Index)

In a stockpot, melt the butter and stir in the flour. Cook over moderate heat until the roux becomes foamy and starts to turn golden.

Add the stock and cook, stirring, until the mixture is smooth and thick. Simmer 20 minutes, skimming off any scum that appears on the surface. Strain through a fine sieve.

Can be frozen.

*Yield: about 7 cups*

## Potage Jacqueline

7 cups fish velouté base (see preceding recipe)
2 egg yolks
1/2 cup heavy cream

1/4 cup diced cooked carrots
1/2 cup cooked peas
1/3 cup cooked rice

In a 3-quart casserole, heat the velouté to boiling.

In a bowl, combine the egg yolks and cream and stir in 1 cup of hot soup, stirring constantly. Return the mixture to the hot soup and heat to just below the boiling point. (Do not boil once the eggs have been added.) Stir in the carrots, peas, and rice and mix well.

*Yield: 8 servings*

## Velouté de Volaille (Cream of Chicken Base)

This base is very useful for making any number of delicious vegetable-flavored cream soups.

4 tablespoons butter
1/2 cup cream of rice
2 quarts chicken stock
4 leeks, chopped

veal knuckle, optional
chicken bones, optional
2 celery stalks, chopped
1 teaspoon salt

In a 3-quart casserole, melt the butter, stir in the cream of rice, and cook until the roux just starts to turn golden. Add the chicken stock and leeks and cook, stirring, until it just comes to a boil. Add the veal, chicken bones, celery, and 1 teaspoon salt. Bring to a boil, stirring often. Skim off any scum and simmer for 2 hours, stirring often.

Strain through a food mill and then through a fine sieve.

Can be frozen up to 6 months. A flavored base can also be frozen before performing the liaison of egg yolks and cream.

*Yield: 1-1/2 quarts of base*

*Note:* Cream of rice is a breakfast cereal. It gives the soup a texture and finish that is not possible when flour is used as a thickening agent. Either instant or regular may be used. Cream of wheat or flour can be used in place of the rice, if necessary.

Be sure to stir the base often while it simmers because the cream of rice tends to settle and stick to the bottom. The double straining helps to give the soup its velvety texture. A food mill is preferable to a processor because it removes the tough fibrous parts of the leeks and celery and any other vegetables used to flavor the soup.

### To Use the Base (Performing the Liaison)

Flavor the base by cooking about 2 cups of a vegetable in the base until very soft. Force the mixture through a food mill and finish with a liaison of 2 egg yolks combined with 1 cup of heavy cream. Beat the eggs with the cream and add about 1 cup of hot soup to the egg mixture. Stir to combine and return it to the soup. Heat almost to boiling, but do not boil. If desired, strain the soup once again.

If the soup is too thick, add another cup of heavy cream. If it is still too thick, thin it with milk or stock. Do not add more cream.

Do not perform the liaison until just before serving.

### Vegetables for the Base

Some vegetables, such as green beans, peas, and carrots, can be added raw to the base. Other vegetables with stronger flavors, such as broccoli, cauliflower, or celery, should be parboiled in boiling salted water to soften their flavor. Sauté mushrooms in butter to bring out their flavor.

Reserve a small amount of the vegetable to be used as a garnish.

Most vegetables for garnish should be cooked in boiling salted water until tender-crisp.

Many of these soups benefit from a dollop of sherry, Madeira, or port added shortly before serving. Add just enough to give a hint of flavor.

## Velouté d'Asperges (Cream of Asparagus Soup)

| | |
|---|---|
| 1 pound asparagus, cut in 1-inch pieces | 2 egg yolks |
| 1-1/2 quarts cream of chicken base (see Index) | 2 cups heavy cream |
| | salt and pepper |
| | Madeira, optional |

Blanch the asparagus in boiling salted water for 5 minutes. Set aside the tips to use as garnish. Combine the remaining asparagus with the chicken base and simmer until the asparagus is very tender.

Strain through a food mill and then through a fine sieve. Combine the egg yolks and 1 cup cream in a bowl. Stir in 1 cup hot soup and mix well. Return the mixture to the soup and heat to just below boiling. Add enough remaining cream to reach the desired consistency. Correct the seasoning with salt, pepper, and Madeira.

Can be frozen. Do not perform the liaison until shortly before serving.

*Yield: 8 servings*

*Note:* The tough stems of asparagus, which are usually discarded, can be used in this soup.

## Crème Calcutta (Creamed Curry Soup)

| | |
|---|---|
| 4 onions, sliced | 1 cup milk |
| 2 tablespoons butter | 3/4 cup cooked rice |
| 2 teaspoons curry powder | 1/2 to 1 cup heavy cream |
| 1 quart cream of chicken base (see Index) | 1 red Delicious apple, cored, unpeeled, and finely diced |

Blanch the onions in boiling salted water for 4 minutes. Drain. In a 3-quart casserole, sweat the onions in the butter until very soft, but not browned. Stir in the curry powder and cook, stirring, for 5 minutes. Add the cream of chicken base and simmer 5 minutes. Stir in the milk, rice, and enough cream to bring the soup to the desired consistency.

Serve hot garnished with the apple. Can be frozen.

*Yield: 6 servings*

## Crème du Barry (Cream of Cauliflower Soup)

1 small head cauliflower, cut into florets
1-1/2 quarts cream of chicken base (see Index)

2 egg yolks
2 cups heavy cream
salt and pepper

Blanch the cauliflower in boiling salted water for 5 minutes. Drain. Set aside about 1 cup of tiny florets for garnish.

Combine the remaining cauliflower and cream of chicken base and simmer until very tender. Force through a food mill.

Combine the egg yolks with 1 cup heavy cream and stir in 1 cup hot soup. Return the mixture to the soup and cook, stirring, until hot, but not boiling. Add enough remaining cream to reach the desired consistency. Correct the seasoning with salt and pepper and garnish with reserved florets.

Can be frozen before performing the liaison.

*Yield: 8 servings*

## Crème Favorite (Cream of Green Bean Soup)

2 cups chopped, fresh green beans
1-1/2 quarts cream of chicken base (see Index)

2 egg yolks
2 cups heavy cream
salt and pepper
1/2 cup diced, cooked green beans

In a 3-quart casserole, simmer the green beans in the cream of chicken base until very tender. Force through a food mill.

In a bowl, combine the egg yolks with 1 cup cream and stir in 1 cup hot soup. Mix well and return the mixture to the soup. Heat, stirring, until very hot, but not boiling. Add enough remaining cream to reach the desired consistency. Correct the seasoning with salt and pepper. Strain.

Serve with cooked beans as a garnish. Can be frozen before performing the liaison.

*Yield: 8 servings*

---

## Crème Forestiere (Cream of Mushroom Soup)

| | |
|---|---|
| 1 onion, minced | 2 egg yolks |
| 1 tablespoon butter | 2 cups heavy cream |
| 1/2 pound mushrooms, minced | salt and pepper |
| | port |
| 1-1/2 quarts cream of chicken base (see Index) | 3/4 cup sliced mushrooms, sautéed in 1 teaspoon butter |

In a 3-quart casserole, sauté the onion in the butter until soft. Add the minced mushrooms and cook until their liquid evaporates. Add the cream of chicken base and simmer 30 minutes, covered. Force through a food mill.

In a bowl, combine the egg yolks with 1 cup cream and mix well. Stir in 1 cup hot soup and mix well. Return the mixture to the soup base and heat, stirring, until hot but not boiling. Strain. Add enough remaining cream to reach the desired consistency. Correct the seasoning with salt, pepper, and port.

Serve garnished with sliced mushrooms. Can be frozen before performing the liaison.

*Yield: 8 servings*

---

## Potage Crème de Laitues (Cream of Lettuce Soup)

| | |
|---|---|
| 4 heads Boston lettuce | 2 egg yolks |
| 1-1/2 quarts cream of chicken base (see Index) | 8 tablespoons butter |
| | 1 teaspoon lemon juice |
| salt and pepper | 1 cup fried croutons cut in 1/2-inch dice (see Index) |
| 1 cup heavy cream | |

Remove 8 to 10 of the greenest leaves from the heads of lettuce. Shred them very finely and plunge into boiling salted water. Bring the water back to a boil. Drain the lettuce, rinse under cold water, and drain again. Dry on paper toweling and set aside.

Shred the remaining lettuce. Rinse in a sink full of cold water, drain, and simmer in the soup base for 1 hour. Force through a food mill and correct the seasoning with salt and pepper.

In a bowl, combine the egg yolks and cream. Mix well and stir in 1 cup hot soup. Mix well and return to the soup. Reheat almost to boiling.

Cream the butter with salt, pepper, and lemon juice and stir teaspoon-size portions into the soup until well blended. Add the reserved lettuce leaves and serve.

Pass the croutons separately. Can be frozen before performing the liaison.

*Yield: 8 servings*

---

## Crème Saint-Germain (Cream of Pea Soup)

| | |
|---|---|
| 1 pound peas, shelled | 2 egg yolks |
| 1-1/2 quarts cream of chicken base (see Index) | 2 cups heavy cream<br>salt and pepper<br>sherry |

In a 3-quart casserole, simmer the peas in the chicken base until tender. Force through a food mill.

In a bowl, combine the egg yolks with 1 cup heavy cream and stir in 1 cup hot soup. Mix well and return to the soup, stirring constantly. Heat, stirring, until hot, but not boiling. Add enough remaining cream to reach the desired consistency.

Correct the seasoning with salt, pepper, and sherry. Strain. Can be frozen before performing the liaison.

*Yield: 8 servings*

The cream soups that follow are quicker to prepare than the preceding recipes because the base does not have to be prepared ahead.

## Potage Vert Pré (Green Meadow Soup)

| | |
|---|---|
| 1/2 cup minced scallion | 1 tablespoon sugar |
| 3 tablespoons butter | 1/2 teaspoon salt |
| 3 tablespoons flour | 6 cups chicken stock |
| 4 cups shelled peas | 1 cup heavy cream |
| 1 head Boston lettuce, shredded | 3 egg yolks |
| | 1/4 teaspoon white pepper |
| 1 cup shredded spinach leaves | 1 cup cooked peas |

In a 3-quart casserole or kettle, sauté the scallions in butter until soft. Add the flour and cook, stirring, for 2 minutes. Add the peas, lettuce, spinach, sugar, salt, and stock. Simmer, covered, for 45 minutes.

Cool slightly and purée in a processor or force through a food mill. Strain through a fine sieve.

In a bowl, combine the cream and egg yolks and stir in 1 cup hot soup. Mix well and return to the soup. Cook, stirring, until hot, but not boiling. Correct the seasoning with pepper. Stir in remaining peas.

Can be frozen before performing the liaison.

*Yield: 6 servings*

## Crème d'Artichauts (Cream of Artichoke Soup)

| | |
|---|---|
| 8 artichokes | 4 cups heavy cream |
| 2 slices lemon | 2 tablespoons butter |
| juice of 1 lemon | 2 tablespoons flour |
| 6 tablespoons olive oil | salt and pepper |

Trim the stems from the artichokes and remove any dried leaves. In a large kettle, combine the artichokes, lemon slices, lemon juice, olive oil, and 1 tablespoon salt. Add 3 cups water and simmer 30 to 45 minutes, or until artichokes are tender. To test for tenderness, pull an outside leaf on an artichoke. It should pull away easily.

Drain the artichokes, discarding the water, and rinse under cold water. When cool enough to handle, remove the leaves, discard the choke, and place the bases in a food processor. With a spoon, scrape the meat from each leaf and add to the processor. Purée.

Bring the cream to a simmer, stir in the purée, and return to a simmer.

In a bowl, mash the butter and flour to a paste (a beurre manie). Stir pea-size pieces into the soup, stirring constantly until the soup is thickened (you may not need all of the beurre manie). Correct the seasoning with salt and pepper.

Can be frozen before or after thickening.

*Yield: 6 servings*

## Crème de Morels (Cream of Morel Soup)

| | |
|---|---|
| 3 ounces dried morels | 1 teaspoon salt |
| 1/2 cup dry white wine | pepper |
| 1/2 cup lukewarm water | 6 cups chicken stock |
| 1/3 cup minced shallots | 2 egg yolks |
| 1/2 cup butter | 2/3 cup heavy cream |
| 1/2 cup flour | |

In a bowl, soak the morels in the wine and water for 2 hours. Drain, saving the liquid and the morels. Strain the liquid through a sieve lined with a paper coffee filter. Remove stems from morels and discard. Halve the caps lengthwise and rinse well to remove any grit. Drain again and cut into 1/4-inch dice.

In a 3-quart kettle, sweat the morels and shallots in the butter until soft, but not brown. Add the flour and cook, stirring, for 3 minutes. Raise the heat and add salt, pepper, chicken stock, and reserved morel liquid, stirring constantly. Cook until boiling and smooth.

Lower the heat to a simmer and cook, uncovered, for 30 minutes, stirring occasionally. Carefully remove any scum that collects on the surface.

In a small bowl, beat the egg yolks and cream until blended. Stir in 1 cup hot soup, mix well, and add to the hot soup. Heat to just below boiling.

Can be frozen before performing the liaison.

*Yield: 8 servings*

## Crème de Champignons (Mushroom Cream Soup)

| | |
|---|---|
| 2 tablespoons minced onion | 1 tablespoon minced parsley |
| 1/2 pound mushrooms, sliced | 1/2 cup heavy cream |
| 2 tablespoons butter | 2 egg yolks |
| 1 teaspoon lemon juice | salt and pepper |
| 3 cups chicken stock | sliced raw mushrooms |

In a 3-quart casserole, sauté the onion, mushrooms, and lemon juice in the butter until soft, but not brown. Add the stock and parsley and simmer 30 minutes. Purée in a blender or processor.

In a small bowl, beat the cream and egg yolks until mixed. Stir in 1 cup hot soup and add the mixture to the soup. Heat until hot, but not boiling. Correct the seasoning with salt and pepper.

Garnish with mushroom slices. Serve hot or cold.

Can be frozen before performing the liaison.

*Yield: 4 to 6 servings*

## Potage Germiny (Cream of Sorrel Soup)

| | |
|---|---|
| 1/2 cup chopped onion | 2 egg yolks |
| 1/4 cup butter | 1 cup heavy cream |
| 1 pound sorrel leaves, shredded | dash of Tabasco sauce |
| 3 cups chicken stock | salt and pepper |

Sauté the onion in the butter until soft, but not brown. Stir in the sorrel and cook until wilted. Add the stock and simmer 10 minutes.

In a bowl, beat the egg yolks and cream thoroughly. Add 1 cup hot soup and mix well. Add the mixture to the soup and heat until hot, but not boiling. Correct the seasoning with Tabasco, salt, and pepper.

Serve hot or cold. Can be frozen before performing the liaison.

*Yield: 6 servings*

*Note:* You can substitute 1 cup of canned sorrel for the fresh.

## Billi Bi (Cream of Mussel Soup)

3 quarts mussels, scrubbed
   and bearded
1 cup dry white wine
3 shallots, minced
4 parsley sprigs
1/2 teaspoon thyme
pepper

1/2 bay leaf
3 tablespoons butter
cayenne pepper
2 cups heavy cream
1 egg yolk
1/4 cup minced parsley

Place the mussels in a large kettle with the wine, shallots, parsley, thyme, pepper to taste, bay leaf, and butter. Cover and bring to a boil. Cook over high heat shaking the pot once or twice, for 5 minutes or until the mussels open. Let mussels cool.

Remove mussels from their shells and set aside for another use, or use some to garnish the soup.

Strain the cooking liquid into a saucepan, taking care not to pour in any of the grit at the bottom of the kettle. (Straining the liquid through a paper coffee filter helps to remove the very fine grit.) Bring the mussel liquor to a boil and season with cayenne to taste. Stir in 1 cup heavy cream.

In a small bowl, combine the egg yolk with the remaining cream and add 1 cup hot soup. Mix well. Pour the mixture into the hot soup and heat until hot, but not boiling.

Serve sprinkled with parsley and some reserved mussels, if desired. Serve hot or cold.

Can be frozen before performing the liaison.

*Yield: 4 to 6 servings*

*Note:* Use the mussel meat as an hors d'oeuvre, a crepe or quiche filling, or in a salad.

## Potage Saint-Jacques (Cream of Scallop Soup)

1 pound sea scallops
2 cups dry white wine
6 mushrooms, minced
2 tablespoons minced
   shallots
2 tablespoons butter

4 parsley sprigs
1/4 teaspoon cayenne pepper
salt and pepper
1 cup heavy cream
3 egg yolks, lightly beaten
dry sherry

In a 2-quart saucepan, combine the scallops, wine, mushrooms, shallots, butter, parsley, cayenne, and salt and pepper to taste. Bring just to a boil and remove scallops immediately. Simmer the cooking liquid for 5 minutes. Strain, discarding the solids.

In a clean saucepan, reheat the liquid.

In a small bowl, combine the cream and egg yolks and mix well. Stir in 1 cup hot soup and mix well. Add to the hot soup and heat through without boiling. Correct the seasoning with salt, pepper, and sherry.

Slice some of the scallops and use to garnish the soup.

Can be frozen before performing the liaison.

*Yield: 4 servings*

*Note:* Use the cooked scallops as an hors d'oeuvre, a crepe or quiche filling, or in a salad.

## CHEESE AND VEGETABLE SOUPS

Soups, vegetable or otherwise, enable the inventive cook to produce quick, interesting, and satisfying meals. They can be as filling as a mixed vegetable soup or as light and clean on the palate as snow pea soup.

Many of the soups in this chapter are meatless; others that have meat as a secondary ingredient are made with chicken or meat stock. For those who wish to avoid meat, these soups can be made with vegetable stock (see Index).

It is possible to interchange soup vegetables, if a particular vegetable is in short supply; this substitution can lead to some exciting variations. If you are making one of the mixed vegetable soups, there is no reason that you cannot proceed if you have most of the ingredients required. Obviously, you cannot make a tomato soup without tomatoes, but if the recipe calls for shallots and you have scallions or onions, make the substitution.

Although the cheese soup recipes in this section specify certain cheeses, these can often be changed to suit your needs or the availability of a specific cheese. There will be a difference in flavor, but you may prefer the change to the original.

## Cheddar Cheese Soup

| | |
|---|---|
| 1/2 cup butter | 1/4 cup flour |
| 1/2 cup minced carrots | 3 cups chicken stock |
| 1/2 cup minced green pepper | 1/2 pound cheddar cheese, |
| 1/2 cup minced onion | grated |
| 1/2 cup minced celery | 3 cups medium cream |

In a 4-quart casserole, melt the butter and sweat the carrots, green pepper, onion, and celery until soft, but not brown. Stir in the flour and cook, stirring, for 5 minutes.

Add the chicken stock, stirring constantly until the mixture comes to a boil and thickens. Lower the heat and stir in the cheese, stirring constantly until the cheese is melted. Stir in the cream and heat until hot but not boiling.

Serve hot or cold. Do not freeze.

*Yield: 8 servings*

*Note:* If desired, strain out the vegetables before adding the cheese for a soup with a smoother texture.

If the soup is too hot, the cheese will "seize" into a lump. If this happens, lower the heat and stir constantly until the cheese melts evenly.


## Swiss Cheese Soup

| | |
|---|---|
| 2 onions, chopped | 1-1/2 cups grated Gruyère |
| 3 tablespoons butter | cheese |
| 3 tablespoons flour | salt and pepper |
| 1-1/2 cups beef stock | |
| 3 cups milk | |

In a 3-quart kettle, sauté the onions in the butter until golden, but not browned. Stir in the flour and cook 2 minutes. Add the beef stock and simmer for 30 minutes, stirring occasionally.

Stir in the milk and simmer 15 minutes longer. Remove from the heat and stir in the cheese until it melts. Correct the seasoning with salt and pepper.

Can be refrigerated and reheated over low heat.

*Yield: 6 servings*

## Potage Printanier (Spring Garden Soup)

3 leeks, minced
1/2 cup minced onion
2 tablespoons butter
2 potatoes, thinly sliced
1 carrot, thinly sliced
2 teaspoons salt
1-1/2 cups hot water

1/4 cup rice
10 stalks asparagus, cut in
    1-inch sections
1/2 pound spinach, chopped
1 cup light cream
pepper

In a 3-quart casserole, sauté the leeks and onions in the butter until soft, but not brown, stirring occasionally. Add the potatoes, carrot, salt, and hot water to the kettle and simmer, covered, for 15 minutes.

Add the rice and simmer 10 minutes. Add the asparagus and simmer 5 minutes longer. Add the spinach and return to a simmer. Stir in the cream and heat until hot. Correct the seasoning with salt and pepper.

Can be reheated, but best if freshly made.
*Yield: 6 servings*

## Soupe Maraichere (Market Garden Soup)

1 cup minced onion
1 cup sliced celery
1/2 cup diced turnip
1/2 cup diced potatoes
3 tablespoons butter
6 cups boiling chicken or
    beef stock
1/2 cup fine noodles
    (vermicelli or angel hair)

2 cups shredded cabbage
1 cup shredded spinach
1 cup shredded lettuce
1-3/4 cups milk
salt and pepper
minced chives
minced chervil

In a 3-quart casserole, cover and sweat the onions, celery, turnip, and potatoes in the butter until they are half cooked. Add the stock and noodles, cover, and simmer until the vegetables are tender.

Add the cabbage, spinach, and lettuce and simmer 5 minutes.

Stir in the milk, correct the seasoning with salt and pepper, and heat until hot.

Serve garnished with chives and chervil. Can be reheated, but best if served immediately.

*Yield: 6 servings*

---

## Soupe Jardiniere (Garden Soup)

---

| | |
|---|---|
| 6 tablespoons olive oil | 2 cups shredded cabbage |
| 1 onion, minced | 10 cups water |
| 4 garlic cloves, minced | 1 cup diced green beans |
| 1 teaspoon oregano | 1 cup diced zucchini |
| 2 tomatoes, peeled, seeded, and chopped | 3 tablespoons minced parsley |
| 2 tablespoons tomato paste | 2 cups basil leaves |
| 2 cups diced potatoes | 1/3 cup grated Parmesan cheese |
| 1 cup diced carrots | salt and pepper |
| 1 cup diced celery | |

In a 3-quart casserole, heat 2 tablespoons oil and sauté the onion, 2 garlic cloves, and oregano until the onion is soft, but not brown. Add the tomatoes and tomato paste and simmer 5 minutes, stirring occasionally.

Add the potatoes, carrots, celery, cabbage, water, salt, and pepper. Simmer 1 hour.

Add the beans and zucchini and simmer for 20 minutes.

In a blender, blend the parsley, basil, and remaining garlic and oil until smooth. Blend in the Parmesan and season with salt and pepper. Serve separately, or stir into the soup just before serving.

Can be frozen.

*Yield: 8 to 10 servings*

*Note:* This soup, also called Soupe au Pistou, qualifies as an Italian minestrone. The basil mixture is known as Pistou, or Pesto. It can be made ahead and frozen. (Do not add the cheese until just before serving.) It is also a wonderful sauce for pasta, eggs, or chicken.

## Soupe aux Legumes (Soup with Vegetables)

1 tablespoon butter
4 tablespoons olive oil
2 onions, sliced
2 turnips, shredded
2 carrots, shredded
2 parsnips, shredded
1 celery stalk, thinly sliced
1 cup green beans, diced

4 cups chicken stock
1/2 cup vermicelli, broken
   into small pieces
salt and pepper
1/2 cup chopped spinach
1/2 cup peas
3 tomatoes, peeled and
   sliced

In a 3-quart casserole, heat the butter and oil. Add the onions, turnips, carrots, parsnips, and celery and cook, stirring, for 5 minutes. Add the beans and cook 3 minutes.

Add the chicken stock and vermicelli and season to taste with salt and pepper. Simmer 15 minutes longer, or until the vegetables are tender.

Add the spinach, peas, and tomatoes and cook until just done, about 5 minutes. Correct the seasoning with salt and pepper.

Can be frozen. Reheat gently.

*Yield: 6 to 8 servings*

## Minestrone di Romagna (Italian Vegetable Soup)

1 cup sliced onions
1/2 cup olive oil
2 tablespoons butter
1 cup diced carrots
1 cup diced celery
2 cups diced potatoes
2 cups diced zucchini
1 cup diced green beans
3 cups shredded savoy
   cabbage

6 cups beef broth
rind from 1 pound Parmesan
   cheese, optional
2/3 cup canned plum
   tomatoes and juice
salt
1-1/2 cups canned cannellini
   beans
1/2 cup grated Parmesan
   cheese

In a large pot, cook the onions in oil and butter until wilted and just golden. Add carrots and cook for 1 minute, stirring once. Repeat the procedure with the celery, potatoes, zucchini, and green beans, cooking each for 2 minutes before adding the next vegetable.

Add the cabbage and cook for 6 minutes, stirring occasionally. Add the broth, cheese rind, if available, tomatoes, and their juice. Season to taste with salt. Cover and simmer slowly for 1-1/2 hours, or until thickened and rich in flavor.

Shortly before serving, remove the Parmesan rind and add the cannellini beans. Swirl in the cheese and remove from the heat.

This soup is best if made a day ahead. Can be frozen.

*Yield: 6 to 8 servings*

---

## Soupe Menerboise

| | |
|---|---|
| 1/2 pound zucchini, cubed | salt and pepper |
| salt | 2 tomatoes, peeled |
| 1/2 cup olive oil | 3 garlic cloves |
| 2 onions, thinly sliced | 1/4 cup fresh basil |
| 3/4 pound tomatoes, chopped | 2 egg yolks |
| 2 small potatoes, cubed | 1/4 cup grated Parmesan |
| 6 cups hot water | cheese |
| 1/2 cup shelled broad beans | |
| 1/2 cup orzo, or other small pasta | |

Sprinkle the zucchini with salt and drain in a colander for 30 minutes.

In a kettle, warm the olive oil and cook onions over low heat until soft, but not brown. Add the zucchini and cook for 10 minutes. Add the chopped tomatoes and cook until they start to give off their moisture.

Add the potatoes and water and simmer for 20 minutes, or until potatoes are almost cooked. Add the beans, pasta, and salt and pepper to taste.

In a processor, combine the peeled tomatoes, garlic, and basil. Blend until smooth. Add the egg yolks and process until thickened slightly.

When the pasta is cooked, combine 1 cup soup with the egg mixture and process for 30 seconds. Add the mixture to the soup and heat gently, stirring constantly, until slightly thickened. Do not boil. Stir in the cheese. Pass additional cheese separately, if desired.

*Yield: 8 servings*

*Note:* This soup is best if eaten fresh. It can be prepared ahead, or frozen, but do not perform the basil-garlic-egg finish until just before serving.

## Portuguese Red Bean Soup

| | |
|---|---|
| 1 cup dried red kidney beans | 6-ounce can tomato paste |
| 6 potatoes, diced | 4 bay leaves |
| 3 onions, sliced | 1 tablespoon allspice |
| 2 garlic cloves, minced | salt and pepper |
| 4 tablespoons bacon fat | |

Soak the beans in water to cover for 12 to 24 hours. Drain.

Put beans into a kettle, add water to cover, and simmer until tender, about 2 hours.

Put the potatoes into a pan, cover with cold water, and simmer 15 minutes. Drain.

In a skillet, sauté the onions and garlic in the bacon fat until golden. Add to the beans with the tomato paste, bay leaves, allspice, and potatoes. Simmer 30 minutes. Correct the seasoning with salt and pepper.

Can be frozen.

*Yield: 6 servings*

*Note:* To prepare the soup more quickly, put the beans into a pot, cover with water, and simmer 5 minutes. Remove from heat, cover, and let stand for 2 hours. Proceed with the recipe.

## Tomato Lentil Soup

| | |
|---|---|
| 2/3 cup dried lentils | 3 tablespoons minced parsley |
| 4 cups water | 2 garlic cloves, minced |
| 4 carrots, chopped | 1/4 teaspoon thyme |
| 2 celery stalks, chopped | 1/4 teaspoon tarragon |
| 1 onion, chopped | 1/8 teaspoon dill weed |
| 1 cup tomato paste | salt and pepper |
| 1/2 cup dry white wine | |

In a 4-quart kettle, combine the lentils, water, carrots, celery, and onion and simmer for 2 hours, or until lentils are tender. It may be necessary to add water as the mixture cooks, to keep the vegetables covered.

Add the tomato paste, wine, parsley, garlic, thyme, tarragon, dill, and salt and pepper to taste. Simmer 30 minutes. Correct seasoning if needed.

Can be frozen.

*Yield: 8 servings*

## Broccoli and Macaroni Soup

| | |
|---|---|
| 2 tablespoons minced salt pork fat | 1 teaspoon salt |
| | 1/4 teaspoon pepper |
| 6 cups water | 3 cups broccoli florets |
| 3 tablespoons tomato paste | 2 cups elbow macaroni |
| 1 tablespoon olive oil | grated Parmesan cheese |
| 1 garlic clove, minced | |

In a 3-quart saucepan, sauté the pork fat until brown. Add the water, tomato paste, olive oil, garlic, salt, and pepper. Simmer 20 minutes.

Add the broccoli and simmer 4 minutes. Add the macaroni and cook 10 minutes, or until just tender. Pass the cheese separately.

Best when freshly made, but can be made a day ahead.

*Yield: 6 servings*

## Potage Purée de Carottes et de Tomates (Purée of Carrot and Tomato Soup)

| | |
|---|---|
| 1 pound carrots, cooked | 4 cups chicken stock |
| 1 cup tomato purée | salt and pepper |
| 4 teaspoons tapioca | |

Purée the carrots and mix with the tomato purée.

Simmer the tapioca in the chicken stock for 20 minutes. Stir in the carrot-tomato mixture. Correct the seasoning with salt and pepper.

Can be frozen.

*Yield: 6 servings*

## Crème Vichy au Pois (Cream of Carrot Soup with Peas)

1 pound carrots, shredded
1 bunch scallions, minced
6 shallots, minced
1 potato, minced
1 garlic clove, minced
1-1/2 teaspoons minced
    tarragon
1-1/2 teaspoons minced
    chervil

3/4 teaspoon minced
    marjoram
1/4 teaspoon minced thyme
1/4 cup butter
2 quarts chicken stock
1 cup peas, cooked
1 cup heavy cream
salt and pepper

In a 4-quart casserole, sweat the carrots, scallions, shallots, potato, garlic, tarragon, chervil, marjoram, and thyme in the butter until the vegetables are softened.

Add the stock and simmer, uncovered, until the potatoes are tender. Purée in a processor or force through a food mill. Return to a clean pot and bring to a simmer. Add the peas and cream and reheat. Correct the seasoning with salt and pepper.

Can be frozen.

*Yield: 8 servings*

*Note:* If you use dried herbs, reduce the quantities by one-third.

## Apple and Celery Soup

2 celery stalks, sliced
1 onion, sliced
1 carrot, sliced
2 tablespoons butter
3 tablespoons peanut oil
6 Cortland apples, unpeeled,
    cored, and sliced

2 cups chicken stock
1 teaspoon meat extract
    (Bovril)
salt and pepper
flour for dredging

In a 2-quart saucepan, sweat the celery, onion, and carrot in the butter and 1 tablespoon oil until they start to wilt. Add 5 of the apples and cook until soft, but not brown. Add the chicken stock and meat extract and season to taste with salt and pepper.

Purée in a processor, food mill, or blender. Return to the pan and reheat.

Dust remaining apple slices with flour and sauté in remaining oil until golden. Serve soup garnished with apple slices.

The soup can be made several days ahead, or frozen. The garnish should be prepared shortly before serving.

*Yield: 6 servings*

## Cucumber Soup

3 cucumbers, peeled and
  seeded
1 leek, split lengthwise
4 cups chicken stock
1 cup raw spinach leaves
1 teaspoon minced dill
1 teaspoon minced chervil

salt and pepper
1/2 cup yogurt, crème
  fraiche, or sour cream
1 small cucumber, scored
  and thinly sliced
minced dill

Cut cucumbers into 2-inch lengths. Simmer cucumbers, leeks, and chicken stock in a 2-quart pot for 30 minutes. Purée in a processor, add the spinach, and purée again.

Return to the pot and season with dill, chervil, and salt and pepper to taste.

Serve hot or cold with a generous dollop of yogurt, crème fraiche, or sour cream, cucumber slices, and dill.

Can be made 2 or 3 days ahead. Can be frozen.

*Yield: 6 servings*

## Ginestrata (Egg and Marsala Soup)

6 egg yolks
1/2 cup dry Marsala wine
3 cups chicken stock
1/4 teaspoon cinnamon

4 tablespoons butter,
  softened
1/4 teaspoon sugar
1/4 teaspoon nutmeg

In a 2-quart saucepan, beat the egg yolks until light colored. Beat in the Marsala, chicken stock, and cinnamon. Cook over low heat, stirring constantly.

Beat in the butter in small bits. When the soup starts to thicken, but before it boils, remove from the heat.

Sprinkle the top of each serving with a mixture of sugar and nutmeg. Serve immediately.

*Yield: 4 servings*

## Zuppa di Scarola alla Siciliana (Sicilian Escarole Soup)

| | |
|---|---|
| 1 pound escarole | 1 cup vermicelli, or melon seed pasta |
| 4 slices lean bacon | |
| 1 teaspoon olive oil | 1 cup cooked chicken, diced |
| 2 garlic cloves, crushed | salt and pepper |
| 8 cups chicken stock | grated Parmesan cheese |

Wash and drain the escarole and cut into 1/4-inch slices.

In a skillet, sauté the bacon in oil until cooked, but not crisp. Remove, drain, and cut into small squares.

In the skillet, sauté the garlic until just golden. (Do not burn the garlic or the soup will be bitter.)

In a 3-quart saucepan, simmer the garlic, bacon, and stock for 1 minute. Add the escarole and simmer, uncovered, for 10 minutes. Add the pasta and cook 10 minutes longer. Add the chicken and heat. Correct the seasoning with salt and pepper.

Pass the cheese separately.

Can be made 1 or 2 days ahead.

*Yield: 6 servings*

*Note:* There are dozens of different pastas for use in soups, such as orzo (rice), farina, stellae (stars), semi di melone (melon seeds), tiny shells, and others. Use whatever you have, or break vermicelli or spaghetti into 1-inch lengths.

## Soupe a l'Ail (Garlic Soup)

| | |
|---|---|
| 1/2 cup garlic cloves, unpeeled | 1/2 teaspoon salt |
| | pinch of cayenne pepper |
| 2 tablespoons butter | nutmeg |
| 4 tablespoons olive oil | 6 slices French bread, toasted |
| 4 cups chicken stock | |
| 6 egg yolks | 1 tablespoon minced parsley |

In boiling water to cover, blanch garlic for 1 minute. Drain and pinch off skins.

In a 3-quart casserole, sweat the garlic in the butter and 1 tablespoon oil until soft, about 15 minutes. Add the stock and simmer 20 minutes.

In a bowl, beat the egg yolks until light. Beat in the remaining oil, a little at a time, until the mixture is as thick as mayonnaise.

Add 1 cup hot soup to the mayonnaise and mix well. Add to the hot soup in a slow stream. Heat almost to boiling. Strain, mashing heavily on the garlic. Add salt, cayenne, and nutmeg to taste.

Place the toast in a tureen and pour on the hot soup. Sprinkle with parsley and serve.

The soup can be prepared 1 or 2 days ahead, or frozen. Add the egg liaison shortly before serving.

*Yield: 6 servings*

---

## Leek and Vermicelli Soup

6 leeks, thinly sliced
1/4 cup butter
2 ounces vermicelli
1 quart chicken stock
1 teaspoon salt

1/4 teaspoon pepper
2 tablespoons flour
water
1 cup milk

In a 3-quart saucepan, sweat the leeks in the butter until soft. Break the vermicelli into 1- to 2-inch lengths and add to the pan with the chicken stock, salt, and pepper. Cover and simmer 10 minutes.

In a bowl, combine the flour and enough water to make a thin slurry. Stir into the soup, whisking constantly. Add the milk and heat until hot and slightly thickened.

Can be made 1 or 2 days ahead. Can be frozen.

*Yield: 6 servings*

## *Lettuce Rice Soup*

| | |
|---|---|
| 2 cups minced scallions | 2 cups shredded Boston |
| 1/4 cup butter | lettuce |
| 3 tablespoons flour | 1 cup peas |
| 6 cups hot chicken stock | salt and pepper |
| 3/4 cup cooked rice | |

In a 3-quart kettle, sweat the scallions in the butter until soft, but not brown. Stir in the flour and cook for 2 minutes. Add the stock, stirring constantly until smooth.

Add the rice and bring to a boil. Add the lettuce and peas and simmer, uncovered, until the peas are cooked, about 3 to 8 minutes. Correct the seasoning with salt and pepper.

Can be made ahead and can be frozen.

*Yield: 4 to 6 servings*

*Note:* If you use frozen peas, the soup will be ready as soon as it returns to a boil. If the peas are fresh, you need to test for doneness.

## Onion Soups

There are many versions of onion soup. Some take only minutes to prepare and others much longer. This collection includes not only familiar versions, but some that are less well known as well.

## *White Wine Onion Soup*

| | |
|---|---|
| 4 large onions, minced | 1/2 cup grated Parmesan |
| 6 tablespoons butter | cheese |
| 3 cups chicken stock | 1/2 cup grated Gruyère |
| 1 cup dry white wine | cheese |
| salt and pepper | minced raw onion, optional |
| 6 large croutons (see Index) | minced parsley, optional |

Preheat the broiler.

In a 3-quart saucepan, sweat the onions in the butter until very soft, but not brown. Stir in the stock and wine and simmer 20 minutes. Correct the seasoning with salt and pepper.

Sprinkle the croutons with the cheeses and brown under the broiler.

Place the soup in a tureen and pass the croutons separately, with bowls of onion and parsley, if desired.

The soup can be made 2 or 3 days ahead. Can be frozen.

*Yield: 6 servings*

## Ouilliat, Tourri, or Toulia (Onion Soup from Béarn)

| | |
|---|---|
| 1/2 cup olive oil | salt and pepper |
| 12 slices French bread | 4 egg yolks |
| 1 cup minced onion | 1/2 pound Gruyère cheese, |
| 1/2° cup flour | grated |
| 2 quarts beef stock | 1/3 cup cognac or Armagnac |

In a large skillet, sauté the bread in 4 tablespoons oil until golden. Drain on paper towels. Pour the skillet oil and remaining oil into a 4-quart kettle and sweat the onions until they just start to turn golden. Sprinkle with the flour and cook, stirring, for 5 minutes.

Add 2 cups stock and bring to a boil, stirring. Add the remaining stock and return to a boil. Simmer, covered, for 30 minutes. Force through a food mill. Correct the seasoning with salt and pepper.

In a soup tureen, beat the egg yolks with half the cheese. Stir in the hot soup, 1 cup at a time. Reheat the bread slices in the oven and add to the soup.

In a small saucepan, warm the cognac or Armagnac. With your face turned away, ignite the liquor. When the flames subside, pour into the soup and mix well. Sprinkle with remaining cheese and serve.

Can be prepared ahead or frozen. Do not finish with the egg yolks and cheese until shortly before serving.

*Yield: 6 servings*

## Thourins, Tourins, or Torrins (Onion Soup from the Bordelais)

| | |
|---|---|
| 3 to 4 large onions, thinly sliced | 6 cups boiling beef stock |
| 2 tablespoons olive oil | 8 slices stale rye bread |
| 1 tablespoon flour | 2/3 cup grated Gruyère cheese |
| 1/2 cup dry white wine | |

In a 3-quart kettle, sauté the onions in the oil until they are golden, but not burned. Sprinkle with flour and stir to blend. Moisten with the wine and stir in the stock. Bring to a full boil, stirring often.

Place a layer of bread in a soup tureen. Sprinkle with a layer of cheese. Continue layering, ending with the cheese. Pour the simmering soup over the bread and cheese. Let stand 5 minutes before serving.

Can be prepared ahead and frozen.

*Yield: 6 servings*

---

## Mediterranean Onion Soup

| | |
|---|---|
| 5 cups thinly sliced onion | 3/4 teaspoon dried oregano |
| 1 teaspoon salt | 1 bay leaf |
| 1 teaspoon sugar | 35 ounces canned Italian |
| 1/4 teaspoon pepper | tomatoes |
| 3 tablespoons olive oil | 1 tablespoon tomato paste |
| 3 garlic cloves, crushed | 5 cups chicken stock |
| 1 parsley sprig | 1/4 cup ditalini, or other |
| 1 teaspoon dried thyme | soup pasta |

In a 3-quart casserole, sauté the onions, salt, sugar, and pepper in the oil until the onions are pale golden, about 15 minutes. Partially cover and sweat until very soft and browned.

Stir in the garlic, parsley, thyme, oregano, and bay leaf. Cook 2 minutes.

Drain the tomatoes and purée in a processor. Strain out the seeds. Stir puréed tomatoes into the onions and add the tomato paste and stock. Simmer, partially covered, for 30 minutes.

Correct the seasoning with salt and pepper. Add the pasta and simmer, uncovered, until tender. Discard the bay leaf and parsley.

Can be made ahead or frozen.

*Yield: 8 servings*

*Note:* Serve with grated Parmesan or Gruyère cheese.

## Zweibelcreme Suppe (Swiss-style Creamed Onion Soup)

6 slices whole-grain rye
  bread
5 tablespoons butter
8 cups thinly sliced onions
2 tablespoons peanut oil
3/4 teaspoon salt
pinch of nutmeg

pinch of pepper
3 cups milk
3 cups light cream
3 egg yolks
2 eggs
minced chives

Cut bread into 1/4-inch cubes. In a skillet, sauté the bread in 4 tablespoons butter until toasted. Drain on paper toweling.

In a 3-quart casserole, sweat the onions in the remaining butter and oil until very soft and just starting to turn golden. Season with salt, nutmeg, and pepper. Add the milk and cream and simmer, stirring, for 10 minutes.

In a 1-quart bowl, beat the egg yolks and eggs until well mixed. Stir in 1 cup hot soup. Slowly stir the egg mixture into the soup over low heat. Cook until thickened, but do not boil. Serve garnished with sautéed bread cubes and chives.

Can be made 2 or 3 days ahead. Can be frozen. Do not add the egg enrichment until shortly before serving.

*Yield: 8 servings*

## Soupe au Mange Tout (Snow Pea Soup)

7 cups chicken stock
2 tablespoons coriander
  leaves
1 tablespoon minced
  gingerroot

1/4 pound snow peas,
  julienned

In a 3-quart casserole, simmer the chicken stock, coriander, and ginger for 10 minutes. Strain.

Bring the stock to a simmer; add the snow peas, and heat 1 minute, or until the snow peas are cooked but still crisp.

Should be served immediately.

*Yield: 6 servings*

## Risi e Bisi, Minestra di Riso e Piselli (Rice and Peas in Broth)

This very thick mixture is a cross between a thick soup and a loose, runny rice dish.

4 pounds fresh peas, in pods
1/4 pound butter
2 tablespoons olive oil
1 onion, minced
3 tablespoons minced parsley

2 ounces minced prosciutto
salt and pepper
1-1/2 cups Arborio rice
6 cups chicken stock
1/3 cup grated Parmesan cheese

Shell the peas.

Place the butter and olive oil in a 2-quart saucepan and add the peas, onion, parsley, ham, salt, and pepper. Cook over low heat until the peas are tender. Add the rice to the vegetables and mix well.

Add 1/2 cup stock to the mixture, stirring, and cook over medium heat until the liquid evaporates. Continue adding stock, 1/2 cup at a time, until the rice is tender, but not mushy (allow each 1/2 cup to evaporate before adding more). If there is remaining stock, add it to the soup. Serve immediately with the cheese on the side.

*Yield: 6 servings*

*Note:* Arborio rice, a short, fat-grained rice, is imported from Italy. Long grain rice is a suitable substitute. If desired, you can add additional stock but, ideally, the soup should be very thick.

## Soupe de Riz a la Provençale (Provençale Rice Soup)

3/4 cup chopped leeks
2 tablespoons olive oil
1/4 cup flour
7 cups beef stock
1 pound tomatoes, peeled and seeded
1 celery stalk
1 bay leaf

2 sprigs thyme
3 sprigs parsley
1 garlic clove
salt and pepper
1/4 cup raw rice
1/8 pound salt pork, minced
small croutons (see Index)

In a 3-quart casserole, sweat the leeks in the oil until soft. Add the flour and cook, stirring, for 2 minutes. Stir in the beef stock and bring to a boil. Add the tomatoes.

Make a faggot with the celery, bay leaf, thyme, and parsley (see Index). Add to the soup with the garlic, salt, and pepper. Simmer 15 minutes. Add the rice and simmer 15 minutes longer, or until the rice is tender.

In a small skillet, render the salt pork until crisp. Drain on paper toweling.

Discard the faggot. Serve the soup garnished with the pork cubes and croutons.

Can be made 1 or 2 days ahead or frozen.

*Yield: 6 servings*

---

## Paparot (Spinach and Cornmeal Soup, Friuli-style)

---

| | |
|---|---|
| 2 pounds spinach, stripped of stems | 2 quarts chicken or beef stock |
| 1 garlic clove, halved | salt and pepper |
| 2 tablespoons butter | 1 cup cornmeal |
| 2 tablespoons olive oil | 1/2 cup sifted flour |

Put the spinach into a kettle with only the water on its leaves. Cook over high heat until wilted, stirring often. Drain, run under cold water, drain again, and squeeze out excess water. Mince.

In a 3-quart kettle, cook the garlic in the butter and oil until golden, but not burned. Discard the garlic. Add the spinach and broth and simmer 2 minutes. Correct the seasoning with salt and pepper.

In a bowl, combine the cornmeal and flour. Cool 1 cup of soup for 5 minutes. Stir into the cornmeal until no lumps remain.

Add to the soup, stirring constantly. Cook, stirring, until the soup is smooth. Simmer for 30 minutes.

Can be made ahead and reheated.

*Yield: 6 servings*

## Potage Provençale (Provençale Vegetable Soup)

4 large potatoes, peeled and
  sliced
2 large onions, sliced
3 celery stalks, sliced
2 leeks, sliced
1/2 cup butter

4 cups cold water
1 teaspoon salt
2 teaspoons white pepper
1 pound spinach, stripped of
  stems
1/2 cup light cream, scalded

In a 3-quart casserole, simmer the potatoes, onions, celery, leeks, butter, water, salt, and pepper until the potatoes are mushy. Remove from the heat and stir in the spinach. Force through a food mill or purée in a processor.

Return to the pan and stir in the cream. The soup can be thinned with water or milk, but it should be thick.

Can be made 1 or 2 days ahead or frozen.

*Yield: 6 servings*

## Soupe Bonne Femme (Hot Potato Soup)

4 leeks, or 2 onions, diced
1 onion, diced
1 tablespoon butter
4 or 5 potatoes, diced
4 cups hot water

2 teaspoons salt
2 cups hot milk
1 tablespoon butter
1 tablespoon minced parsley

Remove green tops and roots from the leeks. Starting 1 inch from the base, slit lengthwise to the tips. Run under cold water, fanning the leaves to remove any grit. Dice.

In a 3-quart kettle, sweat the leeks and onions in the butter until soft. Add the potatoes, water, and salt and simmer until the potatoes are soft. Force through a food mill or process.

Add the milk and remaining tablespoon of butter. Serve hot, garnished with parsley.

This soup can be prepared 2 or 3 days ahead or frozen. Can be served without puréeing.

*Yield: 6 servings*

*Note:* Leeks give the soup its particular flavor. Using only onions makes the soup delicious but different. With further straining and enrichment, this soup becomes Vichyssoise (see Index).

## Soupe de l'Ubac (Potato Soup from Béarn)

2 pounds potatoes, quartered
2 quarts water
2 cups milk
1 veal bone, optional
salt and pepper

3 tablespoons butter
1/4 pound Gruyère cheese, grated
6 slices stale bread

In a 3-quart casserole, simmer the potatoes, water, milk, veal bone, and salt and pepper to taste, for 40 minutes. Discard the veal bone. Force the soup through a food mill or purée in a processor. Return the soup to the kettle and simmer 10 minutes.

Put the butter and cheese in a heated tureen and pour in the hot soup. Garnish with bread slices.

Can be made ahead except for the butter-cheese finish. Keeps 3 to 4 days in the refrigerator. Can be frozen.

*Yield: 6 servings*

## Fresh Tomato Soup with Basil I

3 tomatoes, chopped
1 carrot, sliced
1/4 leek, sliced
1 shallot, sliced
1 garlic clove, sliced
2 tablespoons olive oil
sprig of thyme

1/2 bay leaf
1 tablespoon tomato paste
5 cups chicken stock
1 teaspoon salt
pepper
1 cup fresh basil, packed
2 teaspoons olive oil

In a 2-quart saucepan, sweat the tomatoes, carrot, leek, shallot, and garlic in the oil over low heat until they give off their liquid. Add the thyme, bay leaf, tomato paste, stock, salt, and pepper to taste. Simmer, partially covered, for 20 minutes.

Discard the bay leaf and thyme and purée the soup in a processor or force through a food mill. Return to a clean pot.

In a processor or blender, purée the basil with 2 teaspoons oil to make a smooth paste. Serve the paste separately.

Can be kept in the refrigerator for 3 to 4 days.

*Yield: 6 servings*

## Fresh Tomato Soup II

| | |
|---|---|
| 1 onion, thinly sliced | 1/4 cup flour |
| 1 teaspoon minced dill | 4 cups chicken stock |
| 1 teaspoon minced thyme | 1-1/2 teaspoons sugar |
| 1 teaspoon minced basil | salt |
| 2 tablespoons butter | 1/4 teaspoon white pepper |
| 2 tablespoons olive oil | 1 cup heavy cream |
| 8 tomatoes, peeled, seeded, and chopped | 1/2 cup grated Parmesan cheese |
| 3 tablespoons tomato paste | grated Parmesan cheese |

In a 4-quart kettle, sweat the onion, dill, thyme, and basil in the oil and butter until soft. Add the tomatoes and tomato paste and simmer 20 minutes.

In a small bowl, combine the flour with 1/2 cup chicken stock and mix well. Stir the slurry into the soup. Add the remaining stock, stirring constantly. Simmer, stirring often, for 25 minutes. Correct the seasoning with sugar, salt, and pepper.

Whip the cream until stiff and fold in the grated cheese. Serve the cream mixture separately.

*Yield: 6 servings*

*Note:* You can serve yogurt, sour cream, minced dill, or basil with the soup. Serve the soup hot or cold. For a more dramatic presentation, ladle the soup into a broad, shallow casserole. Dollop the cheese-cream mixture over the surface and brown under a preheated broiler about 1 minute.

## Soupe aux Tomatoes (Fresh Tomato Soup III)

| | |
|---|---|
| 2 leeks, thinly sliced | pinch of thyme |
| 1/4 cup olive oil | bay leaf |
| 1-1/2 tablespoons flour | 1 garlic clove, crushed |
| 2 cups beef or chicken stock | salt and pepper |
| 6 tomatoes, peeled, seeded, and chopped | 2 quarts hot water |
| sprig of parsley | 6 to 12 croutons, sautéed in olive oil (see Index) |
| sprig of celery leaf | |

In a 3-quart casserole, sauté the leeks in the oil until soft and just starting to turn golden. Sprinkle with flour and mix well. Gradually stir in the stock and bring to a boil.

Add the tomatoes, parsley, celery, thyme, bay leaf, garlic, and salt and pepper to taste. Add the water, cover, and simmer 1-1/2 hours. Remove the parsley, celery, and bay leaf.

Place 1 or 2 croutons in each soup plate and ladle in the soup. Can be prepared 3 or 4 days ahead. Can be frozen.

*Yield: 6 servings*

*Note:* The soup can be made with chicken stock, beef stock, or water. Grated Gruyère can be passed with the soup.

## Tomato Saffron Soup

1/2 leek, chopped
1/2 cup chopped carrot
1/3 cup chopped celery
2 tablespoons butter
8 tomatoes, peeled, seeded, and chopped
1-1/2 teaspoons grated lemon rind

pinch of powdered saffron
5 cups beef or chicken stock
salt
1 lemon, thinly sliced, seeds removed
1 tablespoon minced parsley

In a 4-quart kettle, sweat the leek, carrot, and celery in the butter until soft. Add the tomatoes, lemon rind, saffron, stock, and salt. Simmer, partially covered, for 30 minutes.

Purée the soup and return to the kettle. Correct seasoning with salt. Dust one side of each lemon slice with parsley and float on the soup. Serve hot or cold.

Can be prepared 2 or 3 days ahead. Can be frozen.

*Yield: 6 servings*

## Walnut Soup

2 tablespoons butter
2 tablespoons flour
6 cups beef stock
1-1/2 cups finely ground walnuts
1/2 teaspoon salt

pepper
1/4 teaspoon Worcestershire sauce
Tabasco sauce
1/2 cup walnut halves

In a 2-quart saucepan, melt the butter. Stir in the flour and cook, stirring, for 3 minutes, or until it starts to turn golden. Stir in the stock and cook, stirring, until thickened and smooth. Add the walnuts, salt, pepper to taste, Worcestershire, and Tabasco to taste. Simmer 30 minutes.

Serve hot, garnished with walnut halves.

Can be prepared 2 or 3 days ahead. Can be frozen.

*Yield: 6 servings*

# FISH SOUPS

Although many food writers relate any soup made with a variety of fish to Bouillabaisse, the Provençale fish soup made with a tomato base, there are dozens of such soups that are equally delicious but unrelated. The recipes here come from around the world. If a specific fish is not available, you should be able to find another recipe to prepare the fish you do have.

Many fish soups are delicate and require very careful cooking. Generally, fish is easily overcooked; it then becomes tough, rubbery, and unpleasant. It is better to err on the side of undercooking. You can always cook it a minute or two longer if necessary. Shellfish are even more delicate and require closer attention. In fact, many recipes recommend cooking times that are entirely too long. Although the author has tried to give accurate times, many factors are involved. Average shrimp in one locale may be larger or smaller in another. Scallops can vary greatly in size from one batch to the next. The temperature of the fish and the quantity added can affect the time required to cook it properly. The sensitive cook will use the times as guidelines and attend to the soups as they cook. If necessary, remove the fish after it is cooked and return it later.

In many of the recipes, there is a base to which the fish is added during the last minutes before serving. If there is a delay in serving, do not add the fish. Turn off the heat and let the soup cool. Then reheat it quickly, add the fish, cook, and serve. If you try to keep the finished soup warm over low heat, you will certainly have overcooked fish.

One of the most delicious soups in this book, in the author's opinion, is the Soupe de Poissons from France. It is similar to Bouillabaisse in its flavor, but it has no fish in it when it is served. The cost of this soup is extremely reasonable because it is made from fish carcasses, which are usually discarded. It is as delicious as Bouillabaisse but costs a fraction of the amount. If you are inclined to add fish, the selection is up to you. You can add one or a large variety of fish. On the other hand, there is Soupe aux Poissons, which is Bouillabaisse by another name. It is made with the same base and whatever variety of fish you desire or can afford.

## La Soupe de Poissons I (French Fish Soup I)

1 cup sliced onions
1 cup sliced leeks
1/2 cup olive oil
6 tomatoes, chopped
6 garlic cloves, crushed
8 sprigs parsley
1/2 teaspoon thyme
1/4 teaspoon fennel seeds
1/2 teaspoon saffron

1/2 teaspoon dried orange peel
4 pounds fish trimmings (see note)
1-1/2 quarts water
1 tablespoon salt
croutons (see Index)
Rouille (see following recipe)
grated Gruyère cheese

In a 10- to 12-quart kettle, sweat the onions and leeks in the oil until soft. Stir in the tomatoes and garlic and sweat until the tomatoes start to give up their liquid. Add the parsley, thyme, fennel, saffron, orange peel, fish trimmings, water, and salt. Simmer, uncovered, for 30 to 40 minutes.

Strain through a colander, pressing firmly on the ingredients to extract the flavors. Discard the contents of the colander. Strain through a sieve, pressing on any remaining ingredients to extract as much flavor as possible.

Serve the soup with croutons, rouille, and grated cheese.

Can be frozen or refrigerated for 2 to 3 days.

*Yield: about 2 quarts*

*Note:* Fish trimmings include the heads and bodies of white fish, such as haddock, sole, cod, and cusk. Shrimp shells and lobster bodies can also be used.

*Rouille*

2 garlic cloves
2 red peppers, peeled, or 2 roasted peppers
2 egg yolks

6 tablespoons olive oil
Tabasco sauce
salt and pepper

In a processor or blender, purée the garlic and peppers. Add the egg yolks and, with the machine running, add the olive oil in a slow, steady stream. Correct the seasoning with Tabasco, salt, and pepper.

*Yield: about 1-1/2 cups*

---

## La Soupe De Poissons II (French Fish Soup II)

| | |
|---|---|
| 2 onions, minced | 1/2 teaspoon thyme |
| 1/4 cup olive oil | 1/2 teaspoon fennel |
| 2 pounds snapper, perch, | 4 large tomatoes, peeled |
|    cod, and/or black bass, cut | 1/2 teaspoon saffron |
|    in 2-inch cubes | salt and pepper |
| 2 garlic cloves, minced | garlic croutons (see Index) |

In a large pot, sweat the onions in the oil until soft. Turn up the heat and add the fish, garlic, thyme, fennel, and tomatoes. Cook over high heat for 20 minutes, stirring often.

Add cold water to a level twice the depth of the fish. Bring to a boil and cook over high heat for 20 minutes. Force through a food mill and press through a fine sieve, pressing to extract all the juices.

Dissolve the saffron in a little soup. Add to the soup and reheat. Correct the seasoning with salt and pepper.

Serve with croutons. This soup can also be served with rouille (see preceding recipe) or grated Gruyère cheese.

Can be made 2 or 3 days ahead. Can be frozen.

*Yield: 6 servings*

## Soupe De Poisson au Vermicelle et Pernod (Fish Soup with Pasta and Pernod)

2 cups minced onions
1 cup minced celery
1 cup minced leeks
2 tablespoons minced garlic
1/4 cup olive oil
1 teaspoon saffron threads, crumbled
3 pounds fish bones
2-1/2 cups drained canned tomatoes

1 cup white wine
6 tablespoons tomato paste
1 bay leaf
1/4 cup minced parsley
4 sprigs thyme
salt and pepper
3/4 cup vermicelli, broken
1 to 3 tablespoons Pernod
1/4 cup minced basil

In a 10-quart kettle, sweat the onions, celery, leeks, and garlic in the oil until soft. Add the saffron, fish bones, tomatoes, wine, tomato paste, bay leaf, parsley, thyme, and salt and pepper to taste. Simmer over moderately high heat for 20 minutes.

Strain, pressing out as much liquid as possible. Discard the solids.

Bring the soup to a boil, add the vermicelli, and simmer until tender. Add the Pernod to taste. Serve in bowls and sprinkle with the basil. Or serve with croutons, rouille (see Index), or grated Gruyère cheese.

*Yield: 6 to 8 servings*

## Soupe aux Poissons (Soup with Fish)

3 tablespoons minced shallots
1/3 cup olive oil
3 cloves garlic, minced
1/2 cup minced parsley
1 tablespoon crushed saffron
3 cups tomato purée
3-1/2 cups fish stock
1 cup dry white wine
salt and pepper
1 teaspoon crushed, dried mint
1 teaspoon crushed, dried basil

cayenne pepper
3 small lobsters, quartered
1/2 pound scallops
12 shrimp, shelled and deveined
1 pound cod fillets, cut in 6 pieces
12 littleneck clams
2 tablespoons Ricard or Pernod
garlic croutons (see Index)
grated Gruyère cheese

In a 10-quart kettle, sweat the shallot in the oil until soft. Add the garlic and cook until soft. Stir in the parsley, saffron, tomato purée, fish stock, wine, salt, pepper, mint, basil, and cayenne. Boil rapidly for 15 minutes.

Add the lobsters and simmer 10 minutes. Add the scallops, shrimp, cod, and clams and simmer until the clams open, about 4 minutes. Stir in the liqueur.

Pass croutons and Gruyère cheese separately.

*Yield: 6 to 8 servings*

*Note:* The base can be made ahead or frozen. Add the fish just before serving.

## Bouillabaisse (Provençale Fish Soup)

There are dozens of versions of Bouillabaisse, based on the day's catch. In France the soup must have rascasse, a rather ugly looking fish not found in American waters. If you or your guests are purists, call this recipe Bouillabaisse Americaine or Soupe Aux Poissons.

| | |
|---|---|
| 2 leeks, chopped | salt and pepper |
| 1 onion, chopped | 2 lobsters, quartered |
| 1 carrot, chopped | 1 pound eel |
| 1/2 cup olive oil | 2 cups tomato juice |
| 1 pound tomatoes, peeled and seeded | 2 quarts water |
| 2 or 3 garlic cloves, crushed | 1-1/4 pounds striped bass, cut up |
| 2 tablespoons minced parsley | 1-1/4 pounds sea bass, cut up |
| 1 teaspoon saffron | 2 pounds Spanish mackerel, cut up |
| 1 small bay leaf | 2 pounds red snapper |
| pinch of thyme | 2 dozen hard-shell clams, scrubbed |
| pinch of chopped, fresh fennel tips | 2 dozen mussels, scrubbed |

In a large kettle, sweat the leeks, onions, and carrots in the oil until soft. Add the tomatoes, garlic, parsley, saffron, bay leaf, thyme, fennel, salt, and pepper. Arrange the lobster and eel on top of the vegetables and add the tomato juice and water. Bring to a full boil.

Add the bass, mackerel, and snapper. Boil hard for 10 minutes. Add the clams and mussels and cook until the shells open. Correct the seasoning with salt and pepper.

Serve the broth and fish together in large soup bowls, or serve the broth first and then the fish.

*Yield: 6 to 8 servings*

*Note:* This soup must be made and served immediately. Do not try to hold it. If necessary, have your guests wait for the soup. The soup must be boiled rapidly in order to amalgamate the flavors.

## Cacciucco (Italian Fish Soup)

This soup is more fish than liquid and as much a stew as a soup.

| | |
|---|---|
| 1 live lobster | 1-1/4 teaspoons salt |
| 1/2 pound sole or halibut | pinch of crushed red pepper |
| 1 pound sea bass | pinch of sage |
| 1/2 pound scallops | 3/4 cup dry white wine |
| 1/2 cup olive oil | 2 tablespoons tomato paste |
| 2 garlic cloves, minced | 4 cups clam juice |
| 1 tablespoon minced parsley | salt and pepper |

Plunge lobster into boiling, salted water. Cover and cook 6 minutes. Remove lobster and let cool. Remove meat from lobster, reserving the shell. Dice the meat and set aside.

Cut the fish into bite-size pieces.

In a 4-quart casserole, heat the oil and sauté the garlic and parsley for 1 minute. Add the lobster, salt, red pepper, and sage. Cover and cook over low heat for 5 minutes.

Add the wine and cook over high heat for 5 minutes. Add the tomato paste, clam juice, fish, and scallops. Simmer for 5 to 10 minutes, or until the fish is just cooked. Correct the seasoning with salt and pepper.

Serve in deep plates accompanied by Italian bread to soak up the juices.

*Yield: 4 servings*

## Broeto (Venetian Fish Soup)

After poaching, the fish in this recipe are sautéed in garlic oil.

1 quart water
2 pounds mixed small fish
   (see note)
2 tomatoes, chopped
1/2 lemon
1 pound striped bass
1 pound red snapper

2 tablespoons butter
3 tablespoons olive oil
1 garlic clove, crushed
salt
croutons, sautéed in oil (see
   Index)
1 tablespoon minced parsley

Bring the water to a boil. Add the small fish, tomatoes, and lemon. Simmer 30 minutes. Remove fish from the soup and bone. Purée the fish.

Strain the fish broth and combine with the fish purée. Poach the bass and snapper in this broth until cooked. Drain and bone the fish, and cut into large pieces.

In a skillet, heat the butter and oil and sauté the garlic until it starts to turn golden. Remove the garlic and discard. Sauté the fish in the oil until lightly colored on both sides. Add the fish and garlic oil to the soup. Simmer 5 minutes. Correct the seasoning with salt.

Serve in deep dishes with croutons. Sprinkle with parsley.

Can be prepared ahead and reheated.

*Yield: 6 servings*

*Note:* Use butterfish, smelts, or small flounder for the small fish. The fish, including the bass and snapper, should be gutted and used whole.

## Fish Soup in Cream

1 onion, minced
1 cup diced leeks
1/2 cup diced celery
6 tablespoons butter
1 pint clam juice
2 cups dry white wine
2 garlic cloves, crushed
1 bay leaf
1/2 teaspoon dried thyme
1/4 teaspoon black pepper
Tabasco sauce
1/3 cup minced parsley

12 littleneck clams, scrubbed
1 pound red snapper or sea
  bass, cut in 1-1/2-inch
  squares
3/4 pound sole, cut in 2-1/2-
  inch squares
12 shrimp, shelled and
  deveined
1 cup heavy cream, scalded
croutons (see Index)
white pepper

In a 4-quart kettle, sweat the onion, leeks, and celery in the butter until tender. Add the clam juice, wine, garlic, bay leaf, thyme, black pepper, Tabasco to taste, and 1/4 cup parsley. Simmer, uncovered, for 5 minutes.

Add the clams and simmer 3 minutes. Add the snapper and simmer 3 minutes. Add the sole and shrimp and simmer 3 minutes longer, or until the fish is just cooked and clam shells open. Discard the bay leaf.

Add the cream and swirl the pot to mix.

Ladle into soup plates and sprinkle with remaining parsley. Serve the croutons and white pepper separately.

*Yield: 4 to 6 servings*

## Merano Fish Soup

3/4 cup chopped carrot
3/4 cup chopped celery
1 cup chopped onions
1/2 cup chopped leek
1/2 cup olive oil
2 cups dry white wine
3 cups fish stock, or water
2 tablespoons minced
  parsley
1 garlic clove, peeled
salt and pepper

1 teaspoon curry powder
1 pound cod, cut in 1-1/2-
  inch cubes
1/2 pound shrimp, shelled
  and deveined
1/2 pound scallops
1 cup rice, boiled 15 minutes
  and drained
pinch of saffron
2 tablespoons minced chives

In a 4-quart kettle, sweat the carrot, celery, onions, and leek in the oil until soft. Add the wine, fish stock, parsley, garlic, and salt and pepper to taste. Simmer 15 minutes or until vegetables are tender.

In a small bowl, mix the curry powder with 2 tablespoons of soup. Add to the soup with the fish, shrimp, scallops, and rice. Cook over moderate heat for 4 minutes, or until the fish are just cooked. Stir in the saffron and correct the seasoning with salt and pepper.

Serve garnished with chives.

*Yield: 4 to 6 servings*

---

## Cioppino (American Fish Soup)

The Italian name for this soup belies the fact that it was a creation of cooks on the San Francisco waterfront.

1 cup chopped onion
1 green pepper, chopped
2 garlic cloves, minced
1/2 cup olive oil
4 tomatoes, peeled, seeded, and chopped
2 tablespoons tomato paste
2 cups dry white wine
1/2 cup minced, flat leaf parsley

1 teaspoon salt
pepper
1-1/2 pounds lobster, cut up
1-1/2 pounds cod or haddock fillets, cut in 2-inch cubes
1 pound shrimp, peeled and deveined
18 littleneck clams, scrubbed
18 mussels, scrubbed

In an 8-quart casserole, sweat the onion, pepper, and garlic in the oil until soft, but not brown. Add the tomatoes, tomato paste, wine, 1/4 cup minced parsley, salt, and pepper to taste. Simmer, half covered, for 15 minutes.

Add the lobster, baste with the juices, and cook, covered, over low heat for 10 minutes. Add the fish and simmer, covered, for 5 minutes. Add the shrimp, clams, and mussels and simmer 4 to 8 minutes, or until the clams and mussels open their shells.

Serve sprinkled with remaining parsley.

*Yield: 6 servings*

## Soupe aux Langoustines d'Orthez (Soup with Langoustines)

Langoustines in the shell are difficult to find in the United States. You can make this soup very successfully with lobster, crab, or shrimp.

1 pound cooked lobster or langoustines
1 pound cod
2 onions, chopped
2 carrots, sliced
2 potatoes, sliced
1 teaspoon dried thyme
1 tablespoon minced parsley
3 or 4 cloves garlic, crushed
3/4 cup dry white wine or cider

2 lemons
1 pound tomatoes, peeled and seeded
1 pimiento, minced
salt and pepper
1/4 cup rice
2 eggs, beaten
minced parsley

Shell the lobster or langoustines, reserving the meat.

In a 5-quart kettle, combine the lobster shells, 1 onion, carrots, potatoes, thyme, 1 tablespoon parsley, garlic, wine, and 1 thinly sliced lemon. Add 3 quarts water and simmer for 2 hours. Strain into a clean pan.

In a skillet, combine the remaining onion, tomatoes, and pimiento and season to taste with salt and pepper. Cook over low heat until reduced to a pulp. Purée.

Mix the purée into the soup. Add the rice and cook until tender. Dice the reserved lobster meat and stir in.

Grate the peel from the remaining lemon and reserve. In a small bowl, combine the juice of the lemon and the eggs. Mix well.

Add 1 cup hot soup to the egg mixture. Mix well and return the mixture to the soup. Cook over low heat until hot and slightly thickened.

Serve sprinkled with lemon peel and parsley.

The stock can be made ahead and frozen. Do not finish with eggs until almost ready to serve.

*Yield: 6 servings*

## Ttioro (Basque Fish Soup I)

2 cups chopped onion
2/3 cup chopped celery
  leaves
2 garlic cloves, crushed
3 tablespoons butter
56 ounces canned tomatoes
1 cup chicken stock
2/3 cup white wine

2 teaspoons salt
1/2 to 3/4 teaspoon Tabasco
  sauce
1/2 teaspoon dried thyme
1 cup minced parsley
1 pound fish fillets, cut into
  1-inch squares

In a large saucepan, sweat the onion, celery, and garlic in the butter until soft. Add the tomatoes, chicken stock, wine, salt, Tabasco, and thyme. Simmer, uncovered, for 30 minutes.

Add the parsley and fish and cook until the fish is just cooked, about 4 minutes.

The base can be made ahead and refrigerated or frozen. Do not cook the fish until just before serving.

*Yield: 8 servings*

## Ttioro (Basque Fish Soup II)

1-1/2 pound lobster
3 cups chicken stock
2 pounds shrimp
1 bottle dry white wine
3 onions
1 pound celery with leaves,
  chopped
4 cloves
1 red pepper, julienne

1 green pepper, julienne
1 bay leaf
1/4 teaspoon dried red
  pepper flakes
1/4 teaspoon dried thyme
1/2 teaspoon turmeric
1 pound large scallops,
  sliced
chopped celery leaves

Plunge lobster into boiling, salted water. Cover and cook 6 minutes. Remove lobster and let cool. Remove meat from lobster, reserving the shell. Dice the meat and set aside.

Chop the shell and put into an 8-quart pot with the chicken stock and shrimp. Bring to a boil. Remove the shrimp, shell, and return shells to the soup. Add 2 cups wine and simmer 10 minutes. Strain, discarding the shells. Return the stock to the pot.

Cut 2 onions into thin slices and stud the third onion with the cloves. Add the onions, celery, peppers, bay leaf, pepper flakes, thyme, and turmeric to the stock. Add the remaining wine and simmer until the celery is tender, about 30 minutes.

Add the scallops and reserved shrimp and lobster. Bring just to a boil. Discard the clove-studded onion and the bay leaf.

Serve sprinkled with chopped celery leaves.

Can be prepared ahead and reheated.

*Yield: 6 to 8 servings*

## New England Clam Chowder

1/4 pound salt pork, diced
2 cups minced onion
3 cups diced potatoes
1/2 teaspoon dried thyme
2 cups water

4 cups minced chowder
    clams and their liquor
1 quart milk
2 tablespoons butter
salt and pepper

In a 3-quart kettle, render the salt pork until crisp. Remove and drain.

Add the onion to the fat in the kettle and cook, stirring, until soft, but not brown. Add the potatoes, thyme, and water and simmer until the potatoes are tender. Add the clams, the liquor, milk, butter, and salt and pepper to taste. Simmer 10 minutes.

Can be made ahead and reheated. Can be frozen.

*Yield: 6 to 8 servings*

## Manhattan Clam Chowder

1 cup minced onion
1/4 cup minced carrot
1/4 cup minced celery
4 tablespoons butter
4 large tomatoes, peeled,
    seeded, and chopped
2 cups minced clams and
    their liquor

3 cups water
1 bay leaf
1/2 teaspoon dried thyme,
    crumbled
pepper
3 potatoes, diced

In a 4-quart kettle, sweat the onion, carrot, and celery in the butter until soft. Add the tomatoes, clam liquor, water, bay leaf, thyme, and pepper. Simmer 25 minutes. Add the potatoes and simmer 15 minutes, or until tender. Add the clams and cook for 2 to 3 minutes. Discard the bay leaf.

Can be made ahead and reheated.

*Yield: 6 servings*

## New England Fish Chowder

1/4 pound salt pork, diced
1 cup chopped onions
2 cups water
2 potatoes, diced
1 pound cod or haddock
    fillets, cut in 1-inch cubes

1 quart milk
salt and pepper
pinch of dried thyme,
    crumbled

In a 4-quart kettle, render the salt pork until crisp. Drain on paper toweling. Sauté the onions in the fat until soft. Add the water and potatoes and simmer until the potatoes are barely tender.

Add the fish and milk and bring to a boil. Correct the seasoning with salt and pepper. Add thyme if desired.

Can be prepared ahead and reheated.

*Yield: 6 servings*

## Corn and Clam Chowder

4 thick slices bacon, diced
1 cup minced onion
2 potatoes, diced
1 cup clam juice
1 bay leaf
pinch of dried thyme,
    crumbled
1 tablespoon cornstarch

3 cups light cream
2 cups corn kernels
3 tablespoons minced
    parsley
1 cup minced clams
salt and pepper
1 tablespoon minced parsley

In a 3-quart casserole, sauté the bacon until crisp and brown. Remove bacon and drain. Discard all but 2 tablespoons of bacon fat.

Sauté the onions in bacon fat until soft. Add the potatoes and cook, stirring, for 3 minutes. Add the clam juice, bay leaf, and thyme. Simmer until the potatoes are tender.

In a bowl, combine the cornstarch with 2 tablespoons cream. Stir the remaining cream into the potato mixture. Stir in the cornstarch mixture and simmer for 3 minutes. Add the corn and parsley and simmer 5 minutes. Add the clams, salt, and pepper and heat.

Serve garnished with bacon and parsley.

Can be made ahead and reheated.

*Yield: 6 servings*

---

## Cauliflower and Clam Chowder

| | |
|---|---|
| 2 carrots, diced | 8 ounces clam juice |
| 1 small onion, diced | 1/2 cup dry white wine |
| 1 celery stalk, diced | 1 small cauliflower, cut in |
| 1 shallot, minced | florets |
| 2 tablespoons butter | 1/2 cup heavy cream |
| 1-1/2 tablespoons flour | 2 tablespoons sherry |
| 3 6-1/2-ounce cans chopped | 1 teaspoon minced parsley |
| clams | 1/2 teaspoon dried thyme |
| 2 cups water | 1/2 teaspoon dried tarragon |

In a 3-quart kettle, sweat the carrots, onion, celery, and shallot in the butter until soft. Blend in the flour and cook, stirring, for 2 minutes.

Drain and reserve the juice from the clams. Stir the clam juice, water, additional 8 ounces clam juice, and wine into the soup. Bring to a boil, add the cauliflower, and simmer until tender. Stir in the clams, cream, sherry, parsley, thyme, and tarragon. Simmer 5 minutes.

Can be made ahead and reheated. Can be frozen.

*Yield: 6 servings*

## Creamed Crab Soup

2 tablespoons butter
grated rind of 1 lemon
1 tablespoon flour
1 tablespoon Worcestershire
  sauce
pinch of mace
2 hard-cooked eggs, chopped
2 cups cooked crabmeat

3 mushrooms, minced
3 celery stalks, minced
1 scallion, minced
1 tablespoon butter
4 cups milk, scalded
1 cup cream, scalded
salt and pepper
1 cup dry sherry

In a medium-size bowl, mash 2 tablespoons butter to a paste with the lemon rind, flour, Worcestershire, mace, and eggs. Mix with the crabmeat and set aside.

In a 3-quart kettle, sweat the mushrooms, celery, and scallion in the remaining butter until soft. Stir in the milk, cream, and crabmeat paste and heat until hot. Do not boil. Correct the seasoning with salt and pepper. Add the sherry and reheat.

Can be made ahead and reheated.

*Yield: 6 servings*

## Scallop Chowder

3 potatoes, diced
1 carrot, chopped
1 celery stalk, chopped
1 onion, chopped
2 cups chicken stock
1/2 teaspoon salt
1/4 teaspoon pepper
1/2 bay leaf, crumbled
1/2 teaspoon thyme,
  crumbled

1/2 pound mushrooms, sliced
1-1/2 tablespoons butter
1 pound bay scallops
1/2 cup dry white wine
1 cup heavy cream
1 egg yolk, lightly beaten
3 tablespoons minced
  parsley
paprika, optional

In a 6-quart kettle, cover and simmer the potatoes, carrot, celery, onion, chicken stock, salt, pepper, bay leaf, and thyme until tender. Discard the bay leaf. Purée the mixture in a processor or blender. Sauté the mushrooms in the butter. Add the scallops and wine and cook 1 minute.

In a bowl, combine the cream and egg yolk. Add 1 cup hot soup. Return the mixture to the soup and heat gently.

Combine the mushroom-scallop mixture with the soup and heat. Do not boil.

Serve garnished with parsley and paprika.

The soup base can be made ahead and frozen. Prepare the mushroom-scallop mixture just before serving.

*Yield: 4 to 6 servings*

## Shrimp and Feta Cheese Chowder

1 onion, minced
1 garlic clove, crushed
2 tablespoons lard
2 potatoes, diced
1 tomato, peeled, seeded,
  and chopped
1 tablespoon rice
1/4 teaspoon crushed red
  pepper

1/2 teaspoon oregano
salt and pepper
1-1/2 cups water
12 shrimp, shelled
2-1/2 cups milk
1/4 cup feta cheese,
  crumbled

In a 2-quart saucepan, sauté the onion and garlic in the lard until golden. Add the potatoes, tomato, rice, red pepper, oregano, salt and pepper to taste, and just enough water to cover the ingredients. Simmer, covered, for 15 minutes, or until the potatoes are tender.

Cut the shrimp in half lengthwise. Add to the soup with the milk. Simmer 2 minutes and stir in the cheese. Correct the seasoning.

Can be made ahead and reheated.

*Yield: 6 servings*

## Soupe aux Moules du Calvados (Normandy Mussel Soup)

4 onions, thinly sliced
4 carrots, thinly sliced
4 turnips, thinly sliced
2 leeks, sliced
2 celery stalks, thinly sliced
4 potatoes, thinly sliced
4 tablespoons butter
2 quarts chicken stock
5 quarts mussels
2 tomatoes, peeled and
    quartered
2 shallots, minced
2 bunches of parsley
1 teaspoon dried thyme
2 cups white wine
1 cup heavy cream
salt and pepper
1/4 pound Parmesan cheese,
    grated
1 head garlic, peeled
16 croutons, sautéed in
    butter (see Index)

In a 4-quart kettle, sweat the onions, carrots, turnips, leeks, celery, and potatoes in the butter for 20 minutes. Add the stock and simmer 45 minutes.

Scrub the mussels and remove beards. In another kettle, combine the mussels, tomatoes, shallots, parsley, thyme, wine, and cream. Cover tightly and bring to a boil. Cook over high heat until the mussels have opened.

Remove mussels from the shells, discarding the shells and any unopened mussels. Strain the cooking liquid. Add the mussels and cooking liquid to the vegetable mixture and heat. Correct the seasoning with salt and pepper.

In a processor, purée the cheese and garlic and spread on the croutons. Heat in the oven. Serve croutons with the soup.

Can be made 1 or 2 days ahead. Can be frozen.
*Yield: 8 servings*

## Soupe de Moules et Petoncles au Safran (Mussel and Scallop Soup with Saffron)

3 pounds mussels, scrubbed
5 shallots, chopped
2 tablespoons chopped parsley
1 bay leaf
pinch of thyme
pepper
1/2 cup white wine
1 cup water
2 cups fish stock
6 tablespoons butter
5 tablespoons flour

1 cup heavy cream
2 pinches of saffron, brought to a boil in 1/4 cup white wine
1/4 pound bay scallops
1 tablespoon julienne of leek
1 tablespoon julienne of carrot
1 tablespoon julienne of celery
1 cup fish stock
salt and pepper

Soak the mussels in water for 1 to 2 hours to clean them. Drain and place in a 4-quart pot with the shallots, parsley, bay leaf, thyme, pepper, wine, water, and fish stock. Cover and bring to a boil over high heat. Cook until the shells open, about 5 minutes. Remove mussels, reserve meat for another use, and discard the shells.

Strain the broth into a noncorrosive saucepan and reduce over high heat for 5 minutes.

In another saucepan, melt 4 tablespoons butter and stir in the flour. Cook over low heat for 2 minutes. Add the mussel broth and bring to a boil, stirring constantly. Simmer 15 minutes. If too thick, add fish stock to thin. Strain through a fine sieve.

In a clean pot, heat the soup and add the cream, saffron, and scallops. Blanch the leek, carrot, and celery in 1 cup fish stock for 2 minutes. Drain. Add to the soup and swirl in remaining 2 tablespoons butter. Correct the seasoning with salt and pepper.

*Yield: 4 to 6 servings*

*Note:* The mussels can be served with the soup. If prepared ahead or frozen, reheat carefully so the scallops do not overcook.

## Down East Squash and Oyster Soup

| | |
|---|---|
| 2-1/2 cups puréed winter squash | salt and pepper |
| | nutmeg |
| 1 small onion, thinly sliced | 1 cup light cream, scalded |
| 2 cups evaporated milk | 1 pint oysters, drained |
| 1 cup water | 3/4 cup oyster liquor |
| 2 tablespoons butter | paprika |

In a 3-quart kettle, simmer the squash, onion, milk, water, and butter, plus salt, pepper, and nutmeg to taste, for 2 minutes.

Add the cream, oysters, and oyster liquor with a large pinch of paprika. Cook just until the oysters begin to curl.

Can be prepared ahead, but do not add the oysters until just before serving.

*Yield: 6 servings*

## Shrimp Soup with Lemon Grass

| | |
|---|---|
| 1-1/2 quarts chicken stock | 1-1/2 pounds shrimp, shelled |
| 1 tablespoon lemon grass | 4 scallions, minced |
| 1 teaspoon red pepper seeds | 6 sprigs of fresh coriander |
| juice of 1 lemon | (Chinese parsley or |
| dash of Nam Pla (Asian fish sauce) | cilantro) |

Bring the stock to a boil and add lemon grass. Simmer 4 minutes. Add the pepper seeds, lemon juice, and Nam Pla. Lower the heat and add the shrimp. Cook until just done.

Stir in the scallions and coriander.

*Yield: 4 to 6 servings*

*Note:* Lemon grass, Nam Pla, and coriander can be found in Asian markets.

## Fish Ball Soup

1/4 pound fillet of sole
2 ounces ground pork
1 tablespoon cornstarch
1 tablespoon water
4 cups chicken stock

2 scallions, minced
2 tablespoons dry sherry
1 teaspoon salt
1 tablespoon vinegar

In a processor, purée the sole and pork. Add the cornstarch and water and process until combined. Shape into 1-inch balls.

Poach the fish balls in the chicken stock very gently for 15 minutes. Add the scallions, sherry, salt, and vinegar. Heat.

Can be made ahead and reheated. Can be frozen.

*Yield: 4 servings*

*Note:* Do not let the soup boil when poaching or the fish balls may disintegrate.

## Stuffed Flower Soup

1/2 cup Chinese mushrooms,
  soaked
peanut oil
1 pound scallops
1/2 cup water
2 tablespoons sesame oil
1 cup julienne of raw pork
1 onion, minced
1 cup shredded bamboo
  shoots
1/2 cup shredded carrots
1/2 pound shrimp, minced

1/2 pound ground pork
1 tablespoon cornstarch
2 teaspoons sesame oil
2 teaspoons salt
pepper
2 eggs, beaten with
  1 tablespoon milk
8 cups chicken stock
1 tablespoon rice wine or
  sherry
1 tablespoon rice vinegar
1 tablespoon sugar

Shred the mushroom caps.

Oil a 2-quart stainless steel bowl with peanut oil and set aside.

In a small saucepan, poach the scallops in water until just firm, about 1 minute. Set aside and reserve liquid.

Heat the sesame oil in a wok and stir-fry the pork strips and onion until the meat is browned. Remove to a bowl. Stir-fry the mushroom shreds, bamboo shoots, and carrots for 30 seconds.

Remove half the mixture to a bowl and stir in the shrimp, ground pork, cornstarch, sesame oil, salt, and pepper. Mix well. Reserve remaining vegetables.

In a 10-inch skillet, spread about 2 teaspoons peanut oil and heat to the smoking point. Remove the pan from the heat and add the eggs, rotating the pan to spread evenly. Let stand until the eggs are set. They should form a large thin sheet. Slide the egg sheet into the oiled bowl. Repair any tears with pieces of cooked egg.

Shred the scallops and place in the center of the egg-lined bowl. Top with the pork-shrimp mixture, pressing to flatten and smooth the surface. Fold the edges of the egg sheet over the top. Place the bowl in a steamer and steam for 35 to 40 minutes. Remove from the steamer. Invert the bowl over the center of a large, deep serving dish.

In a 3-quart kettle, heat the stock, pork strips, reserved vegetables, wine, vinegar, and sugar until hot. Pour around the egg-scallop ball. With a knife cut the egg sheet into 6 wedges without cutting into the scallop mixture. Fold back the wedges to resemble a flower.

The scallop-egg cake can be made a day ahead. Reheat in steamer before using.

*Yield: 6 servings*

*Note:* To improvise a steamer, see chapter 4.

## MEAT SOUPS

This section contains popular recipes from many countries. Some of the soups are light and almost wistful in flavor; others are among the heartiest and most filling meals. Many of the soups can be prepared in minutes; others take several hours of careful simmering to bring out their superb flavors.

None of the soups is difficult to prepare. With the exception of *Avgolemonou* (Greek egg lemon soup), there are none of the difficulties of the soups presented previously. These soups generally do not have a last-minute enrichment of eggs and cream that can curdle. Furthermore, there is less need to be concerned about overcooking, an important concern with fish soups. Many of these soups can be made a day or two before serving. In fact, they often improve when their flavors have time to meld. Most of them freeze successfully, so you may want to make them in quantity. Freeze them in four- to six-portion containers to make defrosting convenient. They are the perfect solution in case of an emergency or unexpected guests.

## Pasta in Brodo (Pasta in Broth)

Italian households often begin meals with a light first course. Before a substantial dinner, a heavy pasta dish would be inappropriate, but a light, clear tasting broth with a soup pasta floating in it, and possibly a slice of carrot or celery, is the perfect choice.

1/2 cup soup pasta (see note) grated Parmesan cheese
6 to 8 cups broth (see note)

Cook the pasta in boiling stock until al dente. Serve with cheese passed separately.
Can be made ahead and reheated.
*Yield: 6 servings*
*Note:* Soup pasta is any one of a large selection of tiny pastas in various shapes, such as rice, stars, shells, and others. Generally, the tinier the pasta, the less needed. If you use farina, 1 to 2 tablespoons will suffice, whereas you would use about 1/4 to 1/2 cup of tiny shells. However, some people prefer a lot of pasta in relation to the amount of liquid. The broth, and this is true for many Italian soups, can be beef, chicken, or a combination of both. Prepare the broth that appeals to you.

## Tortellini in Brodo, Ravioli in Brodo (Stuffed Pasta in Broth)

1/4 to 1/2 pound tortellini or grated Parmesan cheese
 ravioli
6 to 8 cups broth

In a large kettle, bring 6 quarts salted water to a boil and simmer pasta until al dente. Drain.
Add the cooked pasta to the broth and reheat.
Serve with cheese passed separately.
*Yield: 6 servings*

## Zuppa alla Pavese (Chicken Soup Pavia-style)

6 thick slices Italian bread  
4 tablespoons butter  
8 tablespoons grated  
    Parmesan cheese  
6 eggs  

2-1/2 quarts chicken stock,  
    boiling  
salt and pepper  
grated Parmesan cheese  

Preheat the broiler.

Butter the bread slices, coat with the cheese, and brown under the broiler until golden.

Place a slice of bread into each of 6 soup bowls. Break an egg on top and gently pour on the boiling stock. Pass the remaining cheese.

*Yield: 6 servings*

## Stracciatella alla Romano (Italian Egg-drop Soup)

4 eggs  
1/4 cup grated Parmesan  
    cheese  

8 cups chicken stock  
2 tablespoons minced  
    parsley  

In a bowl, beat the eggs and cheese together until well mixed. Heat the stock to just below the boiling point. Add the egg mixture in a slow, steady stream, stirring constantly, until the eggs separate into shreds. Sprinkle with parsley.

Can be made ahead and reheated.

*Yield: 6 servings*

## Avgolemonou (Greek Egg Lemon Soup)

1/3 cup rice  
6 cups chicken stock  
grated rind of 1 lemon  
5 egg yolks  
juice of 2 lemons  

lemon wedges  
1 to 2 cups heavy cream,  
    optional  
2 tablespoons minced dill,  
    optional  

In a 3-quart kettle, simmer the rice and chicken stock for 30 minutes. Stir in the grated lemon rind.

In a bowl, beat the egg yolks with lemon juice. Add 1 cup hot stock to the mixture. Return the egg mixture to the soup and cook gently until it is thick enough to coat the back of a spoon. Do not boil.

Serve with lemon wedges on the side.

Can be refrigerated for 5 days.

*Yield: 6 servings*

*Note:* To serve cold, purée the soup in a blender or processor and add cream to make desired consistency. Because homemade chicken stock is often gelatinous, it may be necessary to add more cream to thin it. Serve with lemon wedges and minced dill.

---

## Lima Bean and Chicken Soup

3-pound frying chicken, cut up
4 quarts water
bouquet garni of 4 bay leaves, 6 peppercorns, and 1 teaspoon thyme
1 onion stuck with 4 cloves
3 tablespoons flour
5 tablespoons water
2 cups peeled, seeded, and chopped tomatoes

2 potatoes, diced
1 cup cooked corn kernels
2-1/2 cups cooked lima beans
1 teaspoon Worcestershire sauce
1/4 teaspoon cayenne pepper
1 cup heavy cream
salt
2 tablespoons minced parsley

In an 8-quart kettle, simmer the chicken, water, bouquet garni, and onion for 45 minutes, or until the chicken is very tender. Remove chicken, cool, and bone. Dice the meat and set aside.

Strain the stock, put into a pot, and bring to a boil.

In a small bowl, mix the flour and water to form a slurry. Add to the soup, stirring constantly. Add the tomatoes and potatoes and simmer, covered, for 20 minutes.

Add the corn, beans, Worcestershire, and cayenne. Simmer 10 minutes. Add the chicken meat and cream. Correct the seasoning with salt. Serve garnished with parsley.

Can be made ahead. Can be frozen.

*Yield: 6 to 8 servings*

## Tinola (Philippine Chicken Soup)

2 2-1/2-pound chickens, cut up
1-1/2 teaspoons salt
4 tablespoons peanut oil
1 teaspoon gingerroot
1 onion, thinly sliced
2 quarts water
1 cup spinach, shredded

Sprinkle chicken pieces with salt and set aside.

In a 5-quart kettle, heat 2 tablespoons oil and stir-fry the gingerroot for 30 seconds. Add the onion and cook, stirring, until soft, but not brown. Set aside.

Brown the chicken pieces in the kettle, adding more oil if needed. When the chicken is well browned, add the onion and water. Simmer, partially covered, for 40 to 50 minutes, or until the chicken is tender. Just before serving stir in the spinach.

Can be refrigerated for 2 days, or frozen. Do not add spinach until just before serving.

*Yield: 6 servings*

*Note:* Chicken pieces should be about 2 inches. Therefore, the leg and thigh must be cut in two. As the diner eats the soup he chews the meat off the bones. If you wish to avoid serving bones to your guests, bone the cooked chicken and return it to the soup.

## Chicken Corn Soup

2-1/2 pound chicken, cut up
10 cups chicken stock
1/2 cup minced celery
1/4 cup minced parsley
pepper
1 teaspoon salt
1/2 pound egg noodles, broken
2 cups corn kernels
pinch of crumbled saffron
salt and pepper

In a 5-quart kettle, simmer the chicken in the stock until tender, about 30 minutes. Remove the chicken from the stock and cut the meat into 1/2-inch pieces. Set aside.

Add the celery, parsley, pepper to taste, and salt to the stock. Bring to a boil and simmer the noodles, corn, and saffron for 15 minutes, or until the noodles are cooked. Add the chicken to the soup and correct the seasoning with salt and pepper.

Can be prepared ahead. Can be frozen.

*Yield: 6 servings*

*Note:* Cooking the chicken in the stock concentrates the chicken flavor. A less flavorful soup can be made with water.

---

## Minestra di Passatelli d'Urbino (Consommé with Tiny Meatball Dumplings Urbino-style)

1 pound ground beef
3/4 pound spinach, cooked
1-1/2 ounces beef marrow
1 cup grated Parmesan
  cheese
1-1/2 cups soft bread crumbs
3 tablespoons butter,
  softened

5 eggs
nutmeg
salt
2 quarts chicken or beef
  stock
grated Parmesan cheese

The beef must be ground to a smooth paste. If necessary, grind in a processor.

Squeeze excess moisture from the spinach and chop very finely. Chop the marrow very finely.

In a bowl, mix the ground beef, spinach, marrow, Parmesan, bread crumbs, butter, and eggs and work to a smooth paste. Season to taste with nutmeg and salt.

Bring the stock to a full boil. Place the meat in a colander and rub it directly into the soup. Simmer about 5 minutes. Serve additional cheese on the side.

The soup can be frozen.

*Yield: 6 servings*

*Note:* The dumplings should be the size of peppercorns. A *ferro di Passatelli* is used in Urbino, but it is hard to locate here. You can force the mixture through a food mill with the large disk.

---

## Three-color Delicious Soup

1/2 chicken breast, boned
  and skinned
1 egg white
1 tablespoon milk
salt
5 cups chicken stock

3/4 cup cooked peas
1 tomato, peeled, seeded,
  and diced
3 tablespoons cornstarch
1/4 cup water
2 egg whites

In a processor, purée the chicken, 1 egg white, milk, and salt. Fill a pastry bag fitted with a plain #6 large tube.

Bring the stock to a boil and season with salt. Add the peas and tomato. Turn off the heat. Immediately start squeezing the chicken mixture into the broth, cutting off 1/2-inch lengths.

In a small bowl, combine the cornstarch and water and stir into the soup. Beat the remaining egg whites lightly and pour into the soup in a thin, steady stream.

Serve immediately without reheating, if possible. The chicken dumplings should be just cooked.

*Yield: 6 servings*

*Note:* If you do not have a pastry bag and tube, shape the mixture as follows. Rinse your hand under cold water, scoop up a handful of the chicken mixture, and squeeze a small amount through the space between your thumb and index finger. Scoop it off with a teaspoon and add to the soup. This technique is easier than it sounds.

## Woh Mein (Chinese Soup with Noodles)

8 cups chicken stock
1 cup snow peas, shredded
1/4 cup water chestnuts, sliced
1/4 pound small mushrooms, halved
1/2 chicken breast, cooked and shredded
2 chicken gizzards, boiled, peeled, and sliced
1 pound fresh Chinese noodles or vermicelli, cooked and drained

2 chicken livers, blanched and sliced
1/4 pound shrimp, peeled
1/4 pound roast pork, shredded
1 cup thinly sliced abalone, optional
3 scallions, minced
1 teaspoon sesame oil

In a 4-quart casserole, bring the stock to a boil. Add the snow peas, water chestnuts, and mushrooms. Simmer 2 minutes. Add the chicken breasts and gizzards and simmer 2 minutes. Add the noodles, livers, shrimp, and pork. Simmer 2 minutes longer. Add the abalone, remove from the heat, and stir. Sprinkle with scallions and sesame oil.

The various components can be prepared ahead and frozen separately.

*Yield: 6 to 8 servings*

*Note:* This wonderful dish has a large quantity of noodles plus many other ingredients. You can omit one or two ingredients and add others, such as roast duck, crab, Chinese mushrooms, or carrot slices.

You can change the basic flavor by adding 1 teaspoon minced gingerroot and 1 or 2 minced garlic cloves.

## Clouds in Spring Soup

1/2 chicken breast, skinned and boned
1 teaspoon cornstarch
1/2 teaspoon salt
1 teaspoon hot pepper oil
2 cups boiling water
4 cups chicken stock
1-inch piece gingerroot, minced
1-1/2 cups watercress leaves
1/2 cup sliced mushrooms
2 egg whites, lightly beaten
1-1/2 teaspoons salt
1/2 teaspoon sesame oil

Cut the chicken into 1-1/2-inch slices, 1/2 inch wide and 1/4 inch thick.

In a bowl, combine the chicken, cornstarch, salt, and oil and mix well. Let stand for 5 minutes. Poach in boiling water 2 minutes. Drain.

Heat the chicken stock and gingerroot and add the chicken, watercress, and mushrooms. Bring to a boil, remove from the heat, and add the egg whites in a slow, steady stream, stirring constantly. Stir in the salt and sesame oil.

*Yield: 4 servings*

## Potage d'Hiver (Winter Soup)

3 tablespoons olive oil
1/2 cup minced parsley
2 garlic cloves, minced
1 onion, minced
2 ounces ham, chopped
1/2 teaspoon dried basil
1/2 teaspoon dried thyme
8 canned tomatoes
3 tablespoons tomato paste
4 cups beef or chicken stock
2 carrots, sliced
1 potato, chopped or sliced
1 cup cauliflower, in florets

1-1/2 cups lima beans
1 small cabbage, shredded
2 celery stalks, sliced
3 leeks, chopped
2 small zucchini, sliced
10-ounce package frozen fava
 beans
1 cup peas
1 cup chopped mushrooms
1 pound meatballs (see
 following recipe)
grated Parmesan cheese

In a large kettle, sauté the parsley, garlic, onion, and ham in the oil until the onion is soft. Add the basil, thyme, tomatoes, tomato paste, and stock. Simmer 30 minutes.

Purée in a processor or force through a food mill. Return to the kettle and add the carrots, potato, cauliflower, and lima beans. Simmer 20 minutes. Add the cabbage, celery, leeks, zucchini, fava beans, peas, mushrooms, and meatballs. Simmer until vegetables are tender-crisp, about 10 to 15 minutes.

Pass the cheese separately.

*Yield: 6 to 12 servings, depending on the number of vegetables used*

*Note:* From the list of vegetables, select as many or as few as you wish.

### Meatballs

1 pound ground beef
1 egg
3 tablespoons grated
 Parmesan cheese

2 teaspoons dried basil
salt and pepper

In a bowl, combine the beef, egg, Parmesan, basil, and salt and pepper to taste. Mix well.

Shape into 1-inch balls. Poach in the soup, or sauté in butter before adding to the soup.

## Czechoslovakian Beef and Cabbage Soup

2 pounds beef bones
1 cup chopped onion
3 carrots, chopped
2 garlic cloves, chopped
1 bay leaf
2 pounds beef short ribs
2 teaspoons dried thyme
1/4 teaspoon paprika
8 cups water

8 cups shredded cabbage
2 pounds canned tomatoes
salt
Tabasco sauce
1/4 cup minced parsley
3 tablespoons lemon juice
3 tablespoons sugar
1 pound sauerkraut
sour cream

Preheat oven to 450°F.

In a roasting pan, combine the beef bones, onion, carrots, garlic, bay leaf, short ribs, thyme, and paprika. Roast until meat is browned, about 45 minutes.

Transfer the meat and vegetables to a 10-quart kettle. Add the water, cabbage, tomatoes, and salt and Tabasco to taste. Simmer, covered, for 1-1/2 hours. Skim off the fat. Add the parsley, lemon juice, sugar, and sauerkraut. Simmer, uncovered, for 1 hour.

Remove the bones and short ribs from the kettle. Remove meat from the bones and cut into cubes. Return to the kettle. Simmer 5 minutes.

Serve with sour cream.

Can be made 4 or 5 days ahead. Can be frozen.

*Yield: 10 to 12 servings*

## Philippine Hamburger Soup

2 onions, chopped
1 garlic clove, crushed
2 tablespoons butter
1 pound ground beef
2 potatoes, cubed and
  parboiled

2 tomatoes, peeled, seeded,
  and chopped
3 cups beef stock
salt and pepper

Sauté the onions and garlic in the butter until soft. Add the beef and cook, stirring to break up the lumps, until it is no longer pink. Add the potatoes and tomatoes and cook, stirring, for 10 minutes.

Add beef stock and correct the seasoning with salt and pepper. Simmer 20 minutes.

Can be made ahead and reheated. Can be frozen.

*Yield: 4 to 6 servings*

---

## Chinese Bean Curd and Beef Ball Soup

1/2 cup minced scallions
1/2 pound ground beef
2 teaspoons cornstarch
salt
1 cake bean curd

4 to 5 cups chicken stock
2 to 3 leaves iceberg lettuce, shredded
pepper

Pour enough boiling water over the scallions in a cup to just cover.

Place beef in a bowl and add cornstarch and the salt to taste. Strain 1 tablespoon of liquid from scallions and add to the meat. Discard remaining liquid and scallions.

Mix meat until combined. Crumble the bean curd and beat into the meat. Shape the mixture into 16 to 18 1-inch meatballs.

Heat the stock almost to boiling and add the meatballs. Simmer until they rise to the surface. Taste for seasoning and correct with salt.

Put shredded lettuce in bowls and sprinkle with pepper. Pour on the soup and meatballs.

Can be made ahead. Can be frozen.

*Yield: 4 to 6 servings*

## Gulyassuppe (Goulash Soup)

1/4 pound bacon, diced
2 onions, chopped
1 teaspoon Hungarian
   paprika
1/2 teaspoon caraway seeds
pinch of marjoram
1 garlic clove, crushed
6 cups beef stock
1 pound beef chuck, cut in
   1/2-inch cubes

1 teaspoon salt
3 tomatoes, peeled, seeded,
   and chopped
2 potatoes, diced
1/4 cup flour
3/4 cup water
3 beef frankfurters, cooked
salt and pepper
lemon juice

In a 4-quart kettle, heat the bacon until its fat begins to flow. Add the onions and sauté until golden. Stir in the paprika, caraway seeds, marjoram, and garlic. Cook, stirring, for 2 to 3 minutes.

Add the stock, beef, salt, and tomatoes. Simmer 20 minutes or until the meat is almost tender. Add the potatoes and more stock, if needed. Cook until potatoes and meat are tender.

In a bowl, mix the flour and water to make a slurry. Add it to the soup in a stream, stirring constantly. Simmer until thickened.

Skin the frankfurters if necessary and cut into 1/4-inch slices. Add to the soup and simmer for 5 minutes. Correct the seasoning with salt, pepper, and lemon juice.

This soup should preferably be made 2 or 3 days before serving. Can be frozen.

*Yield: 6 to 8 servings*

## Corned Beef and Cabbage Soup

2 cups milk
2 tablespoons cornstarch
1/2 teaspoon salt
1/4 teaspoon pepper
1 cup thinly sliced celery
2 garlic cloves, minced
1/2 cup minced onion

1/4 cup butter
2 cups chicken stock
2 cups shredded cabbage
1 cup thinly sliced carrot
1/4 pound corned beef,
   shredded

In a 1-quart saucepan, stir the cold milk into the cornstarch and season with salt and pepper. Cook, stirring constantly, over medium heat and bring to a boil. Boil 1 minute. Remove from heat and set aside.

In a 2-quart saucepan, sweat the celery, garlic, and onion in the butter until soft. Add the stock, cabbage, carrot, and corned beef. Simmer 20 minutes, or until the vegetables are tender. Stir in the milk and heat through.

Can be made 1 or 2 days ahead and reheated. Can be frozen.

*Yield: 6 servings*

---

## Zuppa di Pomodoro con Polpettine di Vitello (Tomato and Veal Meatball Soup)

4 potatoes, sliced
5 cups peeled, seeded, and chopped tomatoes
1/4 pound prosciutto, chopped
1/2 cup chopped onions
1/4 cup chopped carrots
1/4 cup chopped celery
2 garlic cloves, chopped
2 tablespoons minced parsley
1-1/2 teaspoons salt
1/2 teaspoon pepper
5-1/2 cups chicken stock
1 tablespoon butter
1/2 pound ground veal
2 egg yolks
2 slices white bread (crusts removed), soaked in milk and squeezed dry
2 tablespoons grated Parmesan cheese
pinch of grated nutmeg

Place potatoes, tomatoes, prosciutto, 1/4 cup onion, carrots, celery, garlic, parsley, 1 teaspoon salt, 1/4 teaspoon pepper, and 1 cup stock in a 6-quart kettle. Simmer for 1-1/2 hours, stirring occasionally, and adding more broth if needed. Purée.

In a small saucepan, melt the butter and sauté the remaining onion until soft, but not brown. Remove from the heat and add to the meat with the egg yolks, bread, cheese, 1/2 teaspoon salt, 1/4 teaspoon pepper, and nutmeg. Mix well and shape into 1-inch balls.

In a 2-quart saucepan, bring the remaining chicken stock to a boil. Add the meatballs and poach gently for 20 minutes. Do not boil for the first 10 minutes or the meatballs will disintegrate. Add the meatballs and their poaching liquor to the puréed soup and simmer for 2 minutes. Add more stock, if desired.

Can be made 1 or 2 days ahead. Can be frozen.

*Yield: 6 to 8 servings*

*Note:* If the meatballs disintegrate in poaching, break up any whole pieces and serve the soup as is. It will still taste delicious and no one will be the wiser.

## Scallop and Ham Won Tons in Saffron Stock

2 pounds scallops, minced
1/2 pound pork, ground
1/4 pound ham, ground
8 water chestnuts, minced
6 Chinese mushrooms, soaked and minced (see Index)
1 egg

6 tablespoons minced shallots
2 tablespoons rice wine
salt and pepper
60 won ton skins
2 teaspoons saffron threads
2 quarts chicken stock

In a bowl, mix the scallops, pork, ham, water chestnuts, mushrooms, egg, shallots, and wine.

Place a teaspoon of the filling in the center of a won ton skin. Brush edges with 1 egg, beaten lightly. Fold one side over to meet the other, as if making a turnover, but put the points side by side rather than on top of each other. Take the two points to the right and left of the filling, twist them around, and pinch together. Let rest on a baking sheet while filling the remaining skins.

Bring 3 quarts of water to a full boil and add the won tons. Simmer, stirring occasionally, until the won tons float to the surface and are almost transparent. Strain. Cook the won tons in batches if the kettle is not large enough to cook them all at the same time.

Dissolve the saffron in the chicken stock, bring to a simmer, and add the won tons. Heat until hot.

Can be made ahead. Can be frozen.

*Yield: 6 to 8 servings*

*Note:* It is best to freeze the won tons after poaching. Freeze them on baking sheets and then put into plastic bags. The won tons can also be deep fried at 375°F. until golden and served as an hors d'oeuvre.

Won ton skins are available in Asian markets and many supermarkets.

## Pork and Mushroom Soup

2 pounds pork bones
2 scallions, roots trimmed
8 cups water
1 slice gingerroot
4 Chinese mushrooms, soaked and shredded

1/4 pound pork, cut in julienne
1/4 cup snow peas
6 thin slices lemon peel
salt

In a 3-quart kettle, simmer the pork bones, scallions, water, and gingerroot for 1-1/2 hours.

Strain the broth and add the mushrooms and pork. Simmer 20 minutes. Add the snow peas and simmer 2 minutes. Add the lemon slivers and correct the seasoning with salt.

Can be prepared ahead or frozen. Add the snow peas just before serving.

*Yield: 6 servings*

## Chinese Meatball and Spinach Soup

2 ounces cellophane noodles
1/2 pound pork, ground
1 tablespoon cornstarch
1/2 teaspoon salt
1 tablespoon soy sauce
1/2 egg, lightly beaten

2 tablespoons water
2 cups chicken stock
2 cups water
salt and pepper
2 cups spinach, stripped of stems

Soak the noodles in boiling water for 15 minutes. Drain and cut into 4-inch lengths. Set aside.

In a bowl, combine the pork, cornstarch, salt, soy sauce, egg, and 2 tablespoons water. Mix, stirring in one direction, until the meat holds together. Shape into 1-inch balls.

Bring the broth and remaining water to a boil. Add the meatballs and simmer 2 minutes. Remove any scum. Add the noodles and simmer 2 minutes. Correct the seasoning with salt and pepper. Stir in the spinach and simmer 2 minutes longer.

Can be prepared ahead and frozen. Add the spinach just before serving.

*Yield: 4 to 6 servings*

## Hot and Sour Soup

6 cups chicken stock
1/4 pound raw pork,
  shredded
1/4 cup shredded bamboo
  shoots
1/2 cup shredded bean curd
1/3 cup Chinese mushrooms,
  soaked and shredded
4 teaspoons light soy sauce
1 teaspoon dry sherry

1 teaspoon sugar
2 tablespoons rice vinegar
1/4 teaspoon pepper
1-1/2 tablespoons cornstarch
1/4 cup cold water
2 eggs, beaten
2 teaspoons sesame oil

In a 3-quart kettle, simmer the stock, pork, bamboo shoots, bean curd, and mushrooms for 10 minutes.

In a bowl, combine the soy sauce, sherry, salt, sugar, vinegar, and pepper. Stir into the soup and simmer 1 minute.

In the same bowl, combine the cornstarch and water and stir into the soup. Remove the soup from the heat. Pour the beaten eggs into the soup in a thin, steady stream, stirring rapidly. Pour on the sesame oil and serve.

Can be made a day ahead and reheated. Can be frozen.

*Yield: 6 servings*

## Chinese Stuffed Cucumber Soup

1-1/2 ounces Chinese
    mushrooms, soaked
    and minced
3/4 pound pork, ground
1 tablespoon minced scallion
1 egg, slightly beaten
1/2 teaspoon sesame oil
2 teaspoons dry sherry
1/2 teaspoon salt
2 teaspoons minced Chinese
  parsley, Cilantro, or
  coriander

1/2 teaspoon salt
1/4 teaspoon sugar
pinch of white pepper
3 large cucumbers, cut in
  1-1/2-inch lengths and
  hollowed with an apple
  corer
6 cups boiling chicken stock
scallion shreds

In a bowl, combine the mushrooms, pork, scallion, egg, sesame oil, sherry, parsley, salt, sugar, and pepper. Mix well.

Stuff the cucumbers generously with the mixture. Arrange on a plate in a bamboo steamer and steam for 15 minutes. If you do not have a steamer, see chapter 4 for instructions on improvising a steamer.

Place the cucumbers in a large soup tureen and pour on the boiling stock. Sprinkle with scallion shreds and additional minced Chinese parsley.

The cucumbers can be prepared a day ahead. Reheat in the steamer or in the soup.

*Yield: 6 servings*

---

## Erwtensoep (Dutch Pea Soup)

| | |
|---|---|
| 2 cups dried split peas | 1 celery root, diced |
| 3 quarts cold water | 2 leeks, chopped |
| 1 pig's foot, split | 2 onions, chopped |
| 1 cup diced bacon | 1 bay leaf |
| 1 pound potatoes, thinly sliced | 1 pound smoked sausage, sliced |
| 2 tablespoons salt | minced parsley |
| 1 bunch of celery, leaves only | |

Wash the peas, cover with water, and soak for 12 hours.

Boil 1 hour in soaking water. Add the pig's foot, bacon, potatoes, salt, celery leaves, celery root, leeks, onions, and bay leaf. Simmer 2 hours. Remove the pig's foot and shred the meat. Set aside.

Cook until the soup is smooth and thick and the peas are tender. Discard the bay leaf. Add the shredded meat and sausage and simmer 5 minutes. Serve sprinkled with parsley.

This soup is even better when prepared 2 or 3 days ahead. Can be frozen.

*Yield: 8 servings*

*Note:* This is a basic recipe for pea soup. You can use green or yellow peas, split or whole. The cooking time will be about the same. You can omit the pig's foot and substitute smoked ham hocks or the bone from a smoked ham. You can omit the celery root and use 1/2 pound chopped carrots. You can also omit the leek and use 1 more onion, studded with 4 whole cloves.

## Country Broccoli Soup

2 pounds broccoli
1-3/4 cups minced onions
1 garlic clove, minced
2 tablespoons olive oil
1 tablespoon butter
1/2 pound smoked ham,
   minced

2 quarts beef stock
6 ounces vermicelli, broken
   into 2-inch pieces
salt and pepper

Chop the stems and florets of the broccoli, keeping them separate.

Sauté the onions and garlic in the oil and butter in a 4-quart kettle until golden. Add the ham and cook, stirring occasionally, for 5 minutes. Stir in the stock and bring to a boil.

Add the broccoli stems and simmer, covered, for 25 minutes. Add the broccoli florets and pasta and simmer until the pasta is tender, about 12 minutes. Correct the seasoning with salt and pepper.

Can be prepared ahead. Can be frozen.
*Yield: 8 servings*

## Lebbencs Leves (Hungarian Lebbens Soup)

1/2 cup flour
1 egg
salt
1 pound potatoes, cut in
   1/2-inch cubes
2 quarts beef stock
1/4 pound bacon, diced

1 onion, minced
1 green pepper, cut in
   julienne
1 tablespoon paprika
1 tomato, peeled and
   chopped
pepper

In a bowl, combine the flour, egg, and a pinch of salt. Work into a firm dough. This is easily done in a food processor. Roll the dough to less than 1/8-inch thick and let dry about 2 hours. It should be as stiff as a sheet of paper.

Simmer the potatoes in the stock for 10 minutes.

In a heavy skillet, render the bacon and cook until crisp. Remove the cracklings and set aside.

Break the dried noodle dough into small chips. Sauté the onion and noodle pieces in the bacon fat over low heat for 20 minutes until golden. Add to the soup with salt, green pepper, paprika, and tomato. Add the cracklings and simmer until the potatoes and noodles are done, about 5 minutes. Correct the seasoning with salt and pepper.

Can be prepared ahead. Can be frozen.

*Yield: 8 servings*

---

## Potée Toulousaine (Bean and Sausage Soup from Toulouse)

3 cups dried white beans
4 quarts water
2 ham bones, cut up
salt
4 sweet Italian sausages
5 tablespoons oil
3 onions, chopped

1 cabbage, shredded
5 leeks, sliced
3 carrots, sliced
2 turnips, sliced
3 stalks celery, sliced
bouquet garni (see Index)

Soak the beans in water to cover for 12 hours. Drain.

In a 6-quart kettle, simmer the beans, water, and ham bones until the beans are tender, about 2 hours. Season to taste with salt.

Prick the sausages with a fork. In a large skillet, sauté them in the oil until browned. Remove and slice. In the skillet fat, sauté the onions until golden. Add the cabbage, leeks, carrots, turnips, and celery. Cook, stirring, for 15 minutes.

Add to the bean mixture with the bouquet garni and simmer for about 1 hour, adding more water if required.

Add the sausages and simmer 5 minutes. This soup is better if prepared 1 or 2 days ahead. Can be frozen.

*Yield: 6 servings*

## Polish Sausage Soup

1/2 cup minced carrots
1/2 cup minced celery
1/2 cup butter
3 cups leeks, cut in 1/2-inch sections
2 cups shredded cabbage
2 quarts hot chicken stock
5 tablespoons flour
2 cups chicken stock

2 cups potatoes, cut in 1/2-inch cubes
1/2 teaspoon dried marjoram
1 pound kielbasa, skinned and thinly sliced
salt and pepper
minced parsley
minced dill

In a 4-quart kettle, sauté the carrots and celery in 1/4 cup butter until soft. Add the leeks and cabbage and sauté 3 minutes. Stir in 2 quarts stock and simmer 15 minutes.

In a saucepan, melt the remaining butter. Add the flour and cook, stirring, until it just starts to turn golden. Add the remaining hot stock and cook, stirring, until it boils. Add to the soup with the potatoes and marjoram and simmer 10 minutes. Add the kielbasa and simmer until the vegetables are tender, about 15 minutes.

Correct the seasoning with salt and pepper. Garnish with parsley and dill.

This soup is better if made several days ahead. Can be frozen.
*Yield: 8 servings*

## Spanish Sausage and Lentil Soup

1 pound Chorizo sausage
2 tablespoons olive oil
6 ounces smoked ham, minced
2 onions, minced
1 green pepper, minced
1 carrot, minced
2 garlic cloves, minced
1 bay leaf

3/4 teaspoon minced thyme
1/2 teaspoon ground cumin seed
8 to 9 cups chicken stock
1-pound can tomatoes
1/2 pound dried lentils
salt and pepper
12 leaves spinach, shredded

In a 4-quart kettle, cook the sausage in the oil until browned. Remove sausage and set aside.

Drain all but 2 tablespoons of the fat and add the ham, onion, pepper, and carrot. Cover and sweat over low heat, stirring occasionally, for 15 minutes. Stir in the garlic, bay leaf, thyme, and cumin seed and cook 5 minutes longer.

Thinly slice the sausage and add to the kettle with the stock, tomatoes, and lentils. Partially cover and simmer gently for 2 hours.

Skim any fat off the surface. Correct the seasoning with salt and pepper. Add the shredded spinach and serve.

This soup is better if made ahead. Wait until just before serving before adding the spinach. Can be frozen.

*Yield: 8 to 10 servings*

## COLD SOUPS

Many delicious soups can be served cold. Some recipes were specifically created as cold soups, such as Vichyssoise, Gazpacho, and some cucumber soups. Others that are traditionally served hot are also excellent cold. Some of the tomato soups mentioned previously are delicious when served cold, as are many of the creamed soups. When serving a cream soup cold, it may be necessary to thin it with stock, milk, or cream. Be careful not to use too much cream or the soup will have an unpleasant, cloying effect on the palate. Two of the most delicious hot soups are superb when served cold—Avgolemonou, Greek egg lemon soup, and Billi Bi, the classic mussel soup.

Although cold soups require no special equipment, a food mill is a great help. As stated before, it is possible to purée the soups in a processor or blender, but a food mill removes any hard, fibrous parts in one process. The machines chop these parts and the soup then has to be forced through a very fine sieve if they are to be removed.

Cold soups should be served at a temperature that is cool to the tongue, but not icy. If too cold, they lose their flavor. Generally, the soups taste best at about 45 to 50°F. This temperature is cool to the palate, but still warm enough to retain flavor. Because cold dulls flavors, it is necessary to season cold soups more highly than hot ones. After the food has chilled, check the seasoning again and make any necessary corrections.

Serve the soups in cups or glass soup plates. For a more interesting presentation, use oversize wine glasses. There are special servers for cold soups that have a footed large bowl with a smaller bowl inside. The space between the bowls is filled with crushed ice. Although some manufacturers seem to be making these servers again, you may have more luck finding them in antique shops. You can prepare your own servers by lining small baskets with plastic, filling them with crushed ice, and setting the soup bowls in the center. Large sea shells also make an inventive presentation. Accentuate the clear coolness of the soup by underlining the bowls with leaves or garnishing the soup itself with an edible flower, such as a nasturtium.

## Almond Gazpacho

1-1/4 cups blanched almonds
1 garlic clove, peeled
2 tablespoons olive oil
1 teaspoon salt
5 slices white bread, crusts removed

2 tablespoons wine vinegar
1 egg white
1 to 3 cups ice water
2 or 3 hard-cooked eggs, minced
salt and pepper

Soak the almonds in water to cover for 8 to 12 hours.

In a processor, purée the almonds and garlic, adding olive oil to make a smooth paste. Process until absolutely smooth. If necessary, strain the purée and process any remaining pieces. Return the soup to the processor and add the salt, bread, vinegar, egg white, and 1 cup water. Process until smooth.

Pour into a bowl and add more water until thinned to desired consistency. Correct the seasoning with salt and pepper and chill for 2 hours. Pass the minced egg separately.

Will keep 3 to 4 days in the refrigerator.

*Yield: 6 servings*

*Note:* This soup originally was made in a mortar and pestle. You can prepare it that way also.

## Cold Avocado Soup

2 avocados, peeled and
   seeded
2 tablespoons lime juice
4 cups chicken stock
salt and pepper

1 tablespoon minced green
   chili pepper
1 cup yogurt
paprika

Chop the avocados and purée in a processor until smooth. Add the lime juice, stock, salt and pepper to taste, chili, and yogurt. Process until smooth. Chill.

Serve sprinkled with paprika.

*Yield: 6 servings*

*Note:* Avocados darken when exposed to air. Therefore, the soup should be chilled in a covered container and used within 8 hours.

## Avocado Senegalese Soup

1 onion, minced
1 stalk celery, minced
2 tablespoons butter
1 tablespoon flour
2 teaspoons curry powder
1 tart apple, peeled, cored,
   and chopped
4 cups chicken stock

1 avocado, peeled, seeded,
   and chopped
1 cup light cream
salt
1 avocado, thinly sliced
1/2 cup grated coconut,
   toasted

In a 3-quart saucepan, sweat the onion and celery in the butter until soft. Stir in the flour and curry powder until blended. Add the apple and 2 cups stock. Cook, stirring occasionally, until the apple is soft.

Purée the soup in a processor. Add the chopped avocado and purée again. Put in a container and add the remaining chicken stock and cream. Correct the seasoning with salt. Chill.

Serve garnished with avocado slices and coconut. Serve within 8 hours.

*Yield: 6 servings*

## Russian Borscht

There are many versions of borscht, which may be served either hot or cold.

2 bunches of beets, or
  1-pound can with juices
1/2 cup tomato purée
1 small cabbage, shredded
1/2 cup diced carrots
3/4 cup chopped onion

4 cups beef stock
salt and pepper
2 tablespoons vinegar
2 tablespoons brown sugar
2 bay leaves
sour cream

Cut off the roots and leaves of the beets, leaving 1-inch stalk. Boil in water to cover until tender. Reserve the cooking liquid. Peel and grate the beets. If using canned beets, grate them and reserve the liquid. Mix the liquid with tomato purée.

In a 4-quart saucepan, simmer the cabbage, carrots, onion, stock, salt and pepper to taste, vinegar, brown sugar, and bay leaves, uncovered, for 20 minutes. Add the beets and beet juice. Adjust the flavor with vinegar and brown sugar to develop a sweet and sour taste.

Serve hot or cold. Pass the sour cream separately.

Keeps 3 to 4 days in the refrigerator. Can be frozen.

*Yield: 6 servings*

## Simple Summer Borscht

1-pound can whole beets
2-1/2 cups beef stock
2 teaspoons meat extract
  (Bovril)
1 tablespoon sugar

large bay leaf
juice of 1 large lemon
salt and pepper
1 pint sour cream

Drain the liquid from the beets and combine with the stock and meat extract in a 2-quart saucepan. Stir in 1 tablespoon sugar and the bay leaf. Bring to a boil.

Grate the beets and stir into the soup. Simmer 5 minutes. Correct the seasoning with lemon juice and sugar to achieve a sweet and sour taste. Remove the bay leaf and chill. Add salt and pepper to taste.

Serve with sour cream on the side.
Keeps 3 to 4 days in the refrigerator.
*Yield: 4 servings*

## Cold Cherry and Beet Soup

2-1/2 pounds beets, peeled
    and grated
5 cups water
1 pound cherries, pitted
2 cups water

4 whole cloves
juice of 1 lemon
honey
salt

In a 3-quart saucepan, combine the beets and 5 cups water and simmer 30 minutes. Strain the soup and discard the beets.

In a 2-quart saucepan, simmer the cherries in remaining water with cloves for 10 minutes. Add the lemon juice and honey to taste. Combine with the beet stock and correct the seasoning with salt. Chill.

Serve with dollops of whipped cream seasoned with salt, or with sour cream, or crème fraiche.

Can be prepared 2 to 3 days ahead.
*Yield: 6 servings*

## Jellied Beet Bouillon with Caviar

4 large beets
1 quart hot chicken or beef
    stock
1-1/2 packages unflavored
    gelatin

1/3 cup dry sherry
1 tablespoon lemon juice
1 tablespoon caviar

Cook the beets in boiling water to cover until tender. Cool, peel, and slice. Reduce the cooking liquid to 1 cup and stir in the stock.

Soften the gelatin in the sherry and stir into the hot consommé with the lemon juice. Stir over low heat until the gelatin dissolves. Cool until the consistency of egg white.

In the bottom of bouillon cups or crystal bowls, arrange the beet slices. Pour on the beet bouillon. Chill until set and garnish with caviar.

This soup must be made ahead. Keeps 2 days in the refrigerator.
*Yield: 6 servings*
*Note:* The amount of caviar indicated is small. You may wish to increase the amount considerably. You can garnish the soup with a dollop of sour cream or crème fraiche, and add the caviar or omit it.

## Cold Orange Carrot Soup

1/2 teaspoon minced
  gingerroot
1 pound carrots, thinly
  sliced
1/2 cup sliced leeks
2 tablespoons butter

3 cups chicken stock
1-1/2 cups orange juice
salt and pepper
6 orange slices, peeled
2 tablespoons grated carrot
1 teaspoon minced mint

In a 2-quart saucepan, sweat the gingerroot, carrots, and leeks in the butter until soft. Add 2 cups of stock and simmer until the carrots are very soft, about 30 minutes.

Force through a food mill or purée in a processor. Stir in the remaining stock and orange juice to make a soup of medium consistency. If necessary, add more stock. Correct the seasoning with salt and pepper. Chill.

Serve topped with an orange slice, carrot, and mint.

Can be made 2 or 3 days ahead.

*Yield: 6 servings*

## Crème de Concombres Glacé (Cold Cream of Cucumber Soup)

4 cucumbers
1 large onion, sliced
2 cups water
salt and pepper

2 tablespoons flour
3/4 cup heavy cream
1 tablespoon minced mint

Cut off the ends of the cucumbers. Peel 2-1/2 cucumbers and set aside the peeled half. Slice the 2 peeled and 1-1/2 unpeeled cucumbers.

In a 2-quart saucepan, simmer the cucumber slices with the onion, 1/2 cup water, and salt and pepper to taste until the cucumbers are soft.

In a bowl, combine the remaining 1-1/2 cups water with the flour and mix well. Stir into the soup and bring to a boil. Force through a food mill, or purée in a blender or processor and strain. Discard the seeds. Chill.

Stir in the cream and correct the seasoning with salt and pepper. Cut the reserved cucumber lengthwise into 2 pieces and remove the seeds. Shred finely.

Serve the soup garnished with cucumber shreds and mint.

Can be prepared 2 or 3 days ahead.

*Yield: 6 servings*

---

## Cold Cucumber Soup

2 cucumbers, peeled, seeded, and chopped
4 cups chicken stock
1 cup yogurt
1 teaspoon grated lemon rind
1 teaspoon minced dill
salt and pepper
fresh dill sprigs

In a 2-quart saucepan, simmer the cucumbers in the stock until tender. Force through a food mill or purée in a processor.

Stir in the yogurt, lemon rind, and minced dill. Correct the seasoning with salt and pepper. Chill.

Garnish with dill sprigs.

Can be made 2 or 3 days ahead.

*Yield: 6 servings*

*Note:* You can vary the soup by doubling the amount of yogurt and stirring in 1-1/2 teaspoons curry powder and 1/4 cup raisins.

## Sopa del Sol (Spanish Cucumber Soup)

3 cucumbers, peeled and
  chopped
1/2 cup chopped onion
1 garlic clove, minced
2 cups chicken stock
2 cups sour cream

3 tablespoons white wine
  vinegar
salt and pepper
1 cup peeled, seeded, and
  chopped tomato

Place cucumbers, onion, garlic, and chicken stock in a processor and purée. Strain.

Place the purée in a bowl and stir in the cream, vinegar, and salt and pepper to taste. Chill.

Serve garnished with tomato.

Can be refrigerated for 3 to 4 days.

*Yield: 4 servings*

*Note:* You can substitute medium cream or yogurt for the sour cream.

## Yayla Corbasi (Cold Turkish Yogurt Soup)

1/2 cup raisins
1 hard-cooked egg, chopped
3 cups yogurt
1/2 cup light cream
1 cucumber, chopped
1/4 cup minced scallion

2 teaspoons salt
1/2 teaspoon white pepper
6 ice cubes
1 cup ice water
1 tablespoon minced parsley
1 tablespoon minced dill

Soak the raisins in cold water to cover while preparing the soup.

In a large bowl, mix the egg, yogurt, cream, cucumber, scallions, salt, and pepper. Drain the raisins and add to the yogurt mixture. Stir in the ice cubes, cover, and chill 3 to 4 hours. Stir in ice water.

Serve garnished with parsley and dill.

Can be made 2 or 3 days before serving.

*Yield: 4 servings*

## Iced Cucumber Soup

4 large cucumbers, peeled,
  seeded, and chopped
1 onion, minced
3 tablespoons butter
3 tablespoons flour
2-3/4 cups chicken stock

1 teaspoon curry powder
1 tablespoon lemon juice
2 cups light cream
salt and pepper
1/4 cup minced parsley

In a 2-quart saucepan, sweat the cucumber and onion in the butter until soft. Add the flour, stock, curry powder, and lemon juice. Simmer, stirring, until thickened and smooth. Simmer 10 minutes. Purée in a processor and stir in the cream. Season to taste with salt and pepper. Chill.

Serve sprinkled with parsley.

Can be refrigerated for 2 to 3 days.

*Yield: 6 servings*

## Lettuce Almond Soup

2 heads Boston lettuce,
  shredded
1 cup finely ground almonds
1 teaspoon sugar
1/2 cup sliced onion

1/2 teaspoon dry mustard
2 cups chicken stock
1 to 2 cups medium cream
salt and pepper

In a 2-quart saucepan, simmer the lettuce, almonds, sugar, onion, mustard, and stock for 5 minutes.

Purée in a processor or blender and strain through a fine sieve. Blend the sieved soup until very smooth. Add cream to the desired consistency. Correct the seasoning with salt and pepper. Chill.

Can be prepared 1 or 2 days ahead.

*Yield: 6 servings*

*Note:* This is a delicate soup with a subtle flavor. It is necessary to pulverize the almonds so they are not gritty. It may be necessary to repeat the straining or, better yet, to pound the almond mixture in a mortar and pestle.

## Chilled Cream of Mushroom Soup I

| | |
|---|---|
| 1/4 pound mushrooms, minced | 2 egg yolks |
| 1 tablespoon butter | salt and pepper |
| 1 quart chicken stock | minced dill |
| 1/2 cup heavy cream | lemon slices |

In a 2-quart saucepan, sweat the mushrooms in the butter until soft. Add the stock and simmer 30 minutes. Purée in a processor or blender. Reheat the soup.

In a bowl, combine the cream and egg yolks. Add 1 cup hot soup to warm the mixture. Stir into the hot soup and heat just until hot. Do not boil. Remove from the heat and chill.

Serve garnished with minced dill and lemon slices.

Can be made 2 or 3 days before serving.

*Yield: 6 servings*

## Chilled Cream of Mushroom Soup II

| | |
|---|---|
| 1-1/2 pounds mushrooms | 1 bay leaf |
| 1 onion, chopped | 3 cups dry white wine |
| 1 celery stalk, chopped | 2 tablespoons olive oil |
| 1 carrot, thinly sliced | 2 tablespoons flour |
| 1/2 teaspoon white pepper | 1/2 teaspoon dried thyme |
| 1 teaspoon salt | 2 cups heavy cream |

Remove stems from the mushrooms and reserve caps.

In a 2-quart saucepan, simmer the stems, onion, celery, carrot, pepper, salt, bay leaf, and wine for 20 minutes. Drain; discard the vegetables.

Slice the mushroom caps thinly. In a large skillet, sauté the sliced mushrooms in the oil until the liquid evaporates and they start to brown. Stir in the flour and thyme and cook, stirring, for 3 minutes. Stir reserved vegetable liquor into the skillet. Simmer 10 minutes and taste for seasoning.

Chill and remove any fat from the surface. Stir in the cream.

Can be made 2 or 3 days before serving.

*Yield: 6 servings*

## Cold Mustard Cream Soup

| | |
|---|---|
| 2 tablespoons butter | 1-1/4 cups light cream |
| 2 tablespoons flour | salt and pepper |
| 3 to 4 tablespoons Dijon | 1 tablespoon minced onion |
|    mustard | 2 egg yolks |
| 2-1/2 cups chicken stock | 3 tablespoons heavy cream |

Melt the butter in a 1-1/2-quart saucepan. Stir in the flour and cook, stirring, for 2 minutes. Stir in the mustard. Add the chicken stock, light cream, salt and pepper to taste, and onion. Simmer, stirring often, for 15 minutes.

In a small bowl, combine the egg yolks and heavy cream. Stir in 1 cup of hot soup, then return the egg mixture to the soup. Heat, stirring, until lightly thickened. Do not boil. Strain and chill.

Correct the seasoning with salt, pepper, and additional mustard if desired.

*Yield: 6 servings*

## Iced Pea and Curry Soup

| | |
|---|---|
| 1 onion, thinly sliced | 1 tablespoon flour |
| 1/4 cup peanut oil | 2 cup chicken stock |
| 2 teaspoons curry powder | pinch of nutmeg |
| 1 teaspoon salt | pinch of mace |
| 1-1/2 teaspoons sugar | 1/2 cup light cream |
| cayenne pepper | 1/2 cup heavy cream |
| 2 pounds peas, shelled, or 2 | 1 tablespoon minced chives |
|    10-ounce packages frozen | 3 ounces cooked chicken, |
|    peas |    diced |
| 1-1/2 cups water | |

In a 2-quart saucepan, sauté the onion in the oil until golden. Add the curry powder, salt, sugar, and cayenne to taste. Cook, stirring, over low heat for 5 minutes. Add the peas and 1/2 cup water. Cover and simmer until the peas are tender, about 15 minutes for fresh peas or 3 minutes for thawed frozen peas.

Stir in the flour and cook 2 minutes. Add chicken stock and 1 cup water. Bring to a boil. Add the nutmeg and mace and simmer 10 minutes.

Purée in a processor or force through a food mill. Strain to remove any pea skins. Chill.

Before serving, stir in the light and heavy creams and garnish with chives and chicken.

Can be made 2 or 3 days ahead. Can be frozen.

*Yield: 6 servings*

## Nut Sundi Soup (Cold Peanut Soup)

3 cups chicken or beef stock
1/2 cup dried salted peanuts
1/2 teaspoon chili powder
salt and pepper

1 cup milk
lemon slices or cucumber
  slices

In a 2-quart saucepan, simmer the broth and peanuts for 5 minutes. Purée in a blender or processor. Stir in the chili powder and salt and pepper to taste. Pour into a saucepan, rinse out the blender with the milk, and add to the saucepan. Simmer 5 minutes. Chill.

Serve garnished with lemon or cucumber slices.

Can be made 2 or 3 days ahead.

*Yield: 4 servings*

*Note:* This soup can also be served hot with small croutons.

## Iced Pimiento Soup

1/4 cup chopped onion
2 tablespoons butter
2 tablespoons flour
2-1/2 cups chicken stock

4-ounce jar whole pimientos
1 cup heavy cream
salt and pepper
dill sprigs

In a 1-quart saucepan, sweat the onion in the butter until soft. Stir in the flour and cook 1 minute. Stir in the stock and cook, stirring, until thickened. Add the pimientos and simmer 5 minutes. Purée in a processor or blender.

Stir in the cream and correct the seasoning with salt and pepper. Chill.

Serve garnished with dill.

Can be prepared 1 or 2 days ahead.

*Yield: 4 servings*

*Note:* This soup can be used as a base for many cold soups. Use about 4 ounces of any vegetable in place of the pimientos and simmer until very tender. You can garnish the soup with croutons, lemon slices, cucumber slices, minced tomatoes, or other vegetables.

## Vichyssoise

| | |
|---|---|
| 1-1/2 cups diced leeks | 2 teaspoons salt |
| 1 cup diced onion | 2 cups hot milk |
| 1 tablespoon butter | 2 cups light cream |
| 3 cups diced potatoes | 1 cup heavy cream |
| 4 cups hot water | minced chives |

In a 3-quart kettle, sweat the leeks and onion in the butter until soft. Add the potatoes, hot water, and salt. Simmer, covered, for 30 minutes, or until the potatoes are soft.

Force through a food mill. Return to the kettle, add the hot milk and light cream, and bring to a boil, stirring occasionally to prevent scorching. Strain through a fine sieve, pressing through as much solid matter as possible.

Chill and strain again. Stir in the heavy cream and chill.

Serve garnished with chives.

Can be made 2 or 3 days ahead. Can be frozen.

*Yield: 8 servings*

## Crème Vichyssoise à la Ritz

Combine 1 part tomato juice with 3 parts Vichyssoise. Chill.

## Vichyssoise aux Poires (Cream of Potato Soup with Pears)

Purée 5 peeled and cored ripe pears with the heavy cream and add to the soup.

## Clam Vichyssoise

Add 14 ounces minced clams and their juice to the soup with the milk and light cream.

## Crème de Potiron Glacée (Cold Cream of Pumpkin Soup)

1/2 onion, minced
1/3 cup peanut oil
4 tablespoons flour
3 cups chicken stock
1 2-pound can puréed
   pumpkin
2 teaspoons ground ginger

1 teaspoon salt
1/4 teaspoon white pepper
1 cup light cream
1/2 cup heavy cream,
   whipped
1/2 teaspoon grated nutmeg

In a 2-quart saucepan, sweat the onion in the oil until soft. Add the flour and cook, stirring, for 3 minutes. Add the stock, pumpkin, ginger, salt, and pepper. Cook, stirring, until the mixture comes to a boil and is smooth. Stir in the light cream and simmer 20 minutes.

Correct the seasoning with salt and pepper. Chill.

Serve garnished with dollops of cream sprinkled with nutmeg.

Can be made 2 or 3 days ahead.

*Yield: 6 servings*

## Uncooked Cold Tomato Soup

8 cups peeled, seeded, and
    chopped tomatoes
1/2 cup minced onion
1 cup chicken stock
1 cup white wine

2 teaspoons salt
1 teaspoon sugar
1 teaspoon minced mint
1 teaspoon white pepper
mint sprigs

In a large bowl, combine the tomatoes and onion. Cover and let stand at room temperature for 1 hour. Force through a food mill.

Stir in the stock, wine, salt, sugar, minced mint, and pepper. Cover and chill.

Serve garnished with mint sprigs.

*Yield: 8 servings*

*Note:* This soup must be made with late summer, *fresh* tomatoes.

## Cold Tomato Soup I

1 onion, sliced
1 carrot, sliced
1/3 cup minced parsley
2 garlic cloves, crushed
2 tablespoons olive oil
4 tomatoes, peeled, seeded,
    and chopped

1/2 teaspoon minced fresh
    thyme
1/2 teaspoon minced fresh
    basil
1 teaspoon salt
2 cups chicken stock
lemon or lime wedges

In a 2-quart saucepan, sweat the onion, carrot, parsley, and garlic in the oil until soft. Purée in a blender with the tomatoes, thyme, basil, and salt. Stir in the stock and mix well. Chill.

Serve with lemon or lime wedges.

Can be made 1 or 2 days ahead.

*Yield: 4 servings*

## Cold Tomato Soup II

1-pound, 12-ounce can Italian
  tomatoes and their liquid
4 cups beef or chicken stock
1-1/2 cups minced celery
1 garlic clove, minced
1/2 teaspoon minced dill or
  basil
1/4 teaspoon dried thyme

1/4 teaspoon celery seed
1/2 teaspoon sugar
1/8 teaspoon crushed red
  pepper
salt and pepper
sour cream
minced dill or basil

In a 2-quart kettle, simmer the tomatoes, stock, celery, garlic, parsley, dill, thyme, celery seed, sugar, red pepper, and salt and pepper to taste for 45 minutes, or until celery is tender.

Force through a food mill or purée in a processor. Chill.

Serve with dollops of sour cream sprinkled with dill or basil.

Can be made 2 or 3 days ahead. Can be frozen.

*Yield: 8 servings*

## Soupe de Tomates Fraiches au Pistou (*Cold Tomato Soup III*)

2 carrots, sliced
1 leek, chopped
2 shallots, minced
2 garlic cloves, crushed
2 teaspoons olive oil
6 tomatoes, chopped
1/2 teaspoon dried thyme

1 bay leaf
2 tablespoons tomato paste
1-1/2 quarts chicken stock
salt and pepper
1 cup basil leaves
2 garlic cloves
olive oil

In a 4-quart kettle, sweat the carrots, leek, shallots, and crushed garlic in the oil until soft. Add the tomatoes, thyme, bay leaf, tomato paste, and stock. Simmer for 20 minutes. Discard the bay leaf.

Force the soup through a food mill or purée in a processor. Correct the seasoning with salt and pepper. Chill.

In a processor or blender, purée the basil, remaining garlic, and just enough oil to make a paste as thick as mayonnaise. Serve the soup with the basil mixture (pistou) passed separately.

Can be made 2 or 3 days ahead. Can be frozen.

*Yield: 8 servings*

*Note:* Make substantial quantities of the pistou and freeze in small containers. Use for this and other soups, as well as a sauce for pasta. Before serving, you may wish to add grated Parmesan cheese to taste.

---

## Cold Tomato Soup IV

1 onion, chopped
2 shallots, minced
1 tablespoon butter
6 large tomatoes, peeled, seeded, and chopped
2 cups chicken stock
1 tablespoon tomato paste
1 tablespoon minced fresh thyme

1/2 teaspoon sugar
salt and pepper
3/4 cup heavy cream
1/3 cup sour cream
juice of 1 large lime
Tabasco sauce
parsley sprigs

In a 2-quart saucepan, sweat the onion and shallots in the butter until soft. Stir in the tomatoes, chicken stock, tomato paste, thyme, sugar, and salt and pepper to taste. Simmer, covered, for 20 minutes.

Force through a food mill or purée in a processor. Stir in the heavy cream, sour cream, lime juice, and Tabasco to taste. Strain for a finer texture, if desired. Chill.

Can be made 2 or 3 days before serving. Can be frozen.

*Yield: 6 servings*

*Note:* This soup can be frozen for 2 hours, puréed in a processor, and refrozen. It is like a tomato sherbet. If it is frozen too hard, it may be necessary to process it again.

## Jellied Tomato Consommé

3 cups chicken stock
3 cups tomato juice
1-1/2 cups chopped onion
3 tablespoons chopped celery
3 tablespoons minced chives
4 garlic cloves, crushed
2 whole cloves
1-1/2 teaspoons
   Worcestershire sauce

1-1/2 teaspoons sugar
3 tablespoons lemon juice
3/4 cup beet juice
salt and pepper
1-1/2 packages gelatin
2 tablespoons water
sour cream, optional
heavy cream, whipped and
   salted, optional

In a 3-quart saucepan, simmer the stock, tomato juice, onion, celery, chives, garlic, cloves, Worcestershire sauce, and sugar for 45 minutes.

Stir in the lemon juice, beet juice, and salt and pepper to taste. Stir well. Strain through a very fine meshed strainer. Discard the solids.

Soften the gelatin in the water in a small saucepan and dissolve over low heat. Stir into the consommé and chill until set.

To serve, scoop into clear glass bowls. Top with sour cream or whipped cream, if desired.

Can be kept 2 to 3 days in the refrigerator.

*Yield: 6 servings*

*Note:* For a firmer consommé, double the amount of gelatin and chop it into small cubes.

## Gazpacho (Chilled Tomato Soup with Vegetables)

1-1/2 cups cubed white toast
1 tablespoon salt
1-1/2 teaspoons ground
   cumin
3 tablespoons olive oil
1 to 4 garlic cloves, crushed
3 cups peeled, seeded, and
   chopped tomatoes, or 3
   cups tomato juice
3 cups cold water
black pepper

cayenne pepper
2 to 4 tablespoons vinegar
3 ice cubes
2 to 3 cups sautéed croutons
2 peppers, diced
2 celery stalks, diced
1 cucumber, seeded and
   diced
1 onion, diced
2 tomatoes, peeled, seeded,
   and diced

In a processor, purée the bread, salt, cumin, oil, garlic, and 3 cups tomatoes or tomato juice. Pour into a bowl, add the cold water, black and cayenne peppers to taste, vinegar, and ice cubes. Stir well and chill.

Place the croutons, peppers, celery, cucumber, onion, and remaining tomatoes in separate small bowls. Serve the soup and pass the small bowls of croutons and vegetables so that guests can select their favorites.

The soup can be prepared 2 or 3 days before serving, or frozen. The vegetables should be prepared only a few hours before serving.

*Yield: 6 servings*

*Note:* The vegetables should be diced in 1/4-inch cubes.

## Green Gazpacho

2 tomatoes, peeled and
  chopped
3 celery stalks, chopped
1 cucumber peeled and
  chopped
1 cup chopped romaine
  lettuce

1/4 cup orange juice
1 scallion, chopped
lemon juice
minced parsley

In a processor, purée the tomatoes, celery, cucumber, lettuce, orange juice, scallion, and lemon juice to taste. Chill.

Serve garnished with minced parsley.

Can be made 2 or 3 days before serving.

*Yield: 6 servings*

*Note:* Garlic may be added for a different flavor.

## Cold Zucchini Soup

2 zucchini, sliced
1 green pepper, chopped
1/2 cup chopped onion
3 cups chicken stock

1 cup sour cream or yogurt
1 tablespoon minced parsley
1/2 teaspoon minced dill
salt and pepper

Set aside 4 slices zucchini for garnish.

In a 2-quart saucepan, simmer the remaining zucchini, pepper, onion, and stock for 20 minutes.

Purée in a food processor. Add the sour cream, parsley, and dill. Correct the seasoning with salt and pepper. Chill.

Serve garnished with reserved zucchini slices.

Can be made 2 or 3 days before serving.

*Yield: 4 servings*

---

## Buttermilk Shrimp Soup

1 quart buttermilk
1 pound cooked shrimp, chopped
1 cucumber, peeled, seeded, and chopped
1/2 cup chopped scallion
1/2 green pepper, minced
6 radishes, sliced
salt and pepper
1 tablespoon minced dill

In a large bowl, mix the buttermilk, shrimp, cucumber, scallion, pepper, radishes, and salt and pepper to taste. Chill for 12 hours. Add dill just before serving.

Can be made 2 or 3 days before serving.

*Yield: 6 to 8 servings*

# FRUIT SOUPS

In northern and central Europe, fruit soups are very popular. They are served as a first course, a light lunch, or in some instances as a dessert.

We prefer to serve these soups for a light luncheon followed by platters of fresh fruits and cheeses. They are also appealing as different, cooling desserts, but to our taste they are too sweet to serve before a meal.

The soups generally are quick and easy to prepare. However, they cannot be held for long periods. The soups should be eaten within two days. Otherwise, the fruits can ferment and become sharp flavored and rather unpleasant. Always use fruits that are fresh and unblemished. These soups can be frozen, but they are best when freshly made and chilled.

## Cold Apple and Apricot Soup

1/4 pound dried apricots
2 pounds tart apples, peeled
  and quartered
1-1/2 cups beef stock
1 bay leaf
2 sprigs parsley

2 celery stalks, chopped
salt and pepper
4 cups milk
1/2 cup heavy cream,
  whipped

In a 3-quart saucepan, combine the apricots, apples, stock, bay leaf, parsley, celery, and salt and pepper to taste with enough water to cover. Simmer, covered, for 20 to 30 minutes, or until the fruit is soft.

Force through a food mill or purée in a processor. Add the milk and correct the seasoning with salt and pepper. Thin with more milk if required. Chill completely.

Serve with dollops of whipped cream.

*Yield: 8 servings*

## Cold Fresh Fruit Soup

1 cantaloupe
1 quart strawberries, hulled
1/2 pound green grapes
4 apples, peeled, cored, and
  chopped

3/4 cup lemon juice
1/2 cup sugar
6 cups water
1-1/2 cups orange juice
sour cream

Remove pulp from the cantaloupe and chop coarsely.

In a 6-quart kettle, simmer the cantaloupe, strawberries, grapes, apples, 1/2 cup lemon juice, sugar and water, uncovered, for 15 minutes.

Purée in a processor and add the remaining lemon juice and orange juice. Chill completely.

Serve with sour cream.

*Yield: 8 servings*

## Blueberry Soup

| | |
|---|---|
| 1 cup blueberries | pinch of salt |
| juice of 1/2 lemon | 1/4 cup sugar |
| 1 cinnamon stick | 1 tablespoon cornstarch |
| 2 cups water | 1 cup heavy cream |

In a 2-quart saucepan, simmer the blueberries, lemon juice, cinnamon, and water for 10 minutes, or until soft. Add the salt and sugar.

In a bowl, mix the cornstarch with 2 tablespoons water. Stir into the hot soup and cook, stirring, until thickened and clear. Remove the cinnamon and purée in a blender.

Cool and stir in 1/2 cup heavy cream. Chill. Whip remaining cream until stiff and garnish each serving with a dollop.

*Yield: 4 servings*

## Cold Banana Soup

| | |
|---|---|
| 4 large, ripe bananas, peeled | grated rind of 1 orange |
| 5 cups milk | 1 teaspoon cornstarch |
| sugar | 1 banana, peeled and sliced |
| salt | |

Purée the 4 bananas in a processor. Bring to a boil in a kettle with the milk, sugar and salt to taste, and orange rind.

In a small bowl, combine the cornstarch with 1 tablespoon cold water. Stir into the hot soup and cook, stirring, until slightly thickened. Chill completely.

Serve garnished with fresh banana slices.

*Yield: 4 servings*

## Peach Soup

2 cups puréed peaches
2 tablespoons lemon juice
2 tablespoons sugar
1 bottle dry white wine
1 bay leaf

1 clove
1 cinnamon stick
salt
sour cream

In a bowl, combine the peaches, lemon juice, and sugar. Cover and let stand for 20 minutes.

In a saucepan, simmer the wine, bay leaf, clove, cinnamon, and salt to taste for 3 minutes. Strain and chill.

Stir the chilled wine into the purée and chill. Serve garnished with sour cream.

*Yield: 6 servings*

Soup-making equipment

Crème de Concombres
Glacé; Cold Orange Carrot
Soup; Iced Pea and Curry
Soup

Consommé San Quentin

Soupe aux Moules du Calvados; Pissaladiere

Soupe de Poissons; Caccia con Pesto

Greek Country Salad Loaf

Ham, Egg, and Pepper Croque-Monsieur

Shrimp and Egg Sandwich; Lobster Sandwich; Roast Beef Sandwich

# 2
# SANDWICHES

It is probable that sandwiches have existed since bread was first made. We do know that the English name is attributed to the fourth Earl of Sandwich (1718–1792), an avid card player. Legend has it that the Earl was so fond of card playing that he refused to leave the card table even to eat. He had servants place slices of meat between slices of bread to permit him to play without interruption. In time, any food eaten in that manner was referred to as a sandwich.

Fine sandwiches, like all fine foods, depend on fresh, well-prepared ingredients. Since a principle part of any sandwich is the bread, it must be of fine quality. Unfortunately, quality breads are not easy to obtain. Commercial bread in the United States is generally poor in quality. Large bakeries consistently offer pulpy, flavorless loaves that have no redeeming features. If enough customers left these breads on the shelves, the producers would get the message. In fact, the many "natural" loaves found on today's market shelves are a result of the public asking for better quality bread. Although the large producers have merely added grain and fiber to their original breads, it is a beginning.

It is, however, increasingly possible to buy good bread in many areas. Small bakeries and food shops are making or purchasing quality breads. Unfortunately, the bread is overpriced. The result is that many of us must prepare our own breads. Bread making is not only easy but fun, and the next chapter includes many recipes to guide you.

Although the following sandwich recipes specify a particular bread, you can substitute other breads as desired. Do not be afraid to experiment, but do consider the flavor of both the filling and the bread. Certain breads have a fuller flavor than others and can overwhelm some fillings. Always make the bread and filling complement each other.

Sandwiches should not only taste good, but also look good. A little care can make a sandwich as inviting to look at as it is good to eat. Make your sandwiches neat. Trim the meats to fit the bread slices and arrange the lettuce leaves so that they do not hang over the sides of the sandwich. Use enough filling to reach the edges of the bread and provide a generous flavor, but not so much that it seeps out. Open-faced sandwiches are the exception. Often their coverings are designed to overlap the edges of the bread.

Serve sandwiches in edible portions. Well-filled sandwiches should be cut in half or the ingredients will fall out. Other sandwiches that are made with thinner breads and fillings can be cut into quarters. The exception is the club sandwich, which is quartered and held together with wooden skewers. If the filling is somewhat loose or runny, you must be particularly careful about cutting the portions too small.

Certain sandwiches can be made ahead and refrigerated for up to 24 hours, if covered with a towel wrung out in cold water. Most sandwiches, however, should be made and eaten within a short period of time. The directions will indicate whether the entire sandwich or just the filling can be made ahead.

If you must prepare a large number of sandwiches, it is better to arrange all the ingredients so that you can prepare the sandwiches on an assembly-line basis. Several pairs of hands will speed the process. If you are preparing the sandwiches ahead, be sure to spread the bread generously with softened butter to help seal the bread against moist fillings.

Although many of the sandwiches in this selection were chosen because of their compatibility with soups, others are perfect when served alone. There are many suggestions suitable for lunch boxes, picnics, or quick, nourishing snacks. Particular sandwiches are not linked to particular soups because the possibilities are so numerous. You may choose to consider these sandwiches as fish or meat courses. For example, serve a Soupe de Poisson with a simple ham sandwich on buttered French bread, or a cold Billi Bi with a La Mediatrice. Some soups, such as the Czechoslovakian Cabbage Soup, are so substantial that no sandwich is required. However, one of the Russian rye breads would be a delightful accompaniment.

In addition to hot and cold sandwiches, there are recipes for hot, open-faced sandwiches (called toasts), pain perdu (literally, lost bread), and croque-monsieur (ham-and-cheese-filled French toast). There are also club sandwiches, an American creation, Scandinavian cold, open-faced sandwiches, and sandwiches that we have chosen to call Great Sandwiches. These are often made in whole loaves of bread and include a grand selection of ingredients.

# HOT AND COLD SANDWICHES

## Cheese, Cucumber, and Radish Sandwich

1/4 cup peeled, seeded, and
  minced cucumber
1/2 cup minced radishes
salt

3 ounces cream cheese,
  softened
4 or 8 slices pumpernickel
  bread

In a colander, mix the cucumber, radishes, and salt to taste. Mix well. Drain for 30 minutes. Rinse under cold water, drain, and toss in toweling to dry.

Spread 4 bread slices with cream cheese and cover with a layer of the cucumber-radish mixture. Top with another slice, or serve open-faced. Cut into quarters.

*Yield: 4 sandwiches*

## Herbed Cheese and Alfalfa Sprout Sandwich

8 ounces cream cheese,
  softened
1/3 cup minced chives
2 tablespoons minced thyme
3/4 teaspoon salt

3/4 teaspoon pepper
6 thin slices pumpernickel
  bread
1 cup alfalfa sprouts

In a bowl, cream the cheese, chives, thyme, salt, and pepper. Cover and chill for at least 1 hour.

Spread the cheese on half the bread slices and cover with the sprouts and remaining bread slices.

*Yield: 6 sandwiches*

## Sandwich à la Suisse (Gruyère and Olive Sandwich)

24 large green olives, minced
8 small gherkins, minced
1/4 cup mayonnaise
butter

12 thin slices whole wheat
  bread
6 thin slices gruyère cheese

Use a towel to squeeze the excess moisture out of the olives and gherkins. Put into a bowl and bind with mayonnaise.

Butter the bread slices and spread half the slices with a thin layer of the olive mixture. Add a slice of cheese and cover with remaining bread slices.

*Yield: 6 sandwiches*

## Cheddar and Walnut Sandwich

| | |
|---|---|
| 1/4 pound sharp cheddar cheese, grated | salt |
| | paprika |
| 8 tablespoons butter, softened | 1/4 pound walnuts, chopped |
| | 12 slices whole wheat bread |

In a processor, cream the cheese, butter, and salt and paprika to taste until smooth. Fold in the nuts.

Spread half the bread slices with the cheese. Cover with remaining bread slices.

*Yield: 6 sandwiches*

## Roquefort Cheese and Almond Sandwich

| | |
|---|---|
| 9 ounces Roquefort cheese | 6 tablespoons minced salted almonds |
| 3 tablespoons butter | |
| Tabasco sauce | 12 slices whole wheat bread |

In a processor, purée the cheese, butter, and Tabasco to taste. Spread half of the bread slices with the mixture. Sprinkle with almonds and cover with remaining bread slices.

*Yield: 6 sandwiches*

## Tahini, Sour Cream, and Alfalfa Sprout Sandwich

| | |
|---|---|
| 1/2 cup tahini (see note) | salt |
| 1/2 cup sour cream | 6 slices pumpernickel bread |
| 3 tablespoons lemon juice | 1-1/2 cups alfalfa sprouts |
| 1 garlic clove, crushed | |

In a bowl, combine the tahini, cream, lemon juice, garlic, and salt to taste. Let stand 1 hour.

Spread the bread slices with the mixture and sprinkle with alfalfa sprouts. Serve open-faced.

*Yield: 6 sandwiches*

*Note:* Tahini can be found in Middle Eastern markets and many supermarkets.

## Pepper, Tomato, and Egg Sandwich

3 scallions, minced
3 green peppers, chopped
1/4 cup butter
3 tomatoes, peeled, seeded, and chopped

3 eggs, lightly beaten
salt and pepper
summer savory
6 small pita loaves

In a skillet, sweat the scallions and peppers in the butter until soft. Add the tomatoes and cook, stirring, for 3 minutes. Add the eggs and the salt, pepper, and savory to taste. Cook, stirring, until the eggs are just set.

Cut a slit in the side of the pita loaves, about one quarter of the circumference, or cut the loaves in half and open the cut sides. Fill with the egg mixture.

Can be served warm or at room temperature.

*Yield: 6 sandwiches*

## Tomato, Onion, and Basil Sandwich

3 tomatoes, peeled, seeded, and sliced
salt
1/2 cup mayonnaise
2 tablespoons minced fresh basil

1 Spanish onion, thinly sliced
12 slices white bread

Place the tomato slices on a cake rack, sprinkle with salt, and drain for 30 minutes.

Combine the mayonnaise and basil and spread on the bread slices. Place a thin slice of onion on half the bread slices. Cover with a tomato slice and another slice of onion. Top with remaining bread slices and cut into sections.

*Yield: 6 sandwiches*

*Note:* If desired, use a round cutter the size of the tomato and onion slices to cut the sandwiches into rounds.

## Tomato, Onion, and Coriander Sandwich

3/4 cup butter
5 tablespoons minced fresh
  coriander leaves
1 tablespoon lemon juice
3/4 teaspoon ground
  coriander seed
salt and pepper

18 thin slices white bread
18 slices whole wheat bread
5 large plum tomatoes, cut
  in 1/4-inch thick slices
2 small Bermuda onions,
  thinly sliced

In a processor, cream the butter, minced coriander, lemon juice, ground coriander, and salt and pepper to taste until smooth. Let stand for 1 hour to develop flavor.

Spread the bread slices with the butter. Place the tomato and onion slices on the white bread, cover with the whole wheat bread, and cut into shapes.

*Yield: 18 sandwiches*

*Note:* The butter can be made several days ahead. Can be frozen. If you do not wish to make this many sandwiches, the butter can be used with other fillings.

## Egg, Anchovy, and Shrimp Sandwich

3 hard-cooked eggs
4 anchovy fillets, drained and
  chopped
1/4 cup butter, softened
1 teaspoon minced onion

1 tablespoon mayonnaise
1 teaspoon Dijon mustard
salt and pepper
24 shrimp, cooked
12 slices white bread

In a bowl, mash the eggs, anchovy fillets, butter, and onion to a paste. Fold in the mayonnaise, mustard, and salt and pepper to taste.

Spread 6 bread slices with the egg mixture. Cut the shrimp in

half lengthwise and arrange on the egg. Cover with remaining
bread slices.
*Yield: 6 sandwiches*

---

## Smoked Salmon, Caviar, and Onion Sandwich

12 slices pumpernickel bread      1/4 cup salmon caviar
1/2 cup Russian dressing           1/4 cup minced onion
1/4 pound smoked salmon,
    thinly sliced

Spread the bread with dressing and cover half the slices with
salmon and caviar. Sprinkle with onions and cover with remaining
bread slices.
*Yield: 6 sandwiches*

---

## Sardine and Egg Sandwich

6 sardines                          lemon juice
3 hard-cooked eggs, chopped         salt and pepper
3 tablespoons butter                12 slices Westphalian
1 teaspoon grated lemon rind           pumpernickel
1/2 teaspoon minced onion

In a processor, purée the sardines, eggs, butter, lemon rind,
and onion. Season to taste with lemon juice, salt, and pepper.
   Spread half the bread slices with the sardine mixture and cover
with remaining bread slices.
*Yield: 6 sandwiches*

---

## Cucumber and Shrimp Sandwich

1 cucumber, thinly sliced           2 tablespoons tartar sauce
1/4 cup tarragon wine                  (see Index)
   vinegar                          1/4 pound shrimp, cooked
1 tablespoon sugar                     and peeled
12 slices white toast

In a bowl, combine the cucumber, vinegar, and sugar. Let marinate at least 1 hour.

Spread the toast slices with the tartar sauce and arrange the shrimp on half the toast slices. Drain the cucumbers and arrange on top of the shrimp. Cover with remaining bread slices.

*Yield: 6 sandwiches*

*Note:* The cucumbers can be prepared 2 or 3 days ahead and eaten as a salad.

## Tuna and Egg Pita Sandwich

14 ounces tuna, flaked
2 hard-cooked eggs, chopped
1/4 cup lemon juice
1/4 cup ripe olives, chopped
1/4 teaspoon thyme
salt
6 small pita loaves
1 cup shredded lettuce

In a bowl, mix the tuna, eggs, lemon juice, olives, thyme, and salt to taste.

Cut the loaves in half and open the cut side. Add a layer of lettuce and top with the tuna mixture.

*Yield: 6 sandwiches*

## Tuna and Watercress Sandwich

7 ounces tuna, flaked
1 teaspoon lemon juice
1 teaspoon grated lemon rind
1/2 cup chopped watercress
mayonnaise
butter
8 thin slices white bread

In a bowl, mix the tuna, lemon juice, and rind. Add the watercress and just enough mayonnaise to bind.

Butter the bread slices and spread half the slices with the tuna mixture. Cover with remaining bread slices.

*Yield: 4 sandwiches*

## Chicken and Chutney Sandwich

1 cup minced chicken
1 cup minced chutney
1/2 cup cream cheese
1/2 cup chopped salted
   cashews

12 slices whole wheat bread,
   buttered

In a bowl, mix the chicken, chutney, cheese, and nuts.
Spread half the bread slices with the chicken mixture. Cover
with remaining bread slices.
*Yield: 6 sandwiches*

## Curried Chicken Sandwich

2 cups diced cooked chicken
1/2 cup diced celery
1/2 cup diced tart apple
1/3 cup chopped seedless
   grapes
1/4 cup mayonnaise

1/2 teaspoon salt
1-1/2 teaspoons curry powder
2 teaspoons lemon juice
6 French rolls, split and
   buttered

In a bowl, gently mix the chicken, celery, apple, grapes, mayonnaise, salt, curry powder, and lemon juice.
Fill the rolls generously.
*Yield: 6 sandwiches*
*Note:* For a different presentation, use a whole French bread
cut into 4-inch sections. With the handle of a wooden spoon, hollow
out the center crumb and stuff with the chicken mixture. Wrap
in waxed paper and chill. Serve whole or slice into 1/2-inch sections.

## Chicken, Pork, and Pepper Sandwich

12 slices white bread or toast
mayonnaise
12 slices chicken or roast
   pork

12 roasted sweet peppers
12 Belgian endive leaves
3/4 cup sliced, pitted Greek
   olives

Spread the bread slices with mayonnaise. Arrange 2 slices of meat on half the bread slices. Top with the peppers, Belgian endive, and olives. Cover with remaining bread slices.

*Yield: 6 sandwiches*

## Roast Beef and Cheese Sandwich

6 Kaiser (bulkie) rolls,
  buttered
12 slices rare roast beef

6 slices cheddar cheese
6 tomato slices
12 bacon slices

Arrange the bottoms of the rolls on a board. Put on a slice of beef and top with a slice of cheese and another slice of beef. Cover with tomato and bacon slices and the top of the roll.

*Yield: 6 sandwiches*

## Minced Cold Roast Beef Sandwich I

1/2 pound rare roast beef,
  minced
2 tablespoons minced onion
1 tablespoon grated
  horseradish

salt and pepper
mayonnaise
12 slices Russian rye or
  white bread, buttered

In a bowl, combine the beef, onion, horseradish, and salt and pepper to taste with enough mayonnaise to bind.

Spread half the bread slices with the beef mixture and cover with remaining bread slices.

*Yield: 6 sandwiches*

## Minced Roast Beef Sandwich II

2 cups minced, very rare
  roast beef
1 tablespoon minced celery
  leaves
1 teaspoon Dijon mustard
1 teaspoon onion juice

1 teaspoon Worcestershire
  sauce
salt and pepper
pinch of sugar
6 French rolls, buttered

In a bowl, gently mix the beef, celery leaves, mustard, onion juice, Worcestershire, salt and pepper to taste, and sugar.

Fill the rolls with the mixture.

*Yield: 6 sandwiches*

*Note:* For onion juice, cut an onion in half and use a lemon reamer to squeeze out the juice, just as you would squeeze a lemon.

## Pepitos (Steak and Chili Sandwich)

| | |
|---|---|
| 1 tomato, peeled, seeded, and chopped | 1/2 pound flank steak |
| 1/4 cup minced onion | 2 tablespoons butter |
| 1/4 cup minced Serrano chilies | 4 whole wheat rolls, split |
| | salt and pepper |

In a bowl, mix the tomato, onion, and chilies. Slice the steak 1/4-inch thick.

In a skillet, brown the steak slices quickly in the butter. Set aside.

Dip the cut sides of the rolls into the pan juices and arrange the steak slices on 4 halves. Top with the tomato mixture and season to taste with salt and pepper. Cover with remaining roll halves.

*Yield: 4 sandwiches*

## Minced Veal Sandwich

| | |
|---|---|
| 3/4 cup minced, cooked veal | 2 tablespoons anchovy butter (see Index) |
| salt | 12 thin slices white bread |
| mayonnaise | |

In a bowl, mix the veal, salt to taste, and enough mayonnaise to bind.

Spread the anchovy butter on the bread slices. Spread half the slices with the veal mixture. Cover with remaining bread slices.

*Yield: 6 sandwiches*

## Lamb in Pita Bread with Yogurt Sauce

2 cups yogurt
2 tablespoons lemon juice
2 garlic cloves, minced
1 tablespoon minced mint
salt and pepper
4 loaves pita bread

1/2 pound cooked lamb,
  sliced
2 tomatoes, thinly sliced
1/2 cucumber, thinly sliced
1 red onion, thinly sliced
minced parsley

In a bowl, mix the yogurt, lemon juice, garlic, mint, and salt and pepper to taste and let stand for 1 hour.

Cut the loaves in half and open the pockets.

Fill with layers of lamb, tomatoes, cucumber, and onion. Coat with the sauce and sprinkle with parsley.

*Yield: 4 sandwiches*

*Note:* Broiled, butterflied leg of lamb is best. However, slices of roast leg of lamb can be used.

## Pork and Apple Sandwich

12 thin slices bread, buttered
1 cup thick apple sauce

salt and pepper
12 slices roast pork

Spread the bread slices with apple sauce. Season to taste with salt and pepper and arrange the pork on half of the bread slices.

Cover with remaining bread slices.

*Yield: 6 sandwiches*

## Turkey and Ham Sandwich

12 slices caraway rye bread,
  buttered
4 to 6 tablespoons Russian
  dressing
6 slices turkey

6 slices baked ham
2 tomatoes, thinly sliced
2 hard-cooked eggs, thinly
  sliced

Spread the bread slices with the dressing. Layer slices of turkey, ham, tomato, and egg on half of the bread slices.

Top with remaining bread slices.
*Yield: 6 sandwiches*

## Ham Sandwich

Wonderful ham sandwiches are made from fresh bread, such as white, rye, pumpernickel, or French bread. Ideally, the bread should be cut thin, buttered well, and covered with a few very thin slices of ham. If using French bread, cut off 4-inch sections and split them horizontally to make a sandwich. If possible, weight them for an hour to compress the sandwiches and mingle the ham and butter flavors. Mustard can be added.

There are those who prefer fairly thick slices of ham between thick slices of bread. But do try paper-thin slices of buttered bread and ham. Ham sandwiches made this way have more flavor.

## Tongue Sandwich

2 cups cooked, ground
  tongue
1/2 cup mayonnaise
1/2 cup minced dill pickle
2 tablespoons minced onion
2 teaspoons Dijon mustard

1-1/2 teaspoons
  Worcestershire sauce
1 teaspoon tomato paste
salt and pepper
12 slices bread, buttered

In a bowl, mix the tongue, mayonnaise, pickle, onion, mustard, Worcestershire, tomato paste, and salt and pepper to taste.

Spread on half the bread slices and cover with remaining bread slices.
*Yield: 6 sandwiches*

## Tongue and Roquefort Sandwich

1-1/2 cups cooked, smoked
  tongue, minced
1/3 cup crumbled Roquefort
  cheese

vinaigrette
12 slices bread, buttered

In a bowl, mix the tongue and Roquefort with enough vinaigrette to moisten.

Spread half the bread slices with the tongue mixture and cover with remaining bread slices.

*Yield: 6 sandwiches*

---

## Chicken Liver and Mushroom Sandwich

1/2 pound chicken livers
1 cup chopped mushrooms
4 tablespoons butter
2/3 cup minced red pepper

6 tablespoons minced onion
2 tablespoons mayonnaise
salt and pepper
6 French rolls, buttered

In a skillet, sauté the livers and mushrooms in the butter until the livers are browned, but still pink on the inside.

Purée in a blender or processor with the pepper and onions. Add the mayonnaise. Correct the seasoning with salt and pepper. Chill 1 hour.

Spread on the buttered rolls.

*Yield: 6 sandwiches*

---

## Liverwurst Salad Sandwich

1 pound liverwurst, mashed
1/2 cup minced scallions
1/2 cup shredded lettuce
2 teaspoons Dijon mustard

6 slices white bread
6 slices whole wheat bread
mayonnaise

In a bowl, mix the liverwurst, scallions, lettuce, and mustard.

Spread the bread slices with mayonnaise. Spread the white bread with the liverwurst mixture and cover with the whole wheat bread.

*Yield: 6 sandwiches*

## Bacon and Pimiento Sandwich

24 slices crisp bacon,
  crumbled
1-1/2 cups drained pimiento,
  chopped

6 tablespoons mayonnaise
salt and pepper
12 slices whole wheat bread,
  buttered

In a bowl, mix the bacon, pimiento, mayonnaise, and salt and pepper to taste. Spread on half the bread slices and cover with the remaining bread.
*Yield: 6 sandwiches*


## Corned Beef Sandwich

12 slices bread, buttered
corned beef slices
mustard

12 tomato slices
6 lettuce leaves

Cover half the bread slices with corned beef. Spread with mustard to taste and arrange tomato and lettuce on top.
Cover with remaining bread slices.
*Yield: 6 sandwiches*
*Note:* No quantity is given for the corned beef. Some people prefer one or two thin slices, whereas others want a more generous portion. Moreover, some prefer thick slices and others thin.


## Hot Vegetable Sandwich

1/2 cup minced cabbage
1/2 cup minced carrot
1/2 cup minced green pepper
1/2 cup minced celery
1/2 cup minced radishes
1/2 cup minced onion

6 slices toast, buttered
6 cups grated cheddar cheese
2 cups beer
white pepper
cayenne pepper
dill pickles

Preheat the broiler.
In a bowl, mix the cabbage, carrot, green pepper, celery, radishes,

and onion. Spread the bread slices with 1/2-cup portions of the vegetable mixture and arrange on heatproof serving dishes.

In a saucepan over low heat, melt the cheese in the beer, stirring constantly. Season to taste with white and cayenne peppers.

Coat the vegetable mixture with the sauce and broil until golden. Serve with pickles on the side.

The sandwiches can be prepared for broiling several hours ahead.

*Yield: 6 sandwiches*

## Baked Cheese Soufflé Sandwich

3 eggs, separated
1/4 teaspoon dry mustard
salt and pepper
cayenne pepper

1 cup grated cheddar or
  chevre cheese
6 slices whole wheat toast

Preheat oven to 350°F.

In a bowl, mix the egg yolks with the mustard, and salt, pepper, and cayenne to taste until light and lemon colored. Stir in the cheese.

Beat the egg whites until stiff, but not dry. Fold into the cheese mixture. Spread on the toast and arrange on a baking sheet.

Bake 10 to 12 minutes, or until puffed and golden.

Can be prepared 1 to 2 hours before baking.

*Yield: 6 sandwiches*

*Note:* Any cheese that can be grated or crumbled can be substituted.

## Eggplant Sandwich

6 1/2-inch-thick slices
  eggplant
6 1/4-inch-thick slices tomato
6 1/4-inch thick slices onion

6 tablespoons olive oil
2 tablespoons grated
  Parmesan cheese
12 thin slices French bread

In a large skillet, sauté the eggplant, tomato, and onion slices in the olive oil until golden.

On half the bread slices, arrange layers of eggplant, tomato, and onion. Sprinkle with cheese. Cover with remaining bread slices.

*Yield: 6 sandwiches*

*Note:* If desired, the vegetables can be prepared ahead, cooled, and refrigerated overnight. When ready to serve, heat the vegetables on a baking sheet in a 350°F. oven and assemble sandwiches.

## Onion and Cheese Sandwich

6 French rolls (club)
1/2 cup butter, softened
3 tablespoons Dijon mustard
1/4 teaspoon cayenne pepper

12 thin slices cheddar cheese, halved
12 thin slices onion, halved

Preheat oven to 350°F.

Cut each roll vertically into 1/2-inch-thick slices without cutting all the way through.

In a bowl, cream the butter, mustard, and cayenne.

Spread between the roll sections.

Insert the cheese and onion slices and press the roll together from the ends. Bake 15 minutes, or until heated and the cheese starts to melt.

Can be prepared for baking up to 24 hours before serving.

*Yield: 6 sandwiches*

## Green Pepper and Cheddar Cheese Sandwich

6 tablespoons butter
3 tablespoons sesame seeds
12-inch loaf Italian bread

1/3 cup grated cheddar cheese
1 pepper, thinly sliced

Preheat oven to 400°F.

In a bowl, combine the butter and sesame seeds.

Cut the loaf in half lengthwise and spread the halves with the butter. Sprinkle one half with cheese. Cover with pepper slices and the top half of the loaf. Place on a baking sheet and bake for 10 minutes, or until the cheese starts to melt. Cut into 6 sections.

Can be prepared for baking 24 hours ahead.

*Yield: 6 sandwiches*

## Poppy Seed and Gruyère Sandwich

| | |
|---|---|
| 1/4 cup butter | cayenne pepper |
| 1-1/2 tablespoons minced onion | 6 slices white bread |
| 2 teaspoons poppy seeds | 1/2 cup grated Gruyère cheese |

Preheat oven to 350°F.

In a bowl, mix the butter, onion, poppy seeds, and cayenne to taste.

Toast the bread on one side. Spread the untoasted side with the poppy seed butter. Sprinkle with the cheese and bake until the cheese is melted, about 20 minutes.

*Yield: 6 servings*

*Note:* It is best to toast the bread shortly before serving. The butter will keep for 1 week in the refrigerator.

## Toasted Mushroom Sandwich

| | |
|---|---|
| 8 tablespoons butter, melted | 1/4 teaspoon paprika |
| 1 garlic clove, minced | 1/2 teaspoon salt |
| 4 teaspoons minced onion | pepper |
| 1 pound mushrooms, minced | 12 slices bread |
| 2 tablespoons heavy cream | |

Preheat the broiler.

In a large skillet, sauté the garlic and onion in 2 tablespoons butter until the onion is golden. Add the mushrooms, cream, paprika, salt, and pepper to taste and cook until the mushrooms are tender.

Spread the mixture over 6 slices of bread and top with remaining bread slices. Brush the top of each sandwich with butter and broil until golden. Turn and brush with remaining butter and broil until golden.

Can be prepared for broiling up to 24 hours ahead.

*Yield: 6 sandwiches*

## Horseradish Cheese Croûte

6 thin slices white bread
4 tablespoons butter
3/4 cup grated Gruyère
  cheese
3/4 cup grated Parmesan
  cheese

3 tablespoons heavy cream
1 tablespoon grated
  horseradish
tarragon vinegar
paprika

Preheat oven to 400°F.

Sauté the bread slices in the butter until golden on both sides.

In a bowl, mix the Gruyère and Parmesan cheeses, cream, horseradish, and vinegar to taste. Spread thickly on the toasts.

Bake 4 minutes, or until golden. Sprinkle with the paprika and serve.

*Yield: 6 sandwiches*

## Crab and Mushroom French Rolls

1 cup crabmeat, flaked
1/2 pound mushrooms,
  chopped
12 tablespoons mayonnaise
4 tablespoons grated
  Parmesan cheese
2 tablespoons minced parsley
1 teaspoon lemon juice

1/8 teaspoon rosemary
1/8 teaspoon thyme
1/8 teaspoon sage
6 French or Kaiser rolls
butter
6 tablespoons slivered,
  toasted almonds

Preheat oven to 350°F.

In a bowl, mix the crabmeat, mushrooms, mayonnaise, cheese, parsley, lemon juice, rosemary, thyme, and sage.

Split the rolls in half, spread with butter, and toast.

Spread the bottom halves of rolls with the crab mixture and sprinkle with the almonds. Cover with tops of the rolls.

Wrap each sandwich in foil and bake for 20 minutes, or until thoroughly heated.

Can be prepared for baking 2 to 3 hours ahead.

*Yield: 6 sandwiches*

## Soft-shelled Crab Sandwich

12 tablespoons clarified
   butter
1 garlic clove, thinly sliced
6 slices white bread
6 soft-shell crabs

flour
6 lettuce leaves
6 tablespoons remoulade
   sauce (see Index)

In a large skillet, heat the butter and garlic until the garlic just starts to turn golden. Do not burn. Discard the garlic.

Sauté the bread on both sides in the butter and drain on paper towels.

Dredge the crabs in the flour and sauté in remaining butter until golden, about 3 minutes on each side.

Arrange the lettuce leaves on the toast, top with crabs, and garnish with remoulade sauce. Best if made and served immediately.

*Yield: 6 sandwiches*

## Crabmeat Lorenzo

1 garlic clove, minced
1/4 cup butter
1/3 cup minced scallion
1/4 cup minced green pepper
2 teaspoons flour
1/2 cup milk
1 pound crabmeat, flaked

1/2 cup stale bread crumbs
1/4 cup dry sherry
salt and pepper
6 5-inch toast rounds
12 anchovy fillets
6 tablespoons grated
   Parmesan cheese

Preheat the broiler.

In a skillet, sauté the garlic in the butter until soft, but not brown. Add the scallion and green pepper and simmer, stirring, for 10 minutes, or until soft. Stir in the flour and cook, stirring, 1 minute. Stir in the milk and cook, stirring, until thickened. Fold in the crab, bread crumbs, sherry, and salt and pepper to taste.

Mound the mixture on the toast rounds. Arrange the anchovy fillets on top and sprinkle with the cheese. Broil until golden.

*Yield: 6 sandwiches*

*Note:* The crab mixture can be kept in the refrigerator for 24 hours.

## Broiled Crabmeat Rounds

6 slices white toast
1 cup crabmeat
2 hard-cooked eggs, minced
1/4 cup minced dill pickles
1/4 cup mayonnaise
2 to 3 tablespoons lemon
    juice

salt and pepper
Tabasco sauce
butter
6 tomato slices
6 tablespoons grated
    Parmesan cheese

Preheat oven to 400°F.
Cut crusts from toast.
In a bowl, mix the crab, eggs, pickles, mayonnaise, lemon juice, and salt, pepper, and Tabasco to taste. Spread the toast with butter and then with the crab mixture. Arrange a tomato slice on top and season with salt and pepper.
Sprinkle with the cheese and dot with butter.
Bake for 10 minutes, or until the cheese is melted and lightly browned.
*Yield: 6 sandwiches*
*Note:* If desired, you can cut the bread into small rounds, spread with crab mixture, and top with cherry tomatoes to make 24 canapés.

## Dutch Toast

1/2 pound finnan haddie,
    minced
2 tablespoons butter
3/4 cup béchamel sauce (see
    Index)

12 toast rounds
12 slices hard-cooked egg

Sweat the finnan haddie in the butter until flaky. Fold in the béchamel sauce and spread on the toast rounds.
Top with hard-cooked eggs and serve.
*Yield: 6 sandwiches*
*Note:* The fish mixture can be made a day ahead and reheated. The bread should be toasted just before serving.

## Open-faced Flounder Sandwich

1 pound flounder fillets,
  poached
7 teaspoons tartar sauce (see
  Index)
salt and pepper

8 slices toast, buttered
8 thin slices tomato
12 tablespoons grated
  Gruyère cheese

Preheat the broiler.

Flake the cooked fish and fold in the tartar sauce. Correct the seasoning with salt and pepper.

Spread on the toast slices. Top with tomato and cheese and broil until the cheese is golden.

*Yield: 8 sandwiches*

*Note:* The fish mixture can be made 1 day ahead. Let come to room temperature before using.

## Grilled Lobster Sandwich, Aurora

1/2 cup béchamel sauce (see
  Index)
1-1/2 teaspoons tomato paste
1 teaspoon lemon juice
1-1/2 cups cooked lobster

6 slices white bread, crusts
  removed
6 tablespoons grated Gruyère
  cheese

Preheat the broiler.

In a 1-quart saucepan, reduce the béchamel to 1/3 cup. Stir in the tomato paste, lemon juice, and lobster.

Toast the bread slices on one side. Spread the untoasted side with the lobster mixture and sprinkle with cheese.

Place on a baking sheet and broil until golden.

The lobster can be prepared 2 or 3 days ahead, or frozen.

*Yield: 6 sandwiches*

## Brandied Lobster Sandwich

3/4 cup thick béchamel sauce
1 tablespoon tomato paste
2 tablespoons cognac
2 tablespoons minced parsley
1/2 teaspoon salt
pinch of grated nutmeg
1/4 teaspoon minced tarragon
pepper

1 cup chopped, cooked
  lobster
6 slices white bread, crusts
  removed
butter
1/4 cup grated Gruyère
  cheese

Preheat the broiler.

In a 1-quart saucepan, heat the béchamel, tomato paste, cognac, parsley, salt, nutmeg, tarragon, and pepper to taste.

When hot, fold in the lobster and heat thoroughly.

Toast the bread on one side. Spread the untoasted side with butter. Spread the lobster on the toast and sprinkle with cheese.

Broil until golden.

The lobster mixture can be made 1 day ahead.

*Yield: 6 sandwiches*

## Oyster Sandwich

6 slices rye bread
2 tablespoons butter
2 tablespoons anchovy paste

24 shucked oysters, drained
salt and pepper
12 slices Monterey Jack
  cheese

Preheat oven to 400°F.

Butter the bread slices on one side. Place buttered side down on a baking sheet. Spread anchovy paste on the unbuttered side and arrange 4 oysters on each slice. Sprinkle with salt and pepper.

Cover with cheese slices and bake 10 minutes, or until golden. If needed, brown under the broiler.

*Yield: 6 sandwiches*

## Dieppe Boats

6 slices bread
butter
24 mussels, cooked and
    shelled

8 tablespoons beurre blanc
(see following recipe)

Preheat oven to 400°F.
Sauté the bread slices in butter until golden. Arrange the mussels
on the bread and coat lightly with beurre blanc.
Heat in the oven for 5 minutes.
*Yield: 6 sandwiches*


## Beurre Blanc (White Wine Butter Sauce)

3 tablespoons white wine
    vinegar
3 tablespoons dry white wine

2 shallots, minced
1 cup cold butter, cubed
salt and pepper

In a noncorrosive pan, reduce the vinegar, wine, and shallots
over high heat to about 1 tablespoon. Set the pan over low heat,
or transfer the shallot mixture to the top of a double boiler over
very hot, but not boiling, water.
With a wire whisk, whip in the butter, bit by bit, until the
sauce has thickened. Incorporate each piece of butter before adding
more. Season to taste with salt and pepper.
*Yield: about 1 cup*


## Salmon Soufflé Sandwich

12 slices tomato
6 slices toast, buttered
salt and pepper
1-1/2 cups cooked, flaked
    salmon
1-1/2 cups grated cheddar
    cheese

4 eggs, separated
2 teaspoons Worcestershire
    sauce
2 teaspoons Dijon mustard
1/4 teaspoon paprika

Preheat oven to 350°F.

Arrange 2 tomato slices on each toast slice. Season to taste with salt and pepper. Cover with salmon and place on a lightly buttered baking sheet.

In a bowl, mix the cheese, egg yolks, Worcestershire, mustard, paprika, and salt and pepper to taste.

In a bowl, beat the egg whites until stiff, but not dry. Fold into the cheese mixture and spread on each sandwich.

Bake for 15 minutes, or until puffed and golden.

*Yield: 6 sandwiches*

## Chicken and Grape Toasts

6 slices bread
1 cup minced chicken
1/2 cup green grapes, chopped

3/4 cup béchamel sauce
1/2 cup grated Gruyère cheese

Preheat the broiler.

Toast the bread slices on one side.

In a bowl, mix the chicken, grapes, and béchamel. Spread on the untoasted side of the bread and sprinkle with cheese.

Broil until golden.

Filling can be prepared several days ahead.

*Yield: 6 sandwiches*

## Mary Garden Sandwich

6 slices white toast, buttered
3 small chicken breasts, thinly sliced
12 mushroom caps, sliced
1 tablespoon butter

12 asparagus tips, cooked
1-1/2 cups mornay sauce (see Index)
parsley sprigs

Preheat the broiler.

Place the toast on heatproof serving plates. Arrange the chicken slices on top.

Sauté the mushrooms in the butter until tender. Scatter over the chicken. Arrange the asparagus on top of the mushrooms. Coat the top of each sandwich with sauce and brown under the broiler. Garnish each serving with parsley sprigs.

*Yield: 6 sandwiches*

## Chicken and Gherkin Sandwich

6 slices rye bread
butter
12 thin slices cooked chicken
salt and pepper

3 gherkins, thinly sliced
2 tablespoons grated
   mozzarella cheese

Preheat oven to 400°F.

Toast the bread on one side and lightly butter the untoasted side. Arrange the chicken slices on the untoasted side and season with salt and pepper. Arrange the gherkin slices on the chicken and sprinkle with cheese.

Bake 10 minutes, or until golden.

*Yield: 6 sandwiches*

## Puffed Chicken Sandwich

1-2/3 cups chopped, cooked
   chicken
1/2 cup chopped celery
1/3 cup mayonnaise
1-1/2 tablespoons lemon juice

salt and pepper
6 slices whole wheat bread
3 egg whites
3/4 cup grated cheddar or
   Parmesan cheese

Preheat oven to 450°F.

In a bowl, mix the chicken, celery, mayonnaise, lemon juice, and salt and pepper to taste.

Toast the bread on one side and lightly butter the untoasted side. Spread the chicken mixture on the buttered side.

In a bowl, beat the egg whites with a pinch of salt until stiff, but not dry. Fold in the cheese and spread the mixture on top of the chicken.

Bake 10 minutes, or until puffed and golden.

*Yield: 6 sandwiches*

## Broiled Chicken Sandwich

1-1/2 cups diced, cooked
   chicken
6 tablespoons butter,
   softened
1/4 cup heavy cream
1 tablespoon lemon juice

1/2 teaspoon ground thyme
salt and pepper
6 slices toast, buttered on
   one side
grated Parmesan cheese

Preheat the broiler.
In a bowl, combine the chicken and butter. Fold in the cream,
lemon juice, thyme, and salt and pepper to taste. Spread on the
buttered side of the toast and sprinkle with cheese.
Brown under the broiler.
*Yield: 6 sandwiches*

## Devonshire Sandwich

18 slices crisp bacon
3/4 cup bacon fat, from
   cooking the bacon
1 cup flour
1 quart milk
1 pound sharp cheddar
   cheese, grated
2 teaspoons dry mustard

salt
pinch of sage
6 slices toast
18 thin slices chicken or
   turkey
1/4 cup grated Parmesan
   cheese

Preheat oven to 350°F. or preheat the broiler.
Heat the bacon fat, stir in the flour, and cook 3 minutes. Stir
in the milk and cook, stirring, until thickened and smooth. Stir
in the cheddar cheese and mustard and cook, stirring, over low
heat until the cheese is melted. Season to taste with salt and sage.
Place the toast on a heatproof platter and top with bacon and
chicken. Coat with the cheese sauce and sprinkle with grated
cheese. Bake until hot and bubbly. If desired, brown under the
broiler.
Can be prepared for heating 1 to 2 hours before serving.
*Yield: 6 sandwiches*

## Bacon and Turkey Sandwich

6 slices rye toast
mayonnaise
6 thin slices turkey

12 slices crisp bacon
6 1/2-inch-thick slices tomato
6 slices Gruyère cheese

Prehat oven to 400°F.
Spread the toast with mayonnaise to taste. Arrange turkey, bacon, tomato, and cheese slices on top.
Bake for 10 minutes, or until the cheese is melted.
Can be prepared for heating 2 to 3 hours before serving.
*Yield: 6 sandwiches*

## Turkey Rarebit Sandwich

3 tablespoons butter
3 tablespoons flour
1-1/2 cups cubed cheddar
    cheese
1/4 teaspoon dry mustard
milk

8 slices white toast
1/2 pound turkey, thinly
    sliced
8 slices tomato
16 slices crisp bacon

Preheat the broiler.
In a saucepan, melt the butter, stir in the flour, and cook, stirring, until the mixture is foamy. Lower the heat and stir in the cheese. Cook, stirring, until the cheese is melted. Stir in the mustard and enough milk to make a thin sauce that just coats the back of a spoon. Keep the sauce warm.
Place the toast on a heatproof serving dish and arrange turkey slices on top. Coat with the sauce. Brown under the broiler until golden.
Garnish with tomato slices and bacon strips.
*Yield: 8 sandwiches*
*Note:* The sauce can be prepared 1 day ahead and reheated. The sandwiches can be prepared for heating several hours before serving. Coat with the sauce just before heating. If desired, substitute beer for the milk.

## Stromboli Sandwich

6 1/2-inch-thick slices French
bread, toasted
6 1-1/2-ounce slices
tenderloin
2 tablespoons butter

6 thin slices ham
6 thin slices mozzarella
cheese
6 pitted ripe olives

Preheat the broiler.

Arrange the toast slices on a heatproof platter.

In a skillet, sauté the tenderloin slices in the butter, over high heat, until rare. Place the tenderloin slices on the toast and top with ham and cheese slices. Broil until the cheese begins to melt.

Garnish each sandwich with a ripe olive.

*Yield: 6 sandwiches*

*Note:* Best prepared and served immediately. Leftover roasted tenderloin can be substituted, but the flavor will be different.

## Bœuf Haché aux Chevre et Poivre (Ground Beef, Chevre, and Pepper Sandwich)

3 pounds ground beef
freshly cracked pepper
coarse salt
2/3 cup cognac

butter
6 club rolls, split and toasted
6 ounces chevre cheese

Shape the beef into 6 patties the same shape as the rolls. Press pepper into both sides of the patties.

In a heavy iron skillet, over high heat, sear both sides of the patties. Lower the heat and cook to desired degree of doneness. Sprinkle generously with salt. Remove from the pan.

Add the cognac to the skillet. Stir up any browned bits and reduce the cognac to 3 tablespoons.

Butter the rolls and place the burgers on the bottom halves. Sprinkle with the pan juices. Cover with a slice of cheese and the tops of the rolls.

*Yield: 6 sandwiches*

## Bœuf Haché à Cheval (Hamburgers with Fried Eggs and Anchovies)

6 rare hamburgers
6 toast rounds, sautéed in
  butter

6 fried eggs
12 anchovy fillets

Arrange the hamburgers on the toast rounds. Top with the eggs and crisscross the anchovies on top.
*Yield: 6 sandwiches*

## Hamburgers Provençale

3 pounds ground beef
3 garlic cloves, minced
olive oil
6 hamburger rolls

6 slices eggplant, sautéed
1/4 cup tomato coulis (see
  Index)

In a bowl, mix the beef and garlic and shape into 6 patties.
In a heavy skillet, sauté the patties in the olive oil to desired degree of doneness. Arrange the patties on the bottom halves of the hamburger rolls. Place eggplant slices on the top halves of the rolls and garnish with tomato coulis.
*Yield: 6 sandwiches*

## Reuben Sandwich

6 tablespoons Russian
  dressing
6 slices dark rye toast,
  buttered
1-1/2 pounds thinly sliced
  corned beef

1 pound sauerkraut, rinsed
  and drained
6 slices Gruyère cheese

Preheat oven to 400°F.
Spread the dressing on the buttered toast and cover with slices

of corned beef. Add a generous layer of sauerkraut and cover with cheese slices.

Bake 5 to 7 minutes, or until the sandwiches are heated and the cheese has started to melt.

*Yield: 6 sandwiches*

## Lamb Sandwich

12 slices white bread
4 tablespoons mustard butter
   (see Index)

1-1/2 pounds hot roast lamb,
   thinly sliced
mint sprigs

Spread the bread slices with mustard butter. Cover half the slices with lamb and garnish with mint sprigs. Cover with remaining bread slices.

*Yield: 6 sandwiches*

## Panini Rustici (Italian Country Sandwich)

1 pound ricotta cheese
2 eggs
1/2 teaspoon salt
1/2 pound mozzarella cheese,
   diced
1/4 pound salami, diced
1/4 pound prosciutto, diced

1/2 pound mortadella, diced
6 Italian rolls, halved
1/2 cup grated Parmesan
   cheese
pepper
4 tablespoons butter

Preheat oven to 350°F.

In a bowl, mix the ricotta, eggs, salt, mozzarella, salami, prosciutto, and mortadella. Spread the mixture on both halves of the rolls. Sprinkle with Parmesan and pepper to taste and dot with butter.

Bake 10 to 15 minutes, or until well heated.

If desired, brown the sandwiches under the broiler.

Can be prepared for heating 2 to 3 hours ahead.

*Yield: 6 to 12 sandwiches*

## Crostino Caldo alla Re Guido D'Andrea (Hot Italian Sandwich)

6 slices Italian bread, toasted
6 slices mozzarella cheese
2 tablespoons minced capers
4 ounces anchovies, soaked
  in milk
6 mushrooms, thinly sliced
6 teaspoons minced parsley
1 teaspoon dried basil,
  crumbled

6 slices Gruyère cheese
3 tomatoes, thinly sliced
5 tablespoons grated
  Parmesan cheese
6 slices prosciutto
olive oil
pepper

Preheat oven to 400°F.

On the bread slices, make layers of mozzarella, capers, anchovies, and mushrooms. Sprinkle with parsley and basil. Cover with Gruyère and tomatoes. Sprinkle with Parmesan and cover with prosciutto.

Brush with olive oil and sprinkle with pepper. Bake until the cheese is slightly melted.

Can be prepared for heating 2 to 3 hours ahead.

*Yield: 6 sandwiches*

## Croûtes au Reblochon (Hot Reblochon Cheese Sandwich)

6 slices whole wheat bread,
  toasted and buttered
6 thin slices prosciutto
6 1/4-inch-thick slices
  Reblochon cheese

6 tablespoons bread crumbs
3 tablespoons minced parsley
6 tablespoons heavy cream
salt and pepper

Preheat oven to 375°F.

Cover the bread slices with prosciutto and cheese. Place on a baking sheet.

In a bowl, mix the bread crumbs, parsley, cream, and salt and pepper to taste. Spread over the cheese slices.

Bake until heated and the cheese starts to melt.

Can be prepared for baking 2 to 3 hours ahead.

*Yield: 6 sandwiches*

## Fried Tomato and Bacon Sandwich

6 1/2-inch-thick slices tomato    12 slices crisp bacon
2 tablespoons butter
6 slices whole wheat or rye
  toast, buttered

Sauté the tomato slices in the butter until lightly browned. Arrange the tomato slices on the toast and cover with bacon slices.
*Yield: 6 sandwiches*

## Broiled Bacon, Tomato, and Blue Cheese Sandwich

6 slices bread                    18 thin slices tomato
butter                            6 tablespoons crumbled blue
12 slices crisp bacon               cheese

Preheat the broiler.
Toast the bread on one side and butter the untoasted side. Cover the untoasted side with bacon, tomato, and cheese.
Arrange the sandwiches on a baking sheet and broil until the cheese is just melted and touched with brown.
*Yield: 6 sandwiches*
*Note:* Gruyère, chevre, or cheddar cheese can be substituted for blue cheese.

## Ficelle Picarde (Cheese and Mushroom Sandwich)

2/3 cup duxelles (recipe          1 garlic clove, minced
  follows)                        salt and pepper
1 cup béchamel sauce (see         8 slices white toast
  Index)                          8 slices ham
1 tomato, peeled, seeded, and     grated Gruyère or Parmesan
  chopped                           cheese

Preheat the broiler.
In a bowl, mix the duxelles, béchamel, tomato, garlic, and salt and pepper to taste.

Spread the toast with the mixture and cover with ham slices. Sprinkle generously with cheese. Broil until the cheese is melted.
*Yield: 6 sandwiches*

## Duxelles (Mushroom Spread)

| | |
|---|---|
| 1/2 pound mushrooms, minced | 4 tablespoons butter |
| | salt |
| 2 shallots, minced | 2 teaspoons minced parsley |

In a skillet, sauté the mushrooms and shallots in the butter until the moisture has evaporated.
Season with salt and stir in parsley.
Can be frozen.
*Yield: about 1 cup*

## Broiled Ham and Cheese Sandwich

| | |
|---|---|
| 2 tablespoons butter, softened | 6 slices Italian bread |
| 1/4 teaspoon thyme | 6 slices ham |
| salt and pepper | 6 thin slices Italian fontina cheese |

Preheat the broiler.
In a bowl, beat together the butter, thyme, and salt and pepper to taste.
Toast the bread on one side and butter the untoasted side.
Place the ham and cheese on the toast and arrange on a baking sheet. Broil until the cheese is golden.
*Yield: 6 sandwiches*
*Note:* Italian fontina has a very different flavor from that made in other countries. The Italian variety is recommended.

## Baked Ham, Gruyère, and Roquefort Sandwich

| | |
|---|---|
| 12 slices white toast, crusts removed | 1-1/2 cups crumbled Roquefort cheese |
| 3 tablespoons butter, melted | 2 egg yolks |
| 12 thin slices Gruyère cheese | 3 tablespoons dry white wine |
| 6 thin slices baked ham | |

Preheat oven to 400°F.

Brush one side of the toast with butter.

Place 6 toasts, buttered side up, on a buttered baking sheet. Place a slice of Gruyère, cut to fit, on the toast and cover with a ham slice, cut to fit. Cover with another slice of Gruyère and with remaining toast, buttered side down.

In a bowl, mix the Roquefort, egg yolks, and wine. Spread on top of each sandwich. Bake until the topping is golden.

Can be prepared for baking 2 to 3 hours ahead. Add topping just before baking.

*Yield: 6 sandwiches*

## Derby Toast

1/2 cup walnut halves,
   chopped
1 cup ground ham
1/2 cup warm béchamel
   sauce (see Index)

cayenne pepper
6 slices bread

Preheat oven to 400°F.

In a pie plate, warm the walnuts in the oven for 5 minutes.

In a bowl, mix the walnuts, ham, béchamel, and cayenne to taste. Toast the bread on one side. Spread the untoasted side with the ham mixture. Serve warm.

*Yield: 6 sandwiches*

*Note:* The walnut-béchamel mixture can be prepared 1 or 2 days ahead. Reheat in a saucepan before serving.

## Croûte du Lion d'Or (Mushroom and Ham Toast)

2 shallots, minced
2 tablespoons butter
3/4 pound mushrooms,
   minced
1 cup minced ham
2/3 cup heavy cream

1 teaspoon curry powder
salt
6 slices toast
1/2 cup sauce mousseline (see
   following recipe)

Preheat the broiler.

In a skillet, sauté the shallots in butter until soft.

Add the mushrooms and cook over high heat until the liquid has evaporated. Stir in the ham, cream, curry powder, and salt to taste. Simmer 3 minutes.

Spread on the toast and place on a baking sheet. Coat each slice with a tablespoon of sauce. Brown under the broiler.

*Yield: 6 sandwiches*

*Sauce Mousseline*

| 1 cup warm hollandaise | 1/2 cup whipped cream |
| sauce (see following recipe) | |

Shortly before using, fold the whipped cream into the hollandaise. Yields about 1-1/2 cups.

*Hollandaise Sauce*

| 3 egg yolks | salt |
| 1 tablespoon water | lemon juice |
| 1/2 cup butter | |

In the top of a double boiler over hot water (not boiling), or in a heavy saucepan over low heat, beat the egg yolks and water until light and fluffy.

Beat in the butter, about 1 tablespoon at a time, until each piece is incorporated into the sauce. Beat with a wire whisk for 1 minute after all the butter has been added to lighten the mixture. Season to taste with salt and lemon juice.

If the sauce should curdle, try adding 1 tablespoon of boiling water and beating briskly. If that fails, add 1 tablespoon cold water. If that also fails, put an egg yolk into a warm bowl and beat in some curdled sauce, drop by drop until about a quarter of it has been added. Add remaining curdled sauce in a slow steady stream until everything is incorporated. Hold the sauce over warm water (not boiling) until ready to use.

## Gayolle Toasts

1/2 cup minced ham
1/2 cup minced mushrooms,
   sautéed
1/2 cup grated Gruyère
   cheese

1/2 cup béchamel sauce (see
   Index)
cayenne pepper
8 slices bread

Preheat oven to 400°F.

In a bowl, mix the ham, mushrooms, and cheese together. Add enough béchamel to bind into a thick mixture. Season to taste with cayenne.

Toast the bread on one side. Spread the untoasted side with the ham mixture. Heat about 10 minutes.

*Yield: 8 sandwiches*

## Grilled Curried Ham and Cabbage Sandwich

3 tablespoons mayonnaise
12 tablespoons chutney
curry powder
salt
1-1/2 cups shredded cabbage

1 pound shaved ham
12 slices rye bread, buttered
3 ounces cheddar cheese,
   sliced
2 tablespoons butter

In a bowl, mix the mayonnaise, chutney, and curry powder and salt to taste. Stir in the cabbage.

Place a layer of ham on half the bread slices. Cover with the cabbage mixture and top with a cheese slice. Cover with remaining bread slices. Butter the outside of the sandwiches and brown on both sides in a skillet.

*Yield: 6 sandwiches*

## Bratwurst and Sauerkraut Sandwich

1 quart sauerkraut, washed
   and drained
1 apple, peeled and thinly
   sliced
1 tablespoon caraway seeds,
   crushed
2 tablespoons vegetable oil

1 pound bratwurst
1 tablespoon butter
1/2 cup white wine
6 whole wheat pita loaves, or
   12 slices caraway rye
Dijon mustard

In a skillet, sauté the sauerkraut, apple, and caraway in oil for 3 minutes. Cover and simmer 20 minutes.

In another skillet, sauté the bratwurst in the butter until browned on all sides. Pour off excess fat and add the wine. Simmer until the wine evaporates.

Stuff the pita loaves with sauerkraut and top with bratwurst. Serve mustard on the side.

If using the caraway rye, top half the slices with sauerkraut and slices of bratwurst. Cover with remaining bread slices.

*Yield: 6 sandwiches*

*Note:* Frankfurters, Italian sausage, or almost any other sausage can be substituted for the bratwurst.

## Sausage, Sauerkraut, and Cheese Sandwich

1-1/2 pounds pork sausage
   meat
6 ounces sliced Gruyère
   cheese
1 cup chopped sauerkraut,
   rinsed and drained

1/8 teaspoon caraway seeds
butter
6 Kaiser (bulkie) rolls, or
   poppy seed rolls, split and
   toasted

Shape the sausage meat into 6 patties. Sauté in a skillet until cooked through, or broil. Top each patty with a slice of cheese.

In a 1-quart saucepan, heat the sauerkraut, caraway seeds, and butter.

Place a sausage patty on the bottom of each roll. Cover with sauerkraut and the top of the roll.

*Yield: 6 sandwiches*

## Saucisson en Croûte (Sausages in Bread)

6 Italian sausages        Dijon mustard
6 French rolls

Prick the sausage skin and grill over charcoal, or put into a saucepan with 1/4 inch water and cook until the water evaporates and the sausages are brown on all sides.

Cut off the ends of the rolls. With the handle of a wooden spoon, ream out the center of each roll. Dip the cooked sausages into the mustard and slide them into the rolls.

*Yield: 6 sandwiches*

*Note:* You can use a loaf of French bread cut into sections the same length as the sausage. Chorizo, linquica, or kielbasa can be substituted for the Italian sausage.

## CROQUE-MONSIEUR, PAIN PERDU, OR FRENCH TOAST SANDWICHES

Pain perdu (literally lost bread) or French toast sandwiches are assembled, dipped in egg, and sautéed in butter or deep-fried until golden. In recent years, they have become very popular as lunch offerings, as well as for breakfast or supper. Croque-monsieur—a ham and cheese sandwich—is probably the best known version.

This method is not limited to the sandwiches suggested here. Many sandwiches can be treated in the same manner. The one unifying element in these sandwiches is the cheese. Even though a recipe indicates a particular cheese, you can substitute your favorite.

One advantage is that these sandwiches can be prepared up to 24 hours ahead. Do not dip the sandwiches into the egg until shortly before cooking, or the bread will become soft and break apart in handling. The sandwiches can be sautéed in butter in a skillet, or deep-fried at 375°F. until golden. A special iron can be found in gourmet shops that compresses and shapes the sandwich into a scallop shell. It is fun to use but not necessary for delicious sandwiches.

## Mozzarella in Carrozza (Mozzarella in Wheels)

6 slices white bread, thinly
  sliced
6 1/4-inch-thick slices
  mozzarella cheese
oil for deep frying

2 eggs, lightly beaten
1/2 cup butter
6 anchovy fillets, chopped
1 tablespoon minced parsley

Make the sandwiches with the bread and cheese. Cut into rounds, ovals, or squares, discarding the crusts.

Heat the oil to 375°F.

Dip the sandwiches in the eggs and deep-fry in the oil until golden.

In a small saucepan, melt the butter. Stir in the anchovies and stir until dissolved and the butter is lightly browned. Stir in the parsley.

Serve the sauce separately in small bowls.

*Yield: 6 sandwiches*

## Sautéed Tomato Sandwich

2 tomatoes, peeled
1/2 cup sour cream
1/2 cup grated Gruyère
  cheese
2 tablespoons minced dill
2 tablespoons minced chives
lemon juice

salt and pepper
butter
8 thin slices white bread,
  crusts removed
2 eggs
1/4 cup milk
3 tablespoons clarified butter

Cut tomatoes in 1/4-inch-thick slices and set aside.

In a bowl, mix the sour cream, cheese, dill, chives, and lemon juice, salt, and pepper to taste.

Butter one side of each bread slice. Spread the sour cream mixture on the buttered side of 4 slices, leaving a 1/4-inch border. Arrange tomato slices on top. Cover with remaining bread slices and press gently.

In a shallow dish, beat the eggs and milk. Season to taste with salt and pepper. Dip the sandwiches in the egg mixture, coating both sides. Sauté in clarified butter in a skillet until golden on both sides.

*Yield: 4 sandwiches*

## Grilled Shrimp Sandwich

5 ounces cooked shrimp, chopped
1/2 cup minced celery
1 teaspoon minced onion
1/4 teaspoon salt
1/2 teaspoon chili powder
1/4 teaspoon crushed garlic

1/4 teaspoon ground pepper
1/4 cup mayonnaise
10 slices bread, buttered
3 eggs, lightly beaten
3 tablespoons milk
1/4 teaspoon salt
butter

In a bowl, mix the shrimp, celery, onion, salt, chili powder, garlic, pepper, and mayonnaise. Spread on half the bread slices. Cover with the remaining bread slices and press gently.

In a bowl, combine the eggs, milk, and salt. Dip the sandwiches into the egg mixture and sauté in butter in a skillet until golden on both sides.

Can be prepared for dipping 24 hours ahead.
*Yield: 5 sandwiches*

## Pain Perdu à la Reine (French Toast Chicken Sandwich)

4 eggs
1 cup milk
1/2 teaspoon salt
pinch of cayenne
6 3/4-inch-thick slices bread
6 chicken breasts, skinned, boned, and halved

6 tablespoons butter
salt and pepper
6 tablespoons butter
2 cups mornay sauce (see Index)
1/2 cup grated Gruyère cheese

Preheat oven to 375°F.

Beat the eggs, milk, salt, and cayenne together. Soak the bread slices in the egg mixture for 10 minutes.

In a baking dish, bake the chicken breasts with 6 tablespoons of butter, and salt and pepper to taste for 10 to 12 minutes, or until just cooked.

Cut the bread slices in half diagonally. Sauté the bread slices in 6 tablespoons butter until golden. Overlap the bread and chicken slices on a heatproof platter. Spoon the sauce over and sprinkle with cheese. Glaze under the broiler.

*Yield: 6 sandwiches*

## Milwaukee Sandwich

12 slices white bread,
  buttered
12 thin slices chicken
2 tablespoons crumbled
  Roquefort cheese

paprika
butter

Make 6 sandwiches with the bread, chicken, Roquefort, and paprika to taste.

Butter one side of the sandwich and sauté in a skillet, buttered side down, until golden. Butter the top of the sandwich, turn, and brown the other side.

*Yield: 6 sandwiches*

## Montecristo

6 slices baked ham
12 slices white bread,
  buttered
12 thin slices cooked chicken

6 thin slices Gruyère cheese
3 eggs, lightly beaten
8 tablespoons butter

Place ham slices on half the bread slices. Cover with chicken, cheese, and remaining bread slices. Remove crusts from bread, if desired, and press gently.

Dip the sandwiches in the egg and brown in the butter in a skillet until golden on both sides.

*Yield: 6 sandwiches*

## Croque-Monsieur

12 slices bread, buttered
6 thin slices ham
6 thin slices Gruyère cheese

3 eggs, lightly beaten
butter

Arrange half the bread slices on a board. Cover with ham, cheese, and remaining bread slices. Press gently.

Dip the sandwiches in the eggs and sauté in butter in a large skillet until golden on both sides.

*Yield: 6 sandwiches*

---

## Ham, Egg, and Pepper Croque-Monsieur

| | |
|---|---|
| 1 cup chopped cooked ham | mayonnaise |
| 2 hard-cooked eggs, minced | 8 slices bread |
| 2 tablespoons minced green | 1 egg, lightly beaten |
| pepper | 1/2 cup milk |
| 1/2 teaspoon salt | butter |
| 2 tablespoons minced sour | |
| pickle | |

In a small bowl, mix the ham, eggs, pepper, salt, and pickle with enough mayonnaise to bind. Spread half the bread slices with the mixture and cover with remaining bread. Press gently.

In a bowl, mix the egg and milk. Dip the sandwiches into the mixture and sauté in butter in a large skillet until golden on both sides.

*Yield: 4 sandwiches*

## CLUB SANDWICHES

Club sandwiches are one of the most popular types of sandwiches. They appeal to every appetite and can be found on menus from local diners to four-star restaurants. In addition, they are easy to make at home, requiring ingredients basic to most kitchens.

If you have to make a large number of them, arrange the ingredients like an assembly line on a counter. Toast the bread just before using or it may become soggy. The best method is to make the toast under the broiler so that the bread browns and cooks through. A toaster can leave the inside moist, which causes the toast to become soggy. If you are planning more than a dozen sandwiches, consider getting help.

The perfect club sandwich is made with three slices of crisp dry toast, spread lightly with butter and mayonnaise. The first slice is topped with neatly arranged lettuce leaves, thin slices of chicken breast, another slice of toast, and more neatly arranged lettuce. This is covered with thin slices of tomato and crisp bacon and topped off with the final toast slice. The sandwich is pressed gently and cut into four triangles, each of which is held together with a wooden skewer. The sections are arranged on a plate with one triangle point facing upward.

Some breads will disintegrate if cut into quarters. In that case, cut the sandwiches in half. With some breads, such as rye and pumpernickel, it may be necessary to use thicker bread slices than usual. If so, use two slices of bread for the sandwich instead of three. In fact, there may be some precedent for this. James Beard has written that in his memory the sandwich originally was made with two slices of toast.

The following fillings can be used with any choice of bread. They are equally delicious in French, Kaiser, or poppy seed rolls. In addition to the original club sandwich, we have included several versions with fish and meat.

## Caviar and Onion Club Sandwich

3 slices white toast, buttered
mayonnaise
1/4 cup caviar

1 slice Bermuda onion
2 slices tomato
2 watercress sprigs

Spread a slice of toast with mayonnaise to taste and caviar and cover with a slice of onion. Place a slice of toast on top, spread with mayonnaise, and arrange tomato slices and watercress sprigs on top. Cover with remaining toast slice.

*Yield: 1 sandwich*
*Note:* Use black or red caviar, but the best you can afford.

## Crabmeat Club Sandwich

3 slices toast, buttered
mayonnaise
1/4 cup crabmeat, flaked
2 tomato slices

1/2 cup minced hard-cooked
   egg
1 teaspoon minced celery
watercress sprigs

Spread a slice of toast with mayonnaise to taste. Mix the crabmeat with just enough mayonnaise to bind and spread on the toast slice. Cover with tomato slices and another slice of toast spread with mayonnaise.

Combine the egg and celery with just enough mayonnaise to bind and spread on the toast. Place watercress sprigs on the egg mixture and cover with remaining toast slice.

*Yield: 1 sandwich*

---

## Fried Oyster Club Sandwich

2 slices white toast, buttered
1 slice whole wheat toast, buttered
lettuce leaves
4 large fried oysters (see Index for Peacemaker)
horseradish
3 thin slices white chicken
4 slices crisp bacon
2 tomato slices
1 tablespoon tartar sauce (see Index)

Arrange lettuce leaves neatly on one slice of white toast. Place oysters on top and season with horseradish to taste. Cover with whole wheat toast and arrange chicken, bacon, and tomato slices on top.

Spread lightly with tartar sauce and cover with 1 lettuce leaf. Top with remaining toast slice.

*Yield: 1 sandwich*

---

## Original Club Sandwich

3 slices toast, buttered
mayonnaise
lettuce leaves
2 slices chicken breast
2 slices crisp bacon
2 tomato slices

Spread a slice of toast with mayonnaise. Arrange lettuce leaf neatly on the bread and cover with the chicken slices. Place a slice of toast on the chicken, spread with mayonnaise, and cover with lettuce, bacon, and tomato slices. Spread remaining toast with mayonnaise and cover the sandwich.

*Yield: 1 sandwich*

## Queen Club Sandwich

3 slices toast, buttered
lettuce leaves
1/2 cup minced, cooked
   chicken

mayonnaise
1/4 cup sautéed mushrooms

Cover one slice of toast with lettuce. Mix chicken with enough mayonnaise to bind and spread on the lettuce leaf. Cover with another slice of toast and arrange mushrooms on top. Cover with remaining toast slice.
*Yield: 1 sandwich*

## Bacon, Chicken, and Anchovy Club Sandwich

3 slices toast, buttered
mayonnaise
lettuce leaves
2 slices crisp bacon

2 chicken slices
3 to 4 anchovy fillets
2 tomato slices

Spread the toast slices with mayonnaise to taste. Cover one slice with lettuce, bacon, and another toast slice. Arrange chicken, anchovies, and tomato on top and cover with remaining toast slice.
*Yield: 1 sandwich.*

## Liver, Corned Beef, and Salami Club Sandwich

2 chicken livers
butter
1/4 teaspoon minced onion
Dijon mustard
salt
2 slices rye toast

2 ounces corned beef, thinly
   sliced
lettuce leaves
1-1/2 ounces hard salami,
   sliced

In a small skillet, sauté the livers in the butter until brown on both sides but still pink in the center.

In a processor or blender, purée the livers with the onion and mustard to taste. Correct the seasoning with salt. Spread 1 toast slice with the liver-mustard mixture. Cover with lettuce leaves, corned beef, salami, and the remaining toast slice.

*Yield: 1 sandwich*

---

## Bacon, Chicken Liver, and Tomato Club Sandwich

| | |
|---|---|
| 3 slices white toast, buttered | 2 chicken livers, broiled |
| mayonnaise | medium |
| lettuce leaves | 1 large slice tomato |
| 2 slices crisp bacon | watercress |

Spread the toast with mayonnaise to taste. Arrange lettuce leaves on one slice of toast. Cover with bacon and another slice of toast. Slice the chicken livers and arrange on the toast with the tomato and watercress. Cover with remaining toast slice.

*Yield: 1 sandwich*

## OPEN-FACED SANDWICHES

Although the Scandinavians are given credit for the open-faced sandwich, other nations also serve foods on single slices of bread. Wherever the idea originated, it is most important that these sandwiches look attractive. If you are not careful and precise in the assembly, they can easily look unappetizing. The sandwiches should be prepared shortly before serving to assure that they are fresh and crisp. If desired, you can arrange the ingredients on a baking sheet without the bread. Cover and chill them for two to three hours. When ready to serve, lift them onto a slice of buttered bread. If you are planning to serve a number of people, you can prepare all of the ingredients and put them together with help in assembly-line fashion.

The bread for these sandwiches should be firm textured, such as Westphalian pumpernickel, bauernbrot, or volkenbrot. Flimsy, puffy commercial breads do not hold up under the weight of the fillings, nor do they provide the necessary contrast in texture and flavor.

Open-faced sandwiches often break the rule about keeping the filling within the confines of the bread. They can be arranged with the ingredients draped over the bread like an oversize tablecloth. They are then covered with the garnishing ingredients like a beautifully appointed table. The following recipes are only suggestions, and certainly the garnishes can be selected and arranged as you choose. You can also concoct any combination of ingredients that pleases you. One restaurant in Copenhagen specializes in these sandwiches and its menu features literally hundreds of combinations. Try to incorporate a pleasant surprise to the palate, for example, a combination of grated orange peel and horseradish placed beside roast beef garnished with beets, onion rings, and anchovy fillets.

When preparing sandwiches for a party, plan on two sandwiches for each guest. Make a variety so that your sandwich tray will be colorful and interesting. If you want your guests to be able to sample every sandwich, make them smaller. If they are too small, however, they will be canapés. And remember, the smaller the sandwich, the more difficult it will be to arrange the various garnishes distinctively. Sandwiches that are too busy are not works of art but of confusion.

Always serve these sandwiches with a knife and fork.

## Egg and Tomato Sandwich

1 slice pumpernickel bread
1-1/2 teaspoons anchovy
    butter (see Index)
lettuce leaves

3 thin slices tomato
1 hard-cooked egg, sliced
minced chives

Spread the bread with the butter and arrange the lettuce on top. Arrange tomato and egg slices attractively and sprinkle with chives.

*Yield: 1 sandwich*

## Herring Sandwich

lettuce leaves
1 slice rye bread, buttered
3 pieces pickled herring

2 or 3 raw onion rings
1 tomato wedge

Arrange the lettuce leaves on the bread and top with herring. Garnish with onion rings and tomato wedge.
*Yield: 1 sandwich*

## Lobster Sandwich

1 pound cooked lobster meat, cut into chunks
1/2 cup mayonnaise
1 tablespoon lemon juice
1 teaspoon dry mustard
1/2 teaspoon Worcestershire sauce

Tabasco sauce
8 slices firm white bread
mayonnaise
Boston lettuce leaves
capers

In a bowl, mix the lobster, 1/2 cup mayonnaise, lemon juice, mustard, Worcestershire sauce, and Tabasco to taste.

Toast the bread on one side and cut off the crusts. Spread the untoasted side with mayonnaise and arrange a lettuce leaf neatly on top.

Fill the lettuce leaf with the lobster mixture and garnish with capers.
*Yield: 8 sandwiches*

## Smoked Salmon Sandwich

3 slices smoked salmon
1 slice rye bread, buttered
1/2 cup cold scrambled egg

1 tablespoon salmon caviar
minced chives
freshly ground black pepper

Arrange the salmon slices on the bread. Form a diagonal strip of egg across the salmon. Arrange the caviar on one side of the egg and the chives on the other. Sprinkle the egg generously with ground black pepper.
*Yield: 1 sandwich*

## Wined Sardine Sandwich

1 onion, minced
2 garlic cloves, crushed
2 tablespoons butter
1 3-inch strip lemon peel
1 cup dry white wine
1 bay leaf

2 3-3/4-ounce cans sardines
6 slices toast, buttered
1 cup sliced mushrooms,
sautéed in 2 teaspoons
butter

In a skillet, sweat the onion and garlic in 2 tablespoons butter until soft, but not brown. Add the lemon peel, wine, and bay leaf and simmer 10 minutes.

Drain the oil from the sardines. Arrange in a flat, noncorrosible dish and pour on the hot marinade. Let stand 1 hour or overnight.

Drain the sardines. Arrange on toast slices and scatter the mushrooms over the top.

*Yield: 6 sandwiches*

## Shrimp Sandwich

lettuce leaves
1 slice white bread, buttered
1 cup tiny shrimp, cooked,
peeled, and deveined

lemon wedges

Arrange lettuce on bread and cover neatly with the shrimp. Garnish with lemon wedges.

*Yield: 1 sandwich*

## Shrimp and Egg Sandwich

1/3 cup butter, softened
2 tablespoons mayonnaise
1 teaspoon minced dill
Tabasco sauce
salt
6 slices whole grain rye
bread

2 hard-cooked eggs, sliced
watercress sprigs
1-1/2 pounds shrimp, cooked,
peeled, and deveined
red caviar
minced dill

In a bowl, cream the butter. Beat in the mayonnaise, dill, Tabasco, and salt to taste. Spread the bread with the butter mixture.

Arrange a diagonal row of egg slices on the bread. Place the watercress on one triangle of bread and arrange the shrimp neatly on the remaining triangle of bread. Garnish with caviar and dill.

*Yield: 6 sandwiches*

## Shrimp, Tuna, and Green Bean Sandwich

1 ounce shrimp, chopped
1 ounce dark tuna, flaked
1 teaspoon minced celery
1 tablespoon mayonnaise
1/2 teaspoon lemon juice
1 slice dark rye bread,
    buttered

1/4 cup sliced, marinated
    mushrooms
6 marinated green beans
3 slices hard-cooked egg

In a bowl, mix the shrimp, tuna, celery, mayonnaise, and lemon juice. Spread on the bread. Arrange mushrooms and beans on top and garnish with egg.

*Yield: 1 sandwich*

## Shrimp and Turkey Sandwich

4 slices dark rye or
    pumpernickel bread
6 tablespoons curry butter
    (see Index)
1/2 pound cooked turkey
    breast, sliced
16 shrimp, cooked and
    peeled
4 hard-cooked eggs, thinly
    sliced

5 red radishes, thinly sliced
1 cucumber, thinly sliced
1 avocado
1 tablespoon grated onion
4 ounces cream cheese
1 tablespoon sour cream
lemon juice
Tabasco sauce
dill sprigs

Butter the bread with curry butter. Arrange the turkey, shrimp, eggs, radishes, and cucumbers on the bread.

In a processor, purée the avocado, onion, cream cheese, sour cream, and lemon juice and Tabasco to taste. Pipe onto the sandwich and garnish with dill sprigs.

*Yield: 4 sandwiches*

## Chicken Sandwich Remoulade

1 large slice dark rye bread
escarole leaf
2 tablespoons shredded
  iceberg lettuce
3 tablespoons remoulade
  sauce (see Index)
1 large slice Gruyère cheese

2 slices chicken breast
2 slices crisp bacon
1 tablespoon chopped, hard-
  cooked egg
3 slices green olive
2 tomato quarters

Cover the bread with escarole and sprinkle with shredded lettuce. Spread 1 tablespoon remoulade sauce on the lettuce and arrange cheese and chicken on top. Place bacon on the chicken and sprinkle with egg. Garnish with the olive, tomato, and remaining remoulade sauce.

*Yield: 1 sandwich*

## Turkey Sandwich

2 slices white toast, buttered
4 lettuce leaves
2 or 3 tomato slices
3 or 4 slices cooked turkey

3 or 4 tablespoons lamaze
  dressing (see following
  recipe)
4 or 5 slices crisp bacon

Arrange lettuce leaves on the toast. Top one toast slice with tomato and the other with turkey. Ladle dressing over both slices and garnish with bacon strips.

*Yield: 1 sandwich*

### Lamaze Dressing

1 cup chili sauce
1 cup mayonnaise
1/4 cup minced chutney
1 hard-cooked egg, chopped
2 tablespoons minced celery
1 tablespoon steak sauce

1 teaspoon minced chives
1 teaspoon minced pimiento
1 teaspoon minced green
  pepper
salt and pepper
paprika

In a bowl, mix the chili sauce, mayonnaise, chutney, egg, celery, steak sauce, chives, pimiento, green pepper, and salt, pepper, and paprika to taste. Cover and chill for 2 hours before using.
*Yield: about 2-1/2 cups*
*Note:* Dressing will keep for 4 days in the refrigerator.

## Roast Beef Sandwich

2 slices rare roast beef
1 slice rye bread, buttered
1 slice Danish blue cheese

2 slices mustard pickle
1 gherkin fan

Arrange beef slices on bread and place cheese in the center. Arrange pickles on either side of the cheese and the gherkin fan on top.
*Yield: 1 sandwich*

## English Beef and Cheese Sandwich

2 teaspoons cream cheese, softened
2 teaspoons crumbled blue cheese
1 slice pumpernickel bread, buttered

2 ounces roast beef, thinly sliced
salt and pepper
3 slices pickled beets
2 herring fillets

Mix the cream cheese and blue cheese together and spread on the bread. Arrange the beef on top and season with salt and pepper to taste. Garnish with beets and herring.
*Yield: 1 sandwich*

## Frikadelle Sandwich

1 to 2 cold meatballs, sliced
1 slice rye bread, buttered
2 tablespoons grated pickled beet

cucumber slices

Arrange meatball slices on the bread and garnish with the beets and cucumber slices.

*Yield: 1 sandwich*

*Note:* The meatballs usually are veal, but pork or beef is also delicious.

## Roast Pork Sandwich

3 slices cold roast pork
1 slice rye bread, buttered
1 tablespoon pork cracklings
  (see Index)

2 prunes, soaked in orange
  juice for 6 hours and pitted
1 slice orange
grated gingerroot

Arrange pork slices on the bread and sprinkle with cracklings. Place prunes, separated by a curled orange slice, on the meat. Sprinkle with gingerroot.

*Yield: 1 sandwich*

## Ham and Shrimp Sandwich

1-1/2 tablespoons butter
1/4 cup cooked shrimp,
  chopped
1 teaspoon crumbled blue
  cheese
1/2 teaspoon minced parsley
lemon juice
1/4 teaspoon anchovy paste

cayenne pepper
1 slice dark rye bread
3 thin slices baked ham
3 thin slices Gruyère cheese
3 large ripe olives, pitted
4 cooked shrimp, peeled and
  deveined

In a bowl, mix the butter, 1/4 cup shrimp, blue cheese, parsley, lemon juice, anchovy paste, and cayenne. Spread mixture on the bread.

Sandwich ham and cheese slices together and shape into 3 cornucopias. Arrange on top of the shrimp mixture with the cornucopia points meeting at the center. Put an olive into the opening of each cornucopia. Place a shrimp in front of each olive and the remaining shrimp at the point where the cornucopias meet.

*Yield: 1 sandwich*

## Bacon and Pâté Sandwich

3 slices crisp bacon
1 slice rye bread, buttered
1/2 tomato, thinly sliced
2 slices Danish pâté (see
  following recipe)

1 tablespoon minced aspic
grated horseradish

Arrange bacon slices on the bread alternately with tomato slices. Place pâté slice on top. Garnish with aspic and sprinkle with horseradish.

*Yield: 1 sandwich*

*Note:* Chill a can of beef consommé for a quick aspic if you have none on hand.

*Danish Liver Pâté*

1 pound pork or calves liver,
  chopped
1 pound pork fat, chopped

2 onions, chopped
1/4 cup cognac
salt and pepper

Preheat oven to 325°F.

In a processor, purée the liver, pork fat, and onions in batches. Place in a bowl and beat in the cognac and salt and pepper to taste. (For a smoother texture, force through a sieve.) Pour into a 1-quart loaf pan and bake 1 hour, or until a thermometer registers 165°F.

Cool and chill for at least 12 hours. Unmold and cut into thin slices.

*Yield: about 18 slices*

## Chicken Liver and Apple Sandwich

1 pound chicken livers
6 tablespoons butter
salt and pepper
1 onion, thinly sliced
1 golden Delicious apple,
  peeled and sliced

4 slices whole wheat bread,
  buttered
2 hard-cooked eggs, thinly
  sliced

In a skillet, sauté the livers in 4 tablespoons butter until browned, but still pink in the center. Season with salt and pepper. Transfer livers to a plate with a slotted spoon.

In the same skillet, sauté the onion until soft and lightly browned. Drain and set aside.

In the same skillet, sauté the apple slices in the remaining butter until tender-crisp. Cut livers into thin slices and arrange on bread. Top with onion, apple, and egg slices.

*Yield: 4 sandwiches*

## SUBMARINES, HEROES, GRINDERS, AND OTHER GREAT SANDWICHES

Great sandwiches are composed of a multitude of compatible ingredients piled into whole loaves of bread (sometimes rolls for individual servings) and often allowed to marinate and meld their flavors for thirty minutes or longer before serving. Hot sandwiches of this type, however, have to be served immediately after heating.

Their place of origin is probably around the Mediterranean, where several countries enjoy similar sandwiches. The idea is certainly popular in the United States, where submarine shops abound. In different sections of the country, the sandwiches are called submarines, grinders, heroes, hoagies, poor boys, and mufalettos. The number and variety of fillings offer countless possibilities. However, some shops seem to believe that any Italian meal can be put into a long roll and served. Often, these sandwiches prove less than delightful. The suggestions here are for tried and true, although not necessarily well-known, combinations.

Many of these sandwiches are made in whole loaves of bread that, after a period of melding of flavors, are cut into sections. They are delicious and especially practical for picnics, since one loaf can serve six or more people. Also, these hearty and crusty breads can stand up to a moist filling for a longer period.

In the past people often prepared these sandwiches and wrapped them in tea towels. On the way to the picnic, they would sit on them to compress the sandwich and mingle the flavors. The body heat helped to accomplish this. Today, we recommend that you wrap them securely in foil or plastic wrap, place them on a baking sheet, and cover with another baking sheet weighted with several cans of food or bricks to compress the sandwich. Let them stand for twenty minutes to four hours. If they are meant for a picnic, put them at the bottom of the picnic basket and pile everything else on top to weight the sandwiches.

When ready to serve, cut the sandwiches into wedges or rectangles depending on the shape of the bread. Although these recipes suggest a particular bread, you can certainly use other breads of similar or different shapes. The recipes need not be followed slavishly. If they call for marinated mushrooms and you have marinated green beans, make the substitution. If one salami pleases you more than another, use it. Rely on your imagination to create your own tasteful versions.

We have included a group of sandwiches called La Mediatrice, peacemaker, poor boy, or oyster loaf. They originated in New Orleans. According to legend, a gentleman who had spent the evening carousing would bring one of these sandwiches back to his wife as a peacemaker.

## Sausage and Feta Cheese Sandwich

1 loaf French bread, split
  horizontally
1/2 cup vinaigrette (see
  Index)
4 Italian sausages, cooked
1/4 pound feta cheese,
  crumbled

1/4 cup Spanish olives,
  chopped
1 red onion, thinly sliced
1 avocado, thinly sliced

Pull the inside crumb from both halves of the bread, leaving a 1/2-inch-thick shell. Discard the crumb. Brush both halves generously with vinaigrette.

Chop the sausages coarsely and place in the bottom half of the loaf. Cover with the cheese, olives, onion, and avocado. Cover with the top of the loaf and wrap securely. Weight for about 30 minutes. Cut into sections to serve.

*Yield: 6 sandwiches*

## Ratatouille and Sausage Pita Sandwich

1 pound eggplant, peeled and
   cut into 1-inch cubes
salt and pepper
1 onion, minced
1 green pepper, minced
5 tablespoons olive oil
1/2 pound Italian sausage,
   casing removed and meat
   crumbled
1-pound can Italian plum
   tomatoes

3 garlic cloves, minced
1 bay leaf
1-1/2 teaspoons minced basil
1-1/2 teaspoons minced
   thyme
3 tablespoons minced parsley
2 tablespoons grated
   Parmesan cheese
6 pita loaves

Sprinkle the eggplant with salt and drain in a colander for 15 minutes.

In a skillet, sauté the onion and pepper in 2 tablespoons oil until the onion is soft. Add the sausage and salt and pepper to taste and cook, stirring, until the meat loses its color. Transfer the ingredients to a bowl with a slotted spoon, leaving the fat in the pan.

Add 3 tablespoons oil to the skillet and heat. Pat the eggplant dry with paper toweling and sauté, stirring, for 3 minutes. Add the sausage mixture, tomatoes, garlic, bay leaf, basil, and thyme. Cover and cook over low heat, stirring occasionally, for 30 minutes, or until thickened. Stir in the parsley and cheese. Discard the bay leaf and cool.

Fill pita loaves or, if desired, a whole loaf of white, whole wheat, French, or Italian bread.

*Yield: 6 sandwiches*

## Tomato, Salami, and Mozzarella Cheese Sandwich

1 loaf Italian bread, split
   horizontally
12 slices salami
butter
1/4 pound mushrooms, sliced
1/4 cup flour
1 cup medium cream

1/2 cup white wine
white pepper
celery seed
3 tomatoes, peeled and thinly
   sliced
4 to 6 slices mozzarella
   cheese

Preheat oven to 425°F.

Place bread, cut sides up, on a baking sheet and bake until golden. Remove from the oven, arrange the salami on the bread, and set aside.

In a saucepan, melt 2 tablespoons butter and sauté the mushrooms until golden. With a slotted spoon, scatter the mushrooms over the salami.

Add enough butter to the pan to measure 1/4 cup, stir in the flour, and cook for 3 minutes. Add the cream and celery seed and pepper to taste. Cook until thickened and smooth. Spread the sauce over the mushrooms and cover with overlapping tomato and mozzarella slices. Bake until the cheese melts and the sandwich is heated.

*Yield: 6 sandwiches*

## Mufuletta I

| | |
|---|---|
| 1/2 cup pitted, oil-cured black olives, chopped | 1 teaspoon oregano pepper |
| 1/2 cup chopped Spanish olives | 1 10-inch round bread loaf |
| 1/2 cup chopped mixed marinated vegetables | 1/4 pound salami, thinly sliced |
| 2/3 cup olive oil | 1/4 pound provolone cheese, thinly sliced |
| 1/4 cup minced parsley | 1/4 pound prosciutto, thinly sliced |
| 3 tablespoons lemon juice | |
| 2 garlic cloves, minced | |

In a bowl, mix the olives, vegetables, oil, parsley, lemon juice, garlic, oregano, and pepper to taste. Marinate overnight.

Split the loaf in half horizontally and remove the crumb, leaving 1/2-inch thick shells. Brush the insides with dressing from the vegetable salad. Line the bottom of the loaf with salami slices. Spread on half the salad mixture and place provolone on top. Add remaining salad and top with prosciutto. Cover with the top of the loaf. Wrap in plastic wrap and weight for 30 minutes.

*Yield: 6 sandwiches*

## Baked Sausage and Prosciutto Loaf

1 loaf French bread
1 leek, thinly sliced
2 tablespoons butter
1/4 pound Italian sausage,
  crumbled
1/4 pound spinach, cooked,
  drained, and chopped
1/4 pound prosciutto, thinly
  sliced

1/3 cup minced parsley
1 large egg, lightly beaten
1-1/2 teaspoons minced sage
1/4 pound Gruyère cheese,
  grated
nutmeg
salt and pepper
3 tablespoons butter, melted
1 egg, lightly beaten

Preheat oven to 200°F.

Cut off the top third of the bread and pull out the crumb, leaving 1/2-inch-thick shells. Dry the shells in the oven for 20 minutes. Raise the oven temperature to 350°F.

Spread the crumb on a baking sheet and dry for 20 minutes, or until lightly golden. Pulverize the crumb in a blender or processor.

In a skillet, sauté the leek in butter until soft. Transfer to a bowl. Sauté the sausage until no longer pink. Drain off excess fat and remove sausage to the bowl.

Squeeze the spinach dry and add to the bowl. Chop the prosciutto and add to the bowl with the toasted bread crumbs, parsley, 1 egg, sage, cheese, and nutmeg, salt, and pepper to taste. Mix well.

Brush the insides of the bread with melted butter. Mound the sausage mixture inside the shell and brush the edges of the loaf with remaining egg. Fit the loaf together, wrap in foil, and bake for 30 minutes. Cool to room temperature and cut into 6 sections.

*Yield: 6 sandwiches*

## Prosciutto and Cheese Loaf

1 loaf Italian bread, split
  horizontally
6 to 8 slices Port du Salut or
  Italian fontina cheese
1/4 cup minced leek

12 slices prosciutto or
  pastrami
1 tablespoon capers
2 large eggs, separated
1 cup mayonnaise

Preheat oven to 425°F.

Place the bottom half of the bread on a baking sheet and bake until golden. (Use the top for another recipe or double the remaining ingredients.) Arrange cheese slices on the bread and sprinkle with leeks. Place prosciutto and capers on top.

Beat the egg yolks and fold into the mayonnaise. Beat the egg whites until stiff, but not dry, and fold into the mayonnaise. Spread over the sandwich.

Bake for 8 to 10 minutes, or until the topping is golden.
*Yield: 6 sandwiches*

## Italian Sandwich

1 loaf Italian bread, split horizontally
1/2 garlic clove
1 cucumber, peeled, seeded, and thinly sliced
1/4 pound prosciutto, thinly sliced
1 tomato, peeled and thinly sliced

1 pimiento, sliced
3 green olives, sliced
6 anchovy fillets
olive oil
vinegar
pepper

Rub the insides of the bread with the garlic clove. Discard garlic. Arrange layers of cucumber, prosciutto, tomato, pimiento, olives, and anchovies on the bottom half. Sprinkle with olive oil, vinegar, and pepper to taste.

Cover with the top of the loaf and weight for 30 minutes to 1-1/2 hours.
*Yield: 6 sandwiches*

## Mufuletta II (Olive, Sausage, and Cheese Sandwich)

1-1/2 cups stuffed olives, chopped
1-1/2 cups ripe olives, chopped
2/3 cup olive oil
1/3 cup minced parsley
4 ounces pimiento, drained and chopped
3 anchovy fillets, minced
2 tablespoons capers

1 tablespoon minced garlic
1 tablespoon minced oregano
pepper
1 9-inch round Italian loaf
1/4 pound soppresato sausage, thinly sliced
1/4 pound provolone cheese, thinly sliced
1/4 pound mortadella sausage, thinly sliced

In a bowl, mix the olives, oil, parsley, pimientos, anchovies, capers, garlic, oregano, and pepper to taste. Marinate overnight. Drain the salad, reserving the dressing.

Remove the crumb from the bread, leaving 1/2-inch-thick shells. Brush the insides generously with the reserved dressing. Spoon half the salad into the bottom half and press down firmly. Alternate layers of soppresato, cheese, and mortadella, ending with a layer of mortadella. Mound remaining salad on top and cover with the loaf top.

Wrap in foil or plastic wrap and weight for 30 minutes to 4 hours.

*Yield: 6 sandwiches*

---

## Greek Country Salad Loaf

1 sesame seed, doughnut-
  shaped bread loaf
butter
1 cucumber, peeled and
  sliced
12 cherry tomatoes, sliced
6 ounces feta cheese,
  crumbled
5 ounces salami, cut in
  julienne

24 pitted, ripe Greek olives
1 avocado, peeled and sliced
3 tablespoons capers
8 anchovy fillets
4 tablespoons olive oil
2 tablespoons lemon juice
1/2 teaspoon oregano
salt and pepper

Slice the bread in half horizontally and remove crumb, leaving 1/2-inch-thick shells. Butter shells generously.

Place cucumber, tomatoes, cheese, salami, olives, avocado, capers, and anchovies in a bowl.

In another bowl, mix the oil, lemon juice, oregano, and salt and pepper to taste. Pour over the salad ingredients and toss gently. Spoon into the bottom shell and cover with the top shell. Weight for 30 minutes.

*Yield: 6 sandwiches*

*Note:* Use a round, crusty loaf of bread if the doughnut-shaped bread is not available.

## Pan Bagna I

1-pound loaf French bread, split horizontally
1/2 cup water
1/2 teaspoon salt
1/2 to 1 cup olive oil
2 tomatoes, sliced

4 artichoke hearts, cooked and sliced
1/2 cup sliced mushrooms
1 celery heart, cut in strips
1/4 pound black olives, pitted
8 to 10 anchovy fillets

Place bread halves on a work surface. Combine water and salt and stir until salt is dissolved. Brush bread halves with the salt mixture and sprinkle with oil, to taste.

When the bread is well impregnated, but not soaked, place the tomato, artichoke hearts, mushrooms, celery, olives, and anchovies on the bottom half. Cover with the top half and weight for at least 30 minutes.

*Yield: 6 sandwiches*

## Pan Bagna II

1 loaf French bread, split horizontally
olive oil
1 red onion, thinly sliced
1 green pepper, thinly sliced
1 tomato, thinly sliced
8 anchovy fillets

1 cup tunafish, drained and flaked
1/2 cup pitted ripe olives, sliced
salt and pepper
1 garlic clove, halved

Brush the insides of the loaf with olive oil to taste and let it soak for a few minutes. On the bottom half, place the onion, green pepper, tomato, anchovies, tuna, and ripe olives. Season to taste with salt and pepper.

Rub the inside of the top of the loaf with the garlic, pressing to extract the garlic juices. Discard the garlic. Press the top half onto the sandwich and weight for 2 hours.

*Yield: 6 sandwiches*

## Pan Bagna III

| | |
|---|---|
| 1 tablespoon red wine vinegar | 2 tomatoes, thinly sliced |
| 1/4 teaspoon Dijon mustard | 1 tablespoon minced scallion |
| salt and pepper | 4 anchovy fillets |
| 1/4 cup olive oil | 12 black olives, pitted, sliced |
| 1 loaf French bread, split horizontally | 2/3 cup cooked green beans |
| | 1/2 cup slivered green pepper |
| 1/2 garlic clove | 1/2 cup sliced mushrooms |
| | 2 tablespoons minced parsley |

In a bowl, mix the vinegar, mustard, salt, pepper, and oil.

Rub the cut sides of the bread with the garlic. Discard the garlic. Drizzle half the dressing over the bottom half of the loaf. Layer the tomatoes, scallion, anchovies, olives, beans, green pepper, and mushrooms over the dressing. Sprinkle with parsley, salt, and pepper. Drizzle remaining dressing on the top half of the loaf and cover the sandwich.

*Yield: 6 sandwiches*

## La Mediatrice

| | |
|---|---|
| 1 12-inch loaf French bread, split horizontally | 1 egg, lightly beaten |
| butter, melted | oil for deep frying |
| 36 mussels, scrubbed and bearded | guacamole (see following recipe) |

Preheat oven to 425°F.

Remove the crumb from the loaf, leaving 1/2-inch-thick shells. In a processor, pulverize the crumb and set aside. Brush the shells with butter and bake until golden.

Steam the mussels in 1 inch of water in a covered kettle until they open. Remove the mussels and discard the shells and any unopened mussels.

Dip the mussels into the egg and then into the reserved bread crumbs. Deep-fry at 370°F. until golden. Drain on paper toweling.

Fill the bottom half of the loaf with guacamole and top with mussels. Cover with the top half of the loaf.

*Yield: 6 sandwiches*
*Note:* Add shredded lettuce and chopped tomato to the sandwich, if desired.

## Guacamole

1 ripe avocado, peeled and chopped
1 tomato, peeled, seeded, and chopped
1-1/2 teaspoons minced onion
1-1/2 teaspoons white wine vinegar
1/2 teaspoon lime juice
1/2 teaspoon chili powder
1/4 teaspoon minced garlic
salt and pepper

Prepare about 1 hour before using.
Place avocado, tomato, and onion in a processor with the vinegar, lime juice, chili powder, garlic, and salt and pepper to taste. Chop coarsely with on-off turns.
*Yield: 1-1/2 cups*

---

## Pan Basquaise

4 tablespoons olive oil
4 red peppers, peeled and cut in julienne
1/2 cup tuna packed in olive oil
2 tablespoons red wine vinegar
4 tablespoons minced parsley
3 garlic cloves, minced
salt and pepper
2 loaves French bread, split horizontally
4 hard-cooked eggs, sliced

Preheat the broiler.
In a skillet, heat 3 tablespoons oil and cook the peppers until hot. Add the tuna and cook, stirring, until the tuna is flaked and heated. Add the vinegar, 2 tablespoons parsley, and garlic. Cook until the vinegar has evaporated. Remove from the heat and season to taste with salt and pepper.
Place bread on a baking sheet and toast until warm and crisp, but not brown. Top two bottoms with the tuna mixture and garnish with eggs. Drizzle a little oil on top, sprinkle with remaining parsley, and cover with bread tops.
*Yield: 6 sandwiches*

## La Mediatrice II

| | |
|---|---|
| 6 French rolls | salt and pepper |
| 6 teaspoons melted butter | Tabasco sauce |
| 18 to 24 oysters | hot cream, optional |

Preheat oven to 425°F.

Cut off the tops of the rolls and scoop out the crumb. Brush the insides with butter and bake on a baking sheet until golden.

Sauté the oysters in butter until plump and the edges begin to curl. Season to taste with salt, pepper, and Tabasco. Place the oysters in the rolls, sprinkle with a little hot cream, if desired, and cover with roll tops. Serve hot.

*Yield: 6 sandwiches*

## Peacemaker, Poor Boy, or Oyster Loaf (La Mediatrice III)

| | |
|---|---|
| 1 pint shucked oysters | 1 loaf French bread |
| 1/4 teaspoon cayenne pepper | 4 tablespoons butter, melted |
| black pepper | oil for deep frying |
| 2 eggs | 1/2 cup Creole tartar sauce |
| 1/2 cup evaporated milk | (see following recipe) |
| pinch of salt | 1-1/2 cups shredded lettuce |
| 1 cup cornstarch | 1 tomato, cut in 1/4-inch- |
| 1-1/2 cups soft bread crumbs | thick slices |

Preheat oven to 375°F.

Pat oysters dry on paper towels and season to taste with cayenne and black pepper.

In a bowl, beat the eggs with milk and salt. Spread the cornstarch on a piece of waxed paper and bread crumbs on another sheet. Roll the oysters in cornstarch, dip in eggs, and roll in crumbs. Arrange in one layer on a plate and chill.

Slice the bread in half horizontally and remove the crumb from both sections. Brush the halves with melted butter and bake for 15 minutes, or until crisp and lightly browned.

Heat the oil to 375°F. Deep-fry the oysters until golden. Drain on paper towels.

Spread Creole tartar sauce on bread halves. Scatter lettuce on the bottom half and arrange tomato slices on top. Cover with the oysters and the top of the loaf.

*Yield: 6 sandwiches*

*Note:* Instead of tomatoes and Creole tartar sauce, the loaf can be spread with a mixture of 1/2 cup chili sauce, 2 tablespoons horseradish, 2 teaspoons lemon juice, and 1/4 teaspoon Worcestershire sauce.

### Creole Tartar Sauce

3 egg yolks
1 tablespoon Creole mustard
1/4 teaspoon cayenne pepper
1-1/2 teaspoons salt

1-1/2 cups olive oil
1/2 cup minced scallions
1/2 cup minced parsley
1/2 cup minced dill pickles

In a processor, mix the egg yolks, mustard, cayenne, and salt. With the machine running, pour in the oil in a slow, steady stream. Fold in the scallions, parsley, and pickles.

*Yield: about 2 cups*

## Rump Steak Sandwich

1 2-pound rump steak
salt and pepper
4 tablespoons rosemary or
   garlic butter (see Index)

1 loaf French bread, split
   horizontally

Preheat the broiler.

Broil the steak to desired degree of doneness and let rest for 5 minutes. Season to taste with salt and pepper.

Toast both bread halves and spread with herbed butter. Slice the steak thinly, arrange on the bottom bread half, and cover with the top of the loaf.

*Yield: 4 to 6 sandwiches*

*Note:* For variety, use horseradish butter and garnish with tomato slices.

## Bookmaker Sandwich

1 loaf French bread, split
  horizontally
butter
2 1/2-inch-thick sirloin steaks

salt and pepper
horseradish
dry mustard

Spread both bread halves generously with butter.

Heat a cast-iron skillet until very hot and sear both steaks until rare. Season to taste with salt and pepper and sprinkle both sides with horseradish and mustard. Assemble the sandwich and weight for 20 minutes.

*Yield: 6 sandwiches*

## Beef, Tomato, and Potato Loaf

6-ounce jar marinated
  mushrooms
2 tablespoons tarragon
  vinegar
1/2 teaspoon Dijon mustard
1 garlic clove, minced
salt and pepper
2 shallots, minced
1/4 cup minced parsley

1 pound small potatoes,
  boiled and sliced
2 cups cherry tomatoes,
  halved
1-1/4 pounds rare roast beef,
  or steak, cut into strips
1 10-inch round, crusty bread
  loaf, split horizontally
butter

Drain mushroom juices into a bowl and stir in the vinegar, mustard, garlic, salt and pepper to taste, shallots, and parsley. Add the mushrooms to the dressing with the potatoes, tomatoes, and beef. Mix well.

Remove the crumb from bread, leaving 1/2-inch-thick shells. Butter the bread, generously. Fill the bottom half with the meat-potato mixture, cover with the top, and press down. Weight for at least 30 minutes. Cut into wedges.

*Yield: 6 sandwiches*

## Pita Beef Sandwich

3 cups shredded lettuce
3 cups shredded raw spinach
1/2 cup minced scallions
vinaigrette dressing
6 pita loaves
12 tablespoons cream cheese,
   softened

3/4 pound roast beef, thinly
   sliced
24 large Greek olives, pitted
   and sliced

In a bowl, mix the lettuce, spinach, scallions, and enough vinaigrette to coat lightly.

Cut the loaves in half and open each pocket. Spread the insides with cream cheese. Fill with the lettuce mixture and arrange beef and olives on top.

*Yield: 6 sandwiches*

## Veal and Pepper Submarine Sandwich

1-1/2 pounds veal cutlets, cut
   in 1-inch squares
salt and pepper
1/2 cup flour
8 tablespoons olive oil
1 cup minced onions
1 teaspoon minced garlic

1/2 cup dry white wine
2 red peppers, roasted and
   peeled
2 green peppers, roasted and
   peeled
1 loaf Italian bread, split
   horizontally

Sprinkle the veal with salt and pepper to taste. Dredge in flour and shake off the excess. Heat 4 tablespoons oil in a skillet and sauté the veal in batches until golden. Set aside. Add more oil as needed. Pour off all but 3 tablespoons oil, and sauté the onion and garlic until soft and lightly colored. Pour in the wine and return the veal to the pan.

Cut the peppers into 1-inch squares and add to the pan. Simmer, covered, for 5 minutes. Correct the seasoning with salt and pepper. Fill the bottom half of the loaf with veal and peppers and cover with the top half of the loaf.

*Yield: 2 to 4 sandwiches*

## Syrian Sandwich

4 tomatoes, peeled, seeded,
  and chopped
2-1/2 tablespoons olive oil
1/4 cup pine nuts
2 teaspoons olive oil
1 cup chopped onions
1-1/2 pounds lamb, ground
1/4 cup minced parsley

1/4 cup chopped green
  pepper
1 tablespoon lemon juice
1 tablespoon vinegar
1-1/2 teaspoons salt
1/4 teaspoon cayenne pepper
1/4 teaspoon allspice
6 pita loaves

In a saucepan, cook the tomatoes in 1-1/2 tablespoons oil, covered, for 5 minutes. Uncover and cook, stirring occasionally, for 15 minutes, or until a thick purée.

In a skillet, sauté the pine nuts in 2 teaspoons olive oil. Drain on paper towels. Add 1 tablespoon oil to the skillet and sauté the onions until lightly browned. Add the lamb and cook until it loses its color, breaking it up with a fork.

Add the parsley, green pepper, lemon juice, vinegar, salt, cayenne, and allspice. Cook, stirring, for 3 minutes. Add the tomato purée and cook, stirring, for 2 minutes. Add the pine nuts and let cool to lukewarm. Fill the pita loaves.

*Yield: 6 sandwiches*

# 3
# Breads

Few foods are as satisfying as a well-made bread. Bread can be made from almost any grain, used either alone or in combination with other grains. (Certain grains that lack gluten produce loaves that are delicious but quite heavy.) Some breads (quick breads) are ready to bake in a few minutes; others (yeast breads) must rise for several hours or longer to develop their flavor.

Bread is shaped in many ways, but for sandwiches, the simple shapes are the best, such as, rounds, long loaves, or standard bread pan loaves. Save the braids and rings to serve plain.

The most important point to make about breads is that they are easy to make. Often, writers imply a mystique to bread making that makes a simple activity frightening. In fact, there are few areas in which you can go wrong. (A list of possible trouble spots appears at the end of this introduction.)

Breads are best when served within hours of baking. Few foods are as appealing as a freshly baked loaf of bread. There are times when it is difficult, if not impossible, to prepare a bread to serve fresh from the oven. However, virtually every bread freezes beautifully. Breads can be thawed in a microwave oven, or in a regular oven. They can also be thawed at room temperature, but heating them in the oven brings out the best flavor.

There are a number of things to consider when making breads. Experienced bakers may find that they know most of the following material; new bakers may find the volume overwhelming. But do not be discouraged or you may miss the pleasure of making and eating delicious homemade bread.

After one or two attempts at making bread, you will no longer need to refer to this section, unless something does not work out properly. The following discussion should answer your questions.

Breads can be divided into two general categories: yeast breads and quick breads. Yeast breads are made by leavening the bread with yeast and kneading the ingredients together to develop gluten that holds the air cells formed in the rising process. Once the bread has risen, it is punched down, possibly allowed to rise again, and then shaped. It is usually allowed to rise once more before baking. Although this sounds like a long, tedious process, the dough performs most of the activity and the baker spends only a few minutes working with it.

Quick breads are leavened by using baking powder, or a soured milk product, such as buttermilk, sour milk, yogurt, or sourcream, and baking soda. Because the leavening can lose its potency, the bread is mixed gently and baked almost immediately after assembling. (The "quick" in quick bread refers to the fact that they can be assembled for baking quickly. They take about the same time to bake as yeast breads and in some instances longer.)

## YEAST BREADS

Yeast breads are made of flour, yeast, and a liquid. All the other ingredients are variations on a theme. Salt is often used for flavor; sugar is added to help the yeast grow and to sweeten some breads. (The small amount of sugar added to encourage the growth of the yeast does not make the bread sweet.) Various flours are used alone or in combination to change flavors and textures. Once you understand the techniques of making bread, you can easily create your own recipes.

### Flour

Unbleached white flour with a high gluten content is considered the best for baking white breads. The gluten content allows you to knead the dough to develop elasticity and to create strength to hold the gases created by the yeast. However, you can make wonderful bread using all-purpose flour. You can find unbleached flour and stone-ground wheat flour in many supermarkets and health food stores. Some flours have a high proportion of gluten; others have little or none. Rye flour, for example, will not rise into a light loaf because it lacks gluten. It is therefore often mixed with white flour, which provides the gluten. The greater the proportion of white flour, the lighter the bread will be. Conversely, the bread will have less and less rye flavor.

### Yeast

Yeast can be purchased as a compressed cake or in granular form. Cake yeast is sold in supermarkets in small foil-wrapped squares. Carefully check the date stamp because the corners often dry out, diminishing the amount of viable yeast. In some areas, it is possible to buy 1-pound blocks of compressed yeast. If you plan to bake a lot of bread, you may want to purchase a pound. If you do not use it all within a few days, cut the remainder into tablespoon-size portions, wrap securely in foil or plastic, and freeze until needed. A tablespoon of compressed yeast is the equivalent of a packet of granular yeast.

Granular yeast is sold in paper-foil packets stamped with an expiration date. The author has found that the yeast is still viable well after the stamped date. However, for safety's sake, use the yeast before the expiration date. In some markets, it is possible to buy granular yeast in jars. One tablespoon is the equivalent of a packet of yeast indicated in the recipe. Certain health food stores sell yeast by weight. Experience has shown no difference in the results with any of these yeast forms, and I use them interchangeably.

Compressed yeast must be dissolved. The customary method is to mash the yeast with some sugar in a bowl until it liquefies, before adding the other ingredients. Granular yeast can be used without dissolving, as long as it is fresh. However, I strongly recommend that you prove the yeast before proceeding with the recipe. You will be able to determine within minutes if the yeast is active. It is disappointing to combine all the ingredients for a bread and wait for several hours, only to discover that the bread will not rise because the yeast was not viable.

## To Prove the Yeast

In a bowl, combine the yeast with some warm liquid and a pinch or more of sugar. Cover and let stand about 10 minutes in a warm place, until the yeast starts to grow and look foamy. If it does not start to develop, review what you have done. Check the age of the yeast to make sure it is not too old. Make sure the liquid was not too hot. If you cannot keep your finger in the liquid because it is too hot, it is too hot for the yeast. When it is comfortably warm to your finger, it is fine for the yeast.

## Sponges

In the past, it was common for recipes to require the baker to make a sponge. A sponge is another way of proving the yeast. Sponges are made by combining the yeast with some liquid and enough flour to make a medium-firm ball of dough. Generally, a cross is cut in the surface of the dough and it is allowed to rise.

Some recipes suggest putting the ball of dough into a bowl of warm water to cover, until it floats to the surface. Others suggest putting it into a bowl, covering it generously with warmed flour, and allowing the sponge to rise up through the flour. Still other recipes suggest putting the sponge on a work surface and covering it with a warm bowl until it doubles in bulk. When the sponge has proved that the yeast is viable, it is worked into the remaining ingredients.

The sponge method not only proves that the yeast is active, but also improves the flavor of the bread. You can use the sponge method with any bread recipe. However, unless you are making a number of loaves, it is really unnecessary. Proving the yeast in a bowl before proceeding with the recipe is, on the other hand, a sensible precaution with immediate results.

A sponge can prove very useful. If you have made a bread that is not rising, you can make a separate sponge and work it into the dough. It is an effective method of saving a bread that is not responding. Use a new packet of yeast and make a sponge with the yeast, 1/2 teaspoon sugar, 1 cup flour, and just enough water to make a firm ball. Cut a cross in the top of the sponge and put it into a bowl of lukewarm (100°F.) water to cover. When the sponge floats to the top, drain it in your hands and work it into the dough. You may need to add more flour.

## Liquid

The liquid for yeast bread is usually water or milk. Water saved from boiling potatoes is often used because it helps to keep the baked bread fresh and moist. Generally, the liquid should be warm, but not hot. If it is too hot for your finger, it is too hot for the yeast. A more accurate method is to use an instant-read thermometer, sometimes referred to as a yeast or roasting thermometer. The liquid should register between 90°F. and 110°F. Actually, you can use a cold liquid (it is heat that kills yeast). A cold liquid will slow down the rising action, but not kill the action. Yeast develops and grows between 60°F. and 100°F. The higher the temperature within this range, the faster the bread will rise.

In the past, recipes often instructed the baker to heat the milk almost to a boil and let it cool to lukewarm before using. This was probably required before pasteurization because bacteria in the raw milk could affect the yeast adversely. After the development of pasteurization, custom continued this practice. I often make bread successfully with cold milk that is unheated.

# Kneading

Kneading is a simple procedure. It is necessary to produce the elasticity in the gluten so that the dough can stretch and rise without collapsing. Dough can be kneaded by hand, in an electric mixer fitted with a dough hook, or in a food processor.

Kneading by hand is simple and can be quite relaxing. Once you learn the motion, you never forget. Turn the dough onto a clean work surface that has been dusted lightly with flour. (*Note:* If the work surface is a cutting board that is used regularly to chop onions, garlic, and other strong foods, the kneading may pick up the flavors.) Reach across two-thirds of the dough and, with the heel of your hand, press down and away from you about 4 to 6 inches. Curl your fingertips under the outer edge of the dough and rock back, lifting the edge of the dough on top of itself. Give the dough a partial turn and repeat the pressing and folding. You should quickly develop an even rocking motion using your whole upper body. If you use just your arms you will tire quickly. Continue kneading the dough until it is smooth and elastic. Add just enough flour as you knead to make a medium-firm dough that is no longer sticky. Do not add too much flour or the bread will be dry. Vigorous kneading will work the dough to the desired state. If the dough has been kneaded enough, it will no longer stick to your hands. The time required for kneading depends on your vigor. Generally, recipes say to knead for 8 to 15 minutes. I find that 5 to 10 minutes is usually enough. Since you cannot overwork the dough, it is better to err in terms of kneading it longer. This also creates a finer grained bread. Therapeutically, dough kneading is one way of getting rid of your aggressive feelings. You end up with beautiful bread and a feeling of well-being.

Some electric mixers are equipped with dough hooks and are capable of kneading dough. Do not attempt to knead dough in a machine that is not designed for it. Doughs are heavy and can cause the motor to burn out.

Food processors are capable of kneading doughs, but the capacity of some is too small. If using a processor, mix the dough in a bowl, divide it into 2-cup portions, and knead them separately in the processor. Assemble the finished batches in a bowl and let rise.

# Rising

Once the dough has been kneaded, yeast bread is allowed to rise so that the yeast can grow and provide lightness and the flavor can develop. Very often the instructions advise putting the dough in a warm draft-free area. You do not need to be quite that literal. Many bread-making instructions date to times when buildings had little or no heat, and getting bread to rise was difficult at best. With central heating, this is not a problem. You can simply set the dough to rise on a kitchen counter. The bread can be encouraged to rise faster by putting it in an oven with a pilot light, or in an unlighted oven with a bowl of warm water. Bread rises very well in the refrigerator; it just takes longer. Whenever possible, a longer, slower rising is preferable because it gives the bread a better flavor. However, if it rises too long, it may develop a yeasty flavor.

Dough is allowed to rise until double in bulk. Some breads double in several hours whereas others take a shorter period of time. Rising time depends on the amount of yeast in relation to the amount of flour, the temperature of the room, and the type of flour. Rye breads, for instance, generally take longer to rise.

To determine if the bread has risen enough, poke a finger into the dough. If the hole remains, the dough is ready; if it starts to fill in fairly quickly, it needs to rise longer. This is not a foolproof test, however. If you have time, let the dough continue to rise for about 30 minutes more after it has reached the initial double stage.

## Shaping

The shapes of breads are limited only by the baker's imagination. Certain shapes are the most practical for making sandwiches. Some special recipes, such as pita bread are restricted in shape.

The following shapes are fashioned before the final rising and baking. You should determine the shape according to the bread's use.

*Baguette*: a loaf 2-1/2 inches in diameter and 30 to 36 inches in length.

*Ficelle*: a loaf 1-1/2 inches in diameter and 18 inches in length.

*Round*: any size loaf from 2-1/2 inches to 12 inches in diameter.

*Standard loaf*: A loaf shaped in a loaf pan. The usual sizes are 9 by 6 by 3 inches and 8 by 4 by 2 inches. Individual loaves can be shaped in smaller pans.

To shape standard breads, press the punched down dough into a rectangle as long as desired and approximately three times as wide as required. Roll the bread to form the loaf, pinching all the edges to keep them together. With long loaves, such as a baguette or ficelle, roll the loaves back and forth on the counter, stretching toward the ends. For round loaves, cup the dough with the palms of your hands and press the dough into a ball, turning constantly to even the shape and pulling downward to stretch the top of the dough tautly over the ball.

## Baking Sheet

If the breads are baked on a baking sheet, cover the portion of the sheet under the bread with something to prevent sticking. Do not cover the whole sheet, or the areas not covered by the bread will burn. Cornmeal is traditional for French and some Italian breads. Rye breads and French and Italian breads can be baked on a sprinkle of white flour. Butter can also be used.

If the bread is baked in a mold, such as a loaf pan, the mold should be buttered thoroughly before adding the bread. Fill the mold two-thirds full and allow the dough to rise to the top of the pan before baking.

When buttering pans, use *butter*. The flavor of cooked butter is incomparable. Other fats will help the bread release from the pan, but only butter will give the bread its special flavor.

## Scoring

Many loaves, especially those baked without a mold, are scored to enhance their appearance and to open the surface and provide more space for expansion. Loaves are slashed with a very sharp knife, a razor blade, or a special knife called a *lame*. Long loaves are slashed in long diagonal slices, two or three times. Occasionally, the loaves are snipped with scissors about every 4 inches on opposite sides to create a loaf that looks like a stalk of wheat. One advantage to this cut (called *epee* or "wheat stalk") is that the bread breaks evenly into serving sizes.

Round loaves may be slashed in curves, circles, crosses, or squares. Round loaves are often pressed to flatten them to an overall thickness of about 1 inch. The dough is then brushed with water and decorated with pieces of extra dough to make designs, such as a sheaf of wheat or a bunch of grapes.

Breads are often coated with a wash of salted water, egg white, egg yolk, or whole egg. The wash gives them a deeper color and a sheen. Often, the breads are sprinkled with various seeds, such as caraway or poppy.

If you want a hard crust on the bread, brush it with salted

water or egg white and bake it in the oven with a pan of boiling water on the bottom of the oven. The steam helps to create a crunchy crust. If you want a soft crust, brush the loaf lightly with melted butter before baking and again when you remove the bread from the oven.

## Baking

Bake the loaves until golden brown and crusty. To tell if the loaf is baked, turn it out of its pan or just turn it over and tap the bottom of the loaf. It should sound hollow. If the bread needs further baking, bake it directly on the oven rack.

If desired, you can make your own brown-and-serve loaves by baking the bread just until it starts to turn golden. Remove it from the oven, cool, and freeze. When ready to serve, place the thawed bread in an oven preheated to the original temperature and bake until well-browned.

After the bread is baked, unmold it and cool on racks. Bread slices better if it is allowed to cool completely before serving. However, the wonderful aroma of freshly made bread can be irresistible. If the soup is ready, serve the bread and do not be concerned if the slices are not perfect.

## Storing

When storing breads in the freezer, wrap them securely in plastic wrap or foil. Self-defrosting freezers have a tendency to dry out breads that are poorly wrapped. Bread can be sliced, wrapped in foil, and heated in a 350°F. oven for faster thawing and heating. If there is no great hurry, you can thaw the bread at room temperature, but it will taste much better if warmed in the oven before serving. Breads can also be thawed in a microwave oven. Securely wrapped breads will keep for months in the freezer.

You can prepare bread dough and store it in the freezer, either shaped or unshaped. Let the loaves thaw and double in bulk before baking.

## What Can Go Wrong

The major reason for the failure of yeast bread is that the yeast was killed. Possibly, it may not have been active, but checking the date stamp should avoid that pitfall. Heat kills yeast. If you use warm, not hot, liquids, prove the yeast, and do not try to hurry the rising by leaving it in a hot oven or on a hot radiator, you should be able to produce very good bread. (Remember, if the bread is not rising, make a sponge and add it to the dough as previously noted.)

If you do not knead the dough sufficiently, you may have a heavy loaf. Once the dough is baked, there is nothing you can do except remember to spend a little more time and knead it more vigorously.

Bread that is not given enough time to rise may also be heavy. If in doubt, let it rise longer. If it rises too long and starts to collapse, punch it down and let it rise again. Usually the next rising takes much less time.

Remember that bread making is simple, fun, and gratifying. If your first attempt is not a total success, try again. Soon you will wonder why you were ever concerned about making bread.

## White Bread

This is the standard white loaf suitable for sandwiches, toast, and general consumption. The recipe can be multiplied to produce as many loaves at a time as you need.

| | |
|---|---|
| 1 package yeast | 3 tablespoons butter |
| 1/4 cup warm water | 2 teaspoons salt |
| 1 tablespoon sugar | 6 to 7 cups flour |
| 1-3/4 cups milk | butter |

In a bowl, dissolve the yeast in the water with a pinch of sugar and let prove.

In a saucepan, warm the milk with the remaining sugar, butter, and salt until the butter is melted. If necessary cool to 90°F. Stir into the yeast.

Add 3 cups flour and beat until smooth. Beat in enough additional flour until the dough looks shaggy. Turn out onto a lightly floured board and knead until smooth and elastic, adding just enough additional flour to make a medium-firm dough.

Rub the inside of a bowl with butter. Add the dough and turn it over in the bowl to coat all sides. Cover with a towel wrung out in warm water and let rise until doubled in bulk, about 1-1/2 hours.

Punch down and knead for 2 to 3 minutes to make sure it is fully deflated. Let rise again until doubled in bulk, about 50 minutes.

Butter two 9- by 5- by 3-inch loaf pans. Punch the dough down once more and shape into two loaves. Place the loaves in the pans, brush the tops with a little melted butter, and let rise until doubled in bulk, about 1 hour and 15 minutes.

Preheat oven to 400°F.

Bake loaves about 35 to 40 minutes.

*Yield: 2 loaves*

## French Bread

There are dozens of recipes for French bread. Some involving complicated directions and the addition of tiles and other paraphernalia to your oven. This version produces a delicious loaf easily. It can be made into whole loaves or a variety of differently shaped rolls.

| | |
|---|---|
| 1 package yeast | 2 tablespoons salt |
| 1 tablespoon sugar | 7 to 8 cups flour |
| 2-1/2 cups warm water | cornmeal |

In a bowl, dissolve the yeast and sugar in the water with the salt. Cover with a towel wrung out in warm water and let prove.

Stir in 3 cups flour and beat well. Add enough additional flour, 1 cup at a time, until the dough looks shaggy.

Turn out onto a lightly floured board and knead until smooth and elastic, adding just enough additional flour to make a medium-firm dough. Place the dough in a bowl and dust generously with flour. Cover with a towel wrung out in warm water and let rise until doubled in bulk, about 1 hour.

Punch down and knead about 2 minutes. Return to the bowl, dust again with flour, and cover with a towel. Let rise until doubled in bulk. Punch down and shape as desired.

Sprinkle cornmeal or flour on a baking sheet where the breads are to be placed. Place the dough on the baking sheet, cover with a towel, and let rise until doubled in bulk, about 30 minutes.

Preheat oven to 400°F. Place a pan of boiling water in the bottom of the oven.

Slash the top of the loaves with a sharp knife, brush with salted water, if desired, and let rise 5 minutes longer.

Bake 20 to 40 minutes or until golden and crusty, depending on the size of the loaves.

*Yield: 3 baguettes, 5 ficelles, 24 3-inch rolls, or 2 10-inch round loaves*

*Note:* For variety, sprinkle the top of the loaves with sesame, poppy, or caraway seeds, or coarse salt before baking.

## Whole Wheat French Bread

Use 4 cups whole wheat flour in place of 4 cups white flour, and 2 tablespoons brown sugar in place of 1 tablespoon white sugar.

For crisper loaves, brush with 2 egg whites beaten with 2 tablespoons water when loaves are set to rise, and once again before slashing.

## Kaisersemmeln (Kaiser rolls, Bulkie rolls)

Many delicatessens refer to these as bulkie rolls. It is difficult to achieve the five distinct sections, but once you have the knack, it will be easy. Do not be overly concerned about the shape—they are delicious in any form.

| | |
|---|---|
| 1 package yeast | 3/4 tablespoon salt |
| 1 cup lukewarm water | 6 cups flour |
| 1 tablespoon sugar | Vienna wash (see following |
| 1 cup milk | recipe) |

In a bowl, mix the yeast, water, and sugar. Cover with a towel wrung out in warm water and let prove.

Stir in the milk and salt. Stir in 3 cups flour and beat well. Beat in enough additional flour, 1 cup at a time, until the dough looks shaggy. Turn out onto a lightly floured board and knead until smooth and elastic, adding just enough additional flour to make a medium-firm dough.

Put into a clean bowl and dust generously with flour. Let rise until doubled in bulk. Punch down and let rise again.

Punch the dough down and cut into 24 sections. Roll each section firmly into a ball. In your left hand, place a ball of dough between your thumb and finger tips. With the thumb and index finger of the right hand, pull one edge of the dough out and away from the dough. Bring it back over your thumb and tuck it underneath. Turn the dough slightly and repeat four more times. Pinch the sections under your thumb together and place on a floured baking sheet. Let rise until doubled in bulk.

Preheat oven to 425°F.

Brush the rolls with Vienna wash and bake 10 minutes. Brush with the wash again and bake 2 to 5 minutes longer, or until golden. Cool.

*Yield: about 24 rolls*

*Vienna Wash*

| | |
|---|---|
| 1 egg white | 4 cups cold water |

In a bowl, whisk the egg white with 1/2 cup cold water until well combined. Beat in the remaining water to make a thin wash.

## Finger Rolls

| | |
|---|---|
| 3/4 cup milk | 2 packages yeast |
| 1/4 cup sugar | 3/4 cup warm water |
| 1-1/4 teaspoons salt | 5-1/2 cups flour |
| 4-1/4 tablespoons butter | |

In a small saucepan, mix the milk, sugar, salt, and butter. Heat over low heat until the butter is melted. Cool to lukewarm.

Combine the yeast and water and let prove in a large bowl. Beat in the cooled milk mixture and 2-1/2 cups flour. Beat until smooth. Beat in just enough additional flour, 1 cup at a time, until the mixture looks shaggy. Turn out onto a lightly floured board and knead until smooth and elastic, adding just enough additional flour to make a medium-firm dough.

Put the dough into a buttered bowl and turn it over to coat all sides. Cover with a towel wrung out in warm water and let rise until doubled in bulk, about 1 hour. Punch down and let rise again.

Break off pieces of the dough, about 1-1/2 ounces each, and shape into finger rolls about 3 inches long. Place the rolls on a buttered baking sheet and cover with a towel. Let rise until doubled in bulk.

Preheat oven to 425°F. Bake until golden, about 15 minutes. Remove from the oven and brush with butter.

*Yield: about 16 rolls*

## Pita Bread

1 package yeast                      5 to 6 cups flour
1/2 teaspoon sugar                   2 teaspoons salt
2 cups lukewarm water

In a bowl, dissolve the yeast and sugar in the water. Cover with a towel wrung out in warm water and let prove.

Stir in 3 cups flour and the salt and beat until smooth. Beat in enough additional flour, 1 cup at a time, until the dough looks shaggy. Turn out onto a lightly floured board and knead until smooth and elastic, adding just enough additional flour to make a stiff dough.

Place in a bowl, dust generously with flour, and cover with a towel wrung out in warm water. Let rise until doubled in bulk. Punch down and divide into 12 sections.

With a lightly floured rolling pin, roll each section into a circle about 1/4-inch-thick and place on a buttered baking sheet. Cover with a cloth wrung out in warm water and let rise for 20 minutes.

Preheat oven to 425°F.

Bake until the pitas are lightly browned, puffed, and sound hollow when tapped, about 20 minutes.

*Yield: 12 loaves*

## Processor Crusty Herbed Loaf

1 package yeast                      2 tablespoons chives
1 tablespoon sugar                   1/4 cup butter, softened
1 cup warm water                     1 teaspoon salt
3 cups flour                         black pepper
1 teaspoon salt                      1 large egg
1 garlic clove                       1/2 teaspoon salt
1 cup packed parsley

In the beaker of a processor, combine the yeast, sugar, and water. Let prove.

Add 2 cups of flour and process with on-off turns. Add remaining flour and process until the mixture forms a ball. Turn out onto a counter and knead about 1 minute.

Put the dough into a buttered bowl and turn to coat all sides. Cover with a towel wrung out in warm water and let rise until doubled in bulk, about 1 hour.

In the processor, mince the garlic, parsley, and chives. Add the butter, salt, and pepper to taste and process until smooth.

When the dough has risen, roll on a lightly floured board into a 9- by 12-inch rectangle. Spread with the herb mixture leaving a 1-inch border.

Roll up the short end of the dough, pinching the seams together. Butter a 9- by 5- by 3-inch loaf pan and put the dough into the pan, seam side down.

With a sharp knife, score the bread to reveal the herb layer. Cover with a towel wrung out in warm water and let rise until the dough comes to the top of the pan, about 45 minutes.

Preheat oven to 375°F.

Combine the egg and salt and brush on the dough. Bake 30 to 40 minutes, or until golden and crisp. Remove from the oven and unmold.

*Yield: 1 loaf*

## Herbed French Bread

| | |
|---|---|
| 1 package yeast | 1/4 cup minced parsley |
| 1-3/4 cups warm water | 4 tablespoons onion, sautéed |
| 4 cups flour | 1 teaspoon olive oil |
| salt | |
| 1/2 teaspoon minced | |
| rosemary | |

In a bowl, mix the yeast and water and let prove.

Stir in 2 cups flour and salt to taste and beat well. Add enough additional flour until the dough looks shaggy. Turn out onto a lightly floured board and knead until smooth and elastic, adding just enough additional flour to prevent the bread from sticking.

Cover the bread with a bowl and let rise until doubled in bulk, about 50 minutes. Remove the bowl, knead briefly, and let rise again covered with the bowl. Punch down and pat into a rectangle, 12 by 14 inches.

Sprinkle with rosemary, parsley, and onion. Roll into a loaf. Bring the ends under the loaf and shape into a ball. Place on a baking sheet that is sprinkled with cornmeal or buttered. Brush with olive oil and let rise, uncovered, for 30 minutes.

Preheat oven to 425°F. Put a pan of boiling water on the bottom of the oven.

With a sharp knife or razor blade, cut a tic-tac-toe pattern in the bread. Bake 30 minutes. Lower the heat to 400°F. and bake 15 minutes longer.

*Yield: 1 9-inch round loaf*

*Note:* If desired, you can work the herbs and onion into the dough while punching it down before the second rise. The bread can be baked in a 9- by 5- by 3-inch loaf pan.

For variety, substitute 1/2 teaspoon dried dill weed, a pinch of powdered sage, and a pinch of crumbled marjoram for the herbs listed.

## Cottage Cheese Dill Bread

| | |
|---|---|
| 1 package yeast | 1 teaspoon salt |
| 2 tablespoons sugar | 1/4 teaspoon baking soda |
| 1/4 cup warm water | 1 egg |
| 1 cup cottage cheese | 2-1/2 cups flour |
| 1/4 cup butter | 2 teaspoons butter, melted |
| 1 tablespoon minced onion | dill seed |
| 2 teaspoons dried dill weed | |

In a small bowl, dissolve the yeast with 1 tablespoon sugar in warm water and let prove.

In a saucepan, mix the remaining sugar, cheese, butter, onion, dill weed, salt, and baking soda. Heat just until warm to the touch and the butter is melted. Beat in the egg and the yeast mixture. Beat in just enough flour to make a soft dough that looks shaggy.

Turn out onto a lightly floured surface and knead until smooth and elastic, adding just enough additional flour to keep the dough from sticking. Place the dough in a buttered bowl and turn to coat all sides. Cover the bowl with a towel wrung out in warm water and let rise until doubled in bulk, about 1 hour. Punch down and let rise again.

Shape into a loaf and place in a buttered 8- by 5- by 3-inch loaf pan. Let rise until it reaches the top of the pan.

Preheat oven to 350°F.

Bake 30 minutes, or until golden. Turn out onto a rack to cool. While still warm, brush with melted butter and sprinkle with dill seed.

*Yield: 1 loaf*

## Braided Herb Bread

| | |
|---|---|
| 1 cup milk | 1 teaspoon crumbled |
| 1/2 cup minced onion | rosemary |
| 1/4 cup butter | 1 teaspoon crumbled thyme |
| 1 package yeast | 7 to 8 cups flour |
| 1 cup water | 2 eggs, lightly beaten |
| 3 tablespoons sugar | 1 tablespoon milk |
| 1 tablespoon salt | 1/3 cup sesame seeds |
| 1/4 cup minced parsley | |

In a small saucepan, heat the milk, onion, and butter until the butter is melted. If necessary, let cool to about 100°F.

In a bowl, mix the yeast, water, and sugar and let prove. Stir in the salt, parsley, rosemary, thyme, milk mixture, and 3 cups flour. Mix well. Add just enough additional flour to make the dough look shaggy.

Beat in all but 2 tablespoons of the egg and mix again. Add more flour, if needed, to make a medium-firm dough.

Turn out onto a lightly floured board and knead until smooth and elastic, adding just enough flour to prevent the dough from sticking. Put into a buttered bowl and turn to coat all sides. Cover with a towel wrung out in warm water and let rise until doubled in bulk, about 1-1/2 hours.

Punch down and let rise again. Punch down and divide in half. Divide each half into thirds and roll each third into a 12-inch-long rope. Braid the ropes, pinching the ends together, and place on a buttered baking sheet.

Repeat with the remaining section of dough. Cover both loaves with a towel wrung out in warm water and let rise about 40 minutes, or until doubled in bulk. Brush with reserved egg mixed with 1 tablespoon milk. Sprinkle with sesame seeds.

Preheat oven to 375°F.

Bake loaves 40 minutes, or until golden.

*Yield: 2 12-inch braided loaves*

## Gruyère Herb Bread

2 teaspoons olive oil
1/2 teaspoon dried basil
1/2 teaspoon savory
1/2 teaspoon ground pepper
1/4 teaspoon dried thyme
1 package yeast
2 cups warm water

2 tablespoons sugar
1 tablespoon salt
5 to 6 cups flour
5 ounces Gruyère cheese, grated
1 egg white, lightly beaten

In a small bowl, mix the oil, basil, savory, pepper, and thyme. Let macerate for 1 hour.

In a large bowl, mix the yeast, water, sugar, herb mixture, and salt. Let prove. Stir in 2 cups of flour and beat until smooth. Add more flour, 1 cup at a time, until the dough looks shaggy.

Turn the dough out onto a lightly floured board and knead until the dough is smooth and elastic, adding just enough additional flour to prevent sticking.

Place in a buttered bowl and turn to coat all sides. Let rise until doubled in bulk, about 1 hour. On a work surface, punch down and press into a 20-inch circle. Sprinkle with cheese. Gather the edges together and shape into a ball. Return to the bowl and cover with a towel wrung out in warm water. Let rise until doubled in bulk.

Punch down and roll into a 10- by 24-inch rectangle. Roll up tightly into a long loaf, or coil loosely into a flat circle, or shape into a ring. Let rise until doubled in bulk.

Preheat oven to 425°F.

Brush the loaf with egg white. Snip a design with scissors on the surface of the loaf at 2-inch intervals.

Bake 20 minutes. Lower the heat to 375°F. and bake until golden, about 35 to 40 minutes. Cool on a wire rack.

*Yield: 1 loaf*

## Herb Parmesan Casserole Bread

2 cups water
2 packages yeast
2 teaspoons salt
2 tablespoons butter, softened

1-1/2 tablespoons oregano
1/2 cup plus 1 tablespoon grated Parmesan cheese
4-1/2 cups flour

In a large bowl, mix the water, yeast, and salt and let prove. Stir in the butter, oregano, 1/2 cup cheese, and 3 cups flour. Beat well.

Beat in remaining flour. The dough will be sticky. Cover with a towel wrung out in warm water and let rise until light and bubbly and more than doubled in bulk.

Butter a 1-1/2-quart casserole. Beat the dough vigorously for 2 minutes. Turn into the casserole and sprinkle with remaining cheese. Let stand for 20 minutes.

Preheat oven to 375°F.

Bake 55 minutes, or until golden. Turn onto a rack and cool.

*Yield: 1 loaf*

*Note:* For variety, you can substitute equal amounts of minced dill and grated Gruyère cheese for the oregano and Parmesan cheese.

---

## Garlic Potato Bread

| | |
|---|---|
| 1 large potato, boiled and grated (about 1-1/2 cups) | 1 package yeast |
| 1 teaspoon salt | 2 teaspoons sugar |
| 1 garlic clove, crushed | 2 cups flour |
| 1 cup warm potato water | softened butter |

In a bowl, combine the potato, salt, garlic, potato water, yeast, and sugar. Let prove. Stir in the flour and mix well.

Turn out onto a lightly floured board and knead until smooth and elastic. Place in a buttered bowl and turn to coat all sides. Cover with a towel wrung out in warm water and let rise until doubled in bulk.

Punch down and turn into a buttered 8- or 9-inch cast-iron skillet. Brush the top with butter and let rise until doubled in bulk.

Preheat oven to 450°F.

Bake 25 to 30 minutes, or until golden.

*Yield: 1 loaf*

*Note:* The skillet must have an ovenproof handle. If you do not have a skillet, bake the bread in a 9-inch cake tin.

## Cheese and Garlic Casserole Bread

1 package yeast
1 cup warm water
1 tablespoon sugar
4 cups flour
2 teaspoons salt

1 teaspoon crushed garlic
2 cups grated sharp cheddar
  cheese
1-1/2 cups water

In a bowl, combine the yeast, 1 cup warm water, and sugar. Let prove. Stir in the flour, salt, garlic, cheese, and remaining water. Mix well to make a soft dough.

Lightly oil a bowl and place the dough in it. Let rise until doubled in bulk. Punch down and let rise again.

Butter a 1-1/2- to 2-quart casserole or soufflé dish, or use two 8- by 5- by 2-inch loaf pans. Place dough in pan(s) and let rise until doubled in bulk.

Preheat oven to 400°F.

Bake 30 minutes, or until golden. Brush the loaf with butter and bake 5 minutes longer. Serve warm.

*Yield: 1 round loaf or 2 standard loaves*

## Black Pepper Crackling Bread

This wonderful bread is popular in Italy and the southern states. It is not suitable for sandwiches, but it is excellent with hearty soups.

1 package yeast
1/2 cup lukewarm water
4 teaspoons sugar
1 cup milk
1/3 cup lard
1 tablespoon salt
1 egg

6 cups flour
1/4 cup butter, melted
2 teaspoons freshly ground
  black pepper
3 cups pork cracklings (see
  Index)

In a bowl, mix the yeast, water, and sugar. Let prove.

In a saucepan, heat the milk and lard until the lard is melted. Cool to lukewarm. Stir into the yeast with the salt, egg, and 2 cups flour. Beat until well mixed. Beat in additional flour until the dough looks shaggy.

Turn out onto a lightly floured board and knead until smooth and elastic, adding just enough additional flour to prevent the dough from sticking. Place the dough in a greased bowl and turn to coat all sides. Cover with a towel wrung out in warm water and let rise until doubled in bulk. Punch down.

Form into 2 balls, cover, and let rest 10 minutes. Roll each ball into a 9- by 14-inch rectangle, 1/2-inch-thick. Brush with melted butter and sprinkle with pepper and cracklings. Roll up like a jelly roll and place in buttered 9- by 5- by 3-inch loaf pans. Brush the surface with melted butter and let rise until doubled in bulk, about 1 hour.

Preheat oven to 375°F.

Bake the loaves 40 minutes, or until browned.

*Yield: 2 loaves*

*Note:* Cracklings are available in some markets.

---

## Whole Wheat Bread

| | |
|---|---|
| 1 package yeast | 2 teaspoons salt |
| 1-1/4 cups warm water | 3 cups white flour |
| pinch of sugar | 1 cup whole wheat flour |

In a bowl, mix the yeast, water, and sugar. Let prove. Stir in the salt and flours and mix well.

With your hand, continue to knead the dough in the bowl by picking it up and slapping it against the sides of the bowl. The dough will be very sticky. When it pulls away cleanly from the bowl and your hand, it has been kneaded enough.

Turn into a clean bowl, dust with flour, and cover with a towel wrung out in warm water. Let rise until doubled in bulk.

Turn out onto a board and knead well, adding a little white flour if required to prevent sticking. Shape into an 8-inch ball and place on a pie plate sprinkled with white flour. Cover with a towel and let rise until doubled in bulk.

Preheat oven to 450°F.

Bake for 15 minutes. Lower the heat to 400°F. and bake 30 minutes longer.

*Yield: 1 loaf*

## Fouace aux Noix (Walnut Hearth Bread)

| | |
|---|---|
| 1 package yeast | 1 cup warm milk |
| 1/3 cup warm water | 3 to 4 cups flour |
| 1 tablespoon salt | 1/2 cup whole wheat flour |
| 1 cup chopped walnuts | 2 tablespoons cornmeal |
| 3/4 cup minced onion | |
| 1/2 cup unsalted butter, | |
| softened | |

In a bowl, mix the yeast and water. Let prove. Stir in the salt, walnuts, onion, butter, and milk and mix well. Stir in 3 cups white flour and mix well. Beat in the whole wheat flour until the dough looks shaggy.

Turn out onto a lightly floured board and knead until smooth and elastic, adding just enough additional white flour to make a stiff dough.

Butter a bowl and turn the dough in the bowl to coat all sides. Cover with a towel wrung out in warm water and let rise until doubled in bulk. Punch down and let rise again.

Sprinkle a baking sheet with cornmeal. Shape the dough into a ball and place on the cornmeal. Let rise, uncovered, for 20 minutes.

Preheat oven to 425°F.

Put a pan of boiling water on the bottom of the oven. Bake the bread 30 minutes. Remove the pan of water, lower the heat to 300°F., and bake 30 minutes longer. Cool on a rack.

*Yield: 1 2-pound loaf*

## Honey Bran Bread

| | |
|---|---|
| 2 packages yeast | 1/2 cup honey |
| 1/4 cup warm water | 3 tablespoons sugar |
| 1 cup milk | 1-1/2 cups bran |
| 2 teaspoons butter | 3-1/2 cups flour |
| 1 teaspoon salt | |

In a bowl, mix the yeast and water. Let prove.

Heat the milk, butter, salt, honey, and sugar until the butter is melted. Cool to lukewarm.

In a bowl, stir the milk mixture into the yeast and add the bran. Mix well and let stand for 20 minutes. Stir in 2 cups flour and mix well. Turn out onto a board and knead in just enough additional flour to make a smooth and elastic medium-firm dough.

Place the dough in a buttered bowl and turn to coat all sides. Cover with a towel wrung out in warm water and let rise about 2 hours, or until doubled in bulk. Punch down and let rise again.

Shape into a loaf and put into a buttered 9- by 5- by 3-inch loaf pan. Let rise until the dough comes to the top of the pan.

Preheat oven to 350°F. Bake 50 minutes, or until golden.

*Yield: 1 loaf*

## Soured Rye Bread

This bread is made in two stages. The sponge is a necessary ingredient and must be made at least six hours ahead or up to three days before proceeding with the recipe. The longer the sponge works, the more sour the taste.

### Sponge

| | |
|---|---|
| 1 package yeast | 2 cups rye flour |
| 1-1/2 cups warm water | 1 tablespoon caraway seeds |

In a bowl, mix the yeast and water. Let prove.

Stir in the flour and caraway seeds and stir to blend. Cover with a towel wrung out in warm water and let stand at least 6 hours or up to 3 days. The sponge will get bubbly. Stir it down periodically. After the first day, it can be stored in a screw top jar with the lid loosely applied. Do not put the lid on tightly or it may explode.

### Soured Rye Bread

| | |
|---|---|
| 1 recipe sponge (see preceding recipe) | 1 tablespoon salt |
| 1 package yeast | 1 cup rye flour |
| 1 cup warm water | 3 tablespoons shortening |
| 1/4 cup dark molasses | 5 to 6 cups white flour |
| 2 tablespoons caraway seeds | 1 egg, beaten |
| 1 egg, lightly beaten | 1 tablespoon milk |

Stir down the sponge and stir in the yeast, water, molasses, and 1 tablespoon caraway seeds. Mix well.

Stir in the egg and salt and mix again.

Add the rye flour and beat vigorously for 2 minutes. Beat in the shortening and 2 cups white flour and beat again. Beat in additional flour, 1 cup at a time, until the dough looks shaggy.

Turn out onto a lightly floured board and knead the dough until smooth and elastic, adding just enough additional flour to prevent the dough from sticking.

Butter a bowl and add the dough, turning to coat all sides. Cover with a towel wrung out in warm water and let rise until doubled in bulk, about 1-1/2 hours. Punch down and let rise again.

Divide the mixture and shape into 4 long or round loaves. Or form 2 loaves to fit buttered 9- by 5- by 3-inch loaf pans. Cover with a towel and let rise until doubled in bulk.

Preheat oven to 375°F.

Slash the loaves with a sharp knife or razor blade. Beat the egg with the milk and brush on the tops of the loaves. Sprinkle with remaining caraway seeds.

Bake 40 minutes, or until the crust is crisp and browned.

*Yield: 2 to 4 loaves*

## Russian Rye Bread

| | |
|---|---|
| 1-1/4 cups water | 3 cups rye flour |
| 1 tablespoon sugar | 3 cups white flour |
| 1/2 tablespoon brown sugar | 1/2 tablespoon salt |
| 1-1/2 tablespoons molasses | 2 tablespoons sautéed onion |
| 2 packages yeast | 1 tablespoon caraway seed |

In a bowl, mix the water, sugar, brown sugar, molasses, and yeast. Let prove.

Beat in the rye flour and just enough white flour to make a sticky dough. Beat in the salt, onion, and caraway seeds. Add additional white flour to make a firm dough. Knead until smooth and elastic.

Put into a bowl, sprinkle with white flour, and cover with a towel wrung out in warm water. Let rise until doubled in bulk, about 1-1/2 hours. Punch down and let rise again.

Shape into 1 round loaf. Place on a floured baking sheet and let rise until doubled in bulk.

Preheat oven to 400°F.

Bake about 25 minutes, or until the loaf sounds hollow when tapped on the bottom.

*Yield: 1 2-pound loaf*

---

## Black Bread

7 tablespoons cornmeal
3/4 cup cold water
3/4 cup boiling water
1 tablespoon butter
1 tablespoon salt
2 tablespoons plus 1
  teaspoon brown sugar
1-1/2 teaspoons caraway
  seeds
1 tablespoon unsweetened
  cocoa

1 tablespoon instant coffee
2 packages yeast
1/4 cup warm water
2 cups dark rye flour
1 cup whole wheat flour
2 to 4 cups white flour
1 egg white
2 tablespoons water

In a bowl, mix the cornmeal and cold water.

In a 1-quart saucepan, stir the cornmeal mixture into the boiling water in a slow, steady stream, stirring constantly. Cook until thickened.

Stir in the butter, salt, sugar, caraway seeds, cocoa, and coffee. Let cool to lukewarm.

In a bowl, mix the yeast and warm water and let prove. Stir in the cooled cornmeal mixture and rye and whole wheat flours. Add just enough white flour to make a shaggy dough.

Turn out onto a lightly floured board and knead until smooth and elastic, adding just enough white flour to make a firm dough. Shape into a ball and place in a well-buttered bowl, turning to coat all sides. Cover with a towel wrung out in warm water and let rise until doubled, about 1-1/2 hours.

Punch down and shape into round or oval loaves. Place the bread on a baking sheet sprinkled with white flour or cornmeal, and let rise until almost doubled in bulk. Brush with egg white beaten with cold water.

Preheat oven to 375°F.

Bake 50 to 60 minutes, or until the loaves sound hollow when tapped.

*Yield: 2 10-inch loaves*

## Russian Black Bread

2 packages yeast
2 tablespoons caraway seeds
2 teaspoons instant coffee
2 teaspoons salt
1 teaspoon sugar
1/2 teaspoon fennel seeds, crushed
3 teaspoons warm water
1/4 cup butter
1/4 cup white vinegar
1/4 cup molasses
1 ounce unsweetened chocolate
4 cups rye flour
2 cups bran cereal
2 to 3 cups white flour
1/2 cup water
1 teaspoon cornstarch

In a bowl, mix the yeast, caraway seeds, coffee, salt, sugar, fennel seeds, and 1/2 cup warm water. Let prove.

In a saucepan, mix the remaining water, butter, vinegar, molasses, and chocolate. Heat until the chocolate is melted but the mixture is still lukewarm. Add to the yeast mixture and mix well.

Add the rye flour and bran and beat well for 3 minutes. Beat in enough white flour so that the dough looks shaggy.

Turn out onto a lightly floured board and knead until smooth and elastic, adding just enough white flour to make a medium-firm dough. Place in a buttered bowl, turning to coat all sides. Cover with a towel wrung out in warm water and let rise until doubled in bulk.

Punch down and let rise again. Punch down and shape into 2 balls. Place on a buttered baking sheet, sprinkled with flour or cornmeal.

Preheat oven to 350°F.

Bake 40 minutes.

In a saucepan, combine the remaining water and cornstarch and bring to a boil. Simmer 1 minute. Brush over the bread and bake 10 minutes longer, or until the tops are glazed and the loaves sound hollow when tapped. Cool on racks.

*Yield: 2 1-pound loaves*

## Pumpernickel Bread

3 packages yeast
1-1/2 cups warm water
4 teaspoons salt
1/2 cup molasses
1 to 3 tablespoons caraway
  seeds

2 tablespoons soft butter
3-3/4 cups rye flour
3 to 4 cups white flour

In a bowl, mix the yeast, water, salt, molasses, and caraway seeds. Let prove. Stir in the butter and mix well.

Stir in the rye flour and just enough white flour to make the dough shaggy.

Turn out onto a lightly floured board and knead, adding just enough white flour to make a smooth and elastic medium-firm dough. Place the dough in a buttered bowl and turn to coat all sides. Cover with a towel wrung out in warm water and let rise until doubled in bulk, about 2 hours.

Punch down and let rise again. Punch down and cut into 2 sections. Shape into 2 balls. Place on a floured baking sheet and cover with a towel wrung out in warm water. Let rise 30 to 40 minutes. Brush loaves with cold water.

Preheat oven to 450°F.

Bake 10 minutes.

Lower the heat to 350°F. and bake 30 minutes longer.

*Yield: 2 loaves*

## SPECIALTY BREADS TO ACCOMPANY SOUPS

There are herbed flat breads that are not suitable for sandwiches. They are, in effect, sandwiches themselves and serve as a superb accompaniment to many soups. Versions are found in many European cuisines from Scandinavia to Italy. They have several names, the most common one being pizza. Other names are focaccia, sfinciuni, and pissaladiere.

These breads are made in flat rounds, squares, or rectangles. The flavorings are placed on top (similar to a standard pizza), worked into the dough, or used as a filling between layers of the dough.

## Baking Surface

To achieve a crisp crust on the bottom of the loaves, they should be baked in a preheated oven on preheated cast-iron baking sheets, baking stones, or quarry tiles placed directly on the oven rack. They can be baked on a standard, preheated baking sheet, but the bottom will not be as crisp.

Traditionally, the breads are shaped on a floured surface and slid onto a large, flat wooden board called a *peel*. The peel is used to slide the dough onto the preheated baking surface. There is a knack to sliding the bread off the peel and onto the baking surface. Put the peel into the oven and pull the handle back quickly. The dough should slip off onto the baking surface. You can practice this technique by placing several towels on the peel and slipping them off. If you do not have a peel, a baking sheet without sides or an inverted baking sheet will serve.

These recipes serve only as a starting point. Hopefully, the fillings and flavorings will inspire you to create recipes that suit your needs or the available ingredients. These breads can be as simple or elaborate as you wish. The dough is made from the recipe for French bread (see Index). When you need only a portion of the bread recipe, you can reduce the quantity of the original recipe or make the whole recipe and freeze the remainder, shaped or unshaped. Or use the extra dough to make rolls or loaves.

---

## *Caccia con Pesto (Flat Bread with Pesto)*

1/4 recipe French bread dough (see Index)
1/2 cup Pesto (see Index)
1/2 cup shredded mozzarella cheese
1/3 cup grated Parmesan cheese
1/4 cup grated Italian fontina cheese

Preheat oven to 475°F. and preheat baking surface.

Flour a pizza peel or sideless baking sheet.

Roll and stretch the dough into a 12-inch circle, forming a thicker rim around the edge. Spread the dough evenly with the pesto.

In a bowl, mix the cheeses together and sprinkle over the pesto mixture. Let rise 10 minutes and slip onto the preheated baking surface.

Bake 20 minutes, or until golden brown around the edges.

*Yield: 1 12-inch pizza*

## Caccia a la Nanza (Flat Bread with Garlic and Rosemary)

1/2 recipe French bread
   dough (see Index)
2 garlic cloves, thinly sliced
2 tablespoons chopped fresh
   rosemary

3 tablespoons olive oil
salt and pepper

Preheat oven to 400°F. and preheat baking surface.

Roll the dough 1/2-inch-thick on a lightly floured peel. With your fingers, poke holes all over the surface of the dough.

Roll the garlic in the rosemary and insert the garlic slices into the holes. Rub the surface with olive oil and sprinkle with salt and pepper to taste. Let rise 10 minutes.

Bake 15 minutes, or until golden. Remove garlic before serving, if desired.

*Yield: 1 loaf*

## Focaccia al Salvia, Rosamarino, or Oregane (Sage, Rosemary, or Oregano Flat Bread)

1/2 recipe French bread
   dough (see Index)
5 tablespoons olive oil

2 teaspoons dried sage
   leaves, crumbled, or 2
   tablespoons minced sage
   (or use equal amounts
   rosemary or oregano)

Preheat oven to 400°F. and preheat baking surface.

Knead the dough with 2 tablespoons olive oil and the herb to make a smooth dough and to distribute the herb evenly. Shape into a large, flat loaf, about 1/2-inch-thick, on a lightly floured peel.

With your fingers, press holes into the surface of the dough and sprinkle with the remaining olive oil. Let rest 10 minutes and slide onto the preheated baking surface.

Bake 20 minutes, or until golden.

*Yield: 1 loaf*

---

## Onion Flat Bread

1/2 recipe French bread
    dough (see Index)
8 tablespoons butter

1 cup finely chopped onions
salt and pepper

Preheat oven to 400°F. and preheat baking surface.

Knead 4 tablespoons butter into the dough and knead until smooth. Let rest.

In a skillet, sauté the onions in the remaining butter until golden around the edges, but not burned. Season to taste with salt and pepper. Cool.

Roll the dough 1/2-inch-thick on a lightly floured peel and sprinkle with the onion mixture.

Bake 20 minutes, or until golden and crisp.

*Yield: 1 loaf*

*Note:* Focaccia con le Cipolle, the Italian version of this recipe, substitutes olive oil for the butter. Work half the oil into the dough and scatter thinly sliced, raw onions over the flattened dough. Drizzle with remaining oil and coarse salt.

---

## Pissaladiere (French Pizza)

1/2 recipe French bread
    dough (see Index)
4 tablespoons olive oil
3 large onions, thinly sliced
3 tomatoes, peeled, seeded,
    and chopped

2 garlic cloves, crushed
salt and pepper
12 to 18 anchovy fillets
12 to 18 black olives, pitted

Preheat oven to 400°F. and preheat baking surface.

In a large skillet, heat the oil and cook the onions over low heat until very soft and just pale golden. Do not brown. Add the tomatoes, garlic, and salt and pepper to taste. Cook until well combined and liquid from the tomatoes has evaporated. Cool.

Roll the dough into a large rectangle and spread with the filling. Crisscross the anchovies on top. Fill in the spaces with olives.

Bake 20 minutes, or until golden.

*Yield: 1 large pizza, about a 12-inch circle or a 10- by 12-inch rectangle*

## Focaccia coi Ciccioli (Bacon-flavored Flat Bread)

| | |
|---|---|
| 1/2 recipe French bread dough (see Index) | 1 cup pork cracklings (see Index) |
| 1/4 cup olive oil | coarse salt |

Preheat oven to 400°F. and preheat baking surface.

Knead the dough and olive oil together until smooth. Knead in the cracklings until evenly distributed.

Roll the dough into a square or round bread, 1/2-inch-thick, on a lightly floured peel. Let rise 15 minutes.

Bake 15 to 20 minutes, or until golden.

*Yield: 1 large loaf*

## Pizza alla Marinara (Pizza with Garlic, Tomatoes, and Olive Oil)

| | |
|---|---|
| 1/4 recipe French bread dough (see Index) | 5 tablespoons olive oil |
| | salt |
| 1-1/2 pounds plum tomatoes, peeled, seeded, and chopped | 4 garlic cloves, thinly sliced |
| | 2 teaspoons oregano |

Preheat oven to 450°F. and preheat baking surface.

In a saucepan, cook the tomatoes and 3 tablespoons olive oil until thickened. Cool.

On a lightly floured peel, roll the dough into a 12-inch circle, making the rim thicker than the center. Spread the tomato mixture over the top and sprinkle with salt, garlic, and oregano. Drizzle with remaining oil. Let rise 10 minutes.

Bake 15 to 20 minutes, or until golden.
*Yield: 1 pizza*

---

## Pizza alla Margherita (Pizza with Tomatoes, Mozzarella Cheese, Olive Oil, and Parmesan Cheese)

1-1/2 pounds plum tomatoes,
   peeled
5 tablespoons olive oil
1/4 recipe French bread
   dough (see Index)

6 ounces mozzarella cheese
salt
2 tablespoons grated
   Parmesan cheese

Preheat oven to 450°F. and preheat baking surface.

In a saucepan, cook the tomatoes and olive oil over high heat until most of the liquid has evaporated. Cool.

Roll the dough on a lightly floured peel, making the edges thicker than the center. Spread the tomato mixture on the dough, sprinkle with mozzarella, salt, and Parmesan. Let rise 10 minutes.

Bake 20 minutes, or until golden and crisp.
*Yield: 1 12-inch pizza*

---

## Pizza with Leek and Chevre

4 tablespoons walnut oil
2 cups minced white parts of
   leeks
salt and pepper
1/4 recipe French bread
   dough (see Index)

1/2 pound bucheron cheese,
   crumbled
1 tablespoon minced fresh
   summer savory, or 1
   teaspoon crumbled, dried
   savory

Preheat oven to 450°F. and preheat baking surface.

In a skillet, heat the oil and cook the leeks over low heat until tender, but not brown. Season to taste with salt and pepper. Let cool.

On a lightly floured peel, roll the dough into a 12-inch circle, making the edges thicker than the center. Spread the leek mixture in the center and cover with the cheese and savory. Let rise 10 minutes.

Bake 20 minutes, or until golden.

*Yield: 1 12-inch pizza*
*Note:* Bucheron is one type of chevre (goat) cheese. You may substitute any other chevre.

---

## Sciocco (Tomato, Sausage, and Cheese Flat Bread)

---

1 onion, minced
1 garlic clove, minced
2 tablespoons butter
15 ounces tomato sauce
2 tablespoons heavy cream
pinch of oregano
pinch of basil
1/2 teaspoon salt
pepper
3/4 cup minced parsley

1 pound Italian sausage
1/2 recipe French bread
    dough (see Index)
2 tablespoons olive oil
4 ounces ricotta cheese
3/4 cup shredded provolone
    cheese
cornmeal
olive oil

Preheat oven to 350°F.

In a large skillet, sauté the onion and garlic in the butter until soft, but not brown. Stir in the tomato sauce, cream, oregano, and basil. Simmer until reduced to 3/4 cup. Correct seasoning with salt, pepper, and parsley.

Prick sausage with a fork. In a skillet, simmer sausage in 1/4-inch water until the water is evaporated and the sausage is browned. Cut into 1/4-inch-thick slices.

Knead dough lightly and roll into a 16- by 12-inch rectangle. Brush with olive oil. Spread the tomato sauce on the center third of the dough, lengthwise, scatter sausage on top, and dot with ricotta. Sprinkle with provolone. Fold one uncovered third of dough over the center and then fold over the remaining third of dough. Pinch seams securely.

Place seam side down on a baking sheet sprinkled with cornmeal. Cover the dough with a towel wrung out in warm water and let rise until doubled in bulk, about 45 minutes. Brush the loaf with olive oil. With a sharp knife, cut a series of slits along the top.

Bake 1 hour, or until the dough sounds hollow. Serve in slices.
*Yield: 1 loaf, about 12 1-inch-thick slices*

## Sfinciuni (Meat and Cheese-filled Pie)

4 tablespoons olive oil
1/2 cup thinly sliced onion
1/2 pound lean ground beef
salt and pepper
1/2 cup dry white wine
1/3 cup diced Genoa salami
1/2 cup finely diced Italian
    fontina cheese

1/4 cup ricotta cheese
1/2 recipe French bread
    dough (see Index)
2 tablespoons toasted bread
    crumbs

Preheat oven to 400°F. and preheat baking surface.

In a skillet, heat 3 tablespoons olive oil and sauté the onion until dark golden, but not burned. Add the beef, salt, and pepper. Cook, breaking up the meat with a fork until it loses its color. Add the wine and simmer until the liquid has evaporated. Turn into a bowl and let cool.

Add the salami, fontina, and ricotta to the meat and mix well.

Divide the dough in half and roll 1 piece into a 12-inch circle on a lightly floured peel. Sprinkle the dough with half the bread crumbs and 1 teaspoon olive oil, leaving a 1/2-inch border. Spread the stuffing on top and sprinkle with remaining olive oil and crumbs.

Roll the remaining dough into a 12-inch circle and place over the filling. Press the edges together, fold them up and over to form a rim, and pinch to seal. Brush pastry with remaining olive oil and slide onto the baking surface.

Bake 25 minutes, or until crisp and brown. Allow to rest 20 to 30 minutes before serving.

*Yield: 1 12-inch pie*

## Pizza Calabrese (Tomato, Tuna, and Olive Pizza)

7 tablespoons lard, softened
1/2 recipe French bread
    dough (see Index)
4 tablespoons olive oil
2-1/2 pounds tomatoes,
    peeled, seeded, and
    chopped

salt and pepper
8 ounces tunafish, drained
4 anchovy fillets, chopped
1 cup pitted ripe olives,
    chopped
1 tablespoon capers
melted lard

Preheat oven to 375°F.

On a lightly floured board, knead the lard into the dough until smooth and elastic. Set aside.

In a saucepan, heat the oil and cook the tomatoes with salt and pepper to taste until most of the liquid has evaporated. Stir in the tunafish, anchovies, olives, and capers. Correct the seasoning with salt and pepper. Cool 10 minutes.

Divide the dough into two-third and one-third portions. Roll the larger piece into a 14-inch circle and place in a 9-inch springform pan brushed with melted lard. Place the tuna mixture in the center and level the top.

Roll the remaining pastry into a 9-inch circle. Fold the edges of the pastry in the pan over the top of the filling and wet with cold water. Place the 9-inch pastry round on top and seal the edges by pinching. Cut steam vents in the surface and brush the top with melted lard.

Bake 1 hour, or until golden. Serve hot or cold.

*Yield: 1 9-inch pie*

# QUICK BREADS

These breads are quick to assemble and although they take about an hour to cook, they are truly a quick accompaniment for soup. They are not difficult but you must blend the ingredients together carefully for perfect results.

Because of the leavening agent, these recipes are actually chemical formulas. Be careful to measure the liquid and particularly the leavening agent (baking powder or baking soda) carefully. If you use too much or too little, you will have a bread that is less than appetizing. However, you can adjust the quantity of salt and sugar without difficulty. You can also substitute flours and flavoring ingredients to suit your wishes. Use any cheese you prefer and interchange ham, salami, and Italian sausage freely. You can use herbs that you have on hand, or those that are more appealing to you.

When preparing the breads, put the dry ingredients in a bowl and mix well. Very often, recipes suggest sifting, a most uninteresting chore. Over the years, I have found that mixing the dry ingredients with a wire whisk performs the job with less trouble.

For quick breads, the fat is softened or melted; for muffins, the butter is cold. When adding the liquid, stir it in until just moistened. Do not beat vigorously. If you overwork the mixture, the bread will be tough and you may diminish the leavening power. Do not delay the baking or again you will lose leavening power.

Place the bread in a buttered mold and bake in a preheated oven. To test for doneness, insert a wooden or metal skewer into the bread. It should come out clean. If there is any dough on the skewer, bake a few minutes longer. When the bread is baked, unmold it onto a cooling rack and let cool to lukewarm or room temperature. Serve immediately. Quick breads lose their fresh quality fairly quickly. If they are not to be served within a few hours, it is better to freeze them as soon as possible. If they have been frozen, thaw and warm them in an oven or microwave oven to enhance their flavor.

## Anchovy Mozzarella Bread

2-2/3 cups flour
4 teaspoons baking powder
1/2 teaspoon salt
4 anchovies, chopped
6 ounces mozzarella cheese,
  grated

2 eggs
1 cup milk
2 tablespoons sugar

Preheat oven to 350°F.
Butter a 9- by 5- by 3-inch loaf pan.
In a bowl, whisk together the flour, baking powder, and salt. Add the anchovies and mozzarella and toss to coat with dry ingredients.
Make a well in the dry ingredients and add the eggs, milk, and sugar. Mix until the ingredients are well moistened.
Pour the batter into the prepared pan and bake 1 hour, or until done. Unmold and let cool.
*Yield: 1 loaf*

## Basil Onion Bread

1 large Spanish onion,
  minced
1/2 cup plus 2 tablespoons
  salad oil
2 cups flour
1 tablespoon baking powder
1-1/2 teaspoons salt
1 teaspoon baking soda
2 scallions, minced
1 tablespoon minced basil
3 eggs
1/4 cup sugar
1/4 cup buttermilk
2 tablespoons cider vinegar

Preheat oven to 350°F.

Butter a 12- by 4-inch loaf pan, or two 8- by 5- by 3-inch loaf pans. Dust with flour and shake off the excess.

In a 1-quart saucepan, sweat the onion in the oil, over low heat, until very soft, about 24 minutes.

In a bowl, whisk together the flour, baking powder, salt, and soda.

Add the scallions and basil to the cooked onion and stir in the eggs, sugar, buttermilk, and vinegar. Mix into the dry ingredients until they are well moistened. Turn into the prepared loaf pan.

Bake 40 to 45 minutes, or until done. Cool in the pan for 10 minutes. Unmold onto a cooling rack and let cool.

*Yield: 1 or 2 loaves*

## Hot Cheese Cornbread

1 cup yellow cornmeal
1 cup sifted flour
1/4 cup sugar
1/2 teaspoon salt
4 teaspoons baking powder
1-1/2 cups shredded cheddar
  cheese
1 egg
1 cup milk
1/2 cup melted shortening

Preheat oven to 400°F.

Butter an 8-inch-square cake pan.

In a bowl, mix the cornmeal, flour, sugar, salt, and baking powder. Stir in the cheese. Make a well in the center.

In the well, combine the egg, milk, and shortening. Stir until well moistened and pour into the prepared pan.

Bake 30 minutes. Cool in the pan for 10 minutes. Unmold onto a cooling rack and let cool. Cut into squares.

*Yield: 1 8-inch bread*

## Jalapeno Cornbread

1 cup cornmeal
1/2 cup flour
salt to taste
1/2 teaspoon baking soda
1 cup canned creamed-style
corn

1 tablespoon jalapeno pepper
1 cup grated sharp cheddar
cheese
1/2 cup peanut oil
2 eggs, lightly beaten
1 cup buttermilk

Preheat oven to 425°F.

Butter an 8-inch-square cake pan or black cast-iron skillet.

In a bowl, whisk together the cornmeal, flour, salt, and baking soda. Add the creamed corn, jalapeno pepper, and cheese. Stir to blend.

Stir in the oil, eggs, and buttermilk to moisten. Pour into the prepared pan. Bake 25 minutes, or until golden and done. Serve hot.

*Yield: 1 8-inch bread*

## Buttermilk Cheese Loaf

2 cups flour
1-1/2 teaspoons baking
powder
1/2 teaspoon baking soda
2 teaspoons dry mustard

1 teaspoon salt
1 cup grated cheddar cheese
1 cup buttermilk
1/4 cup salad oil
2 eggs

Preheat oven to 375°F.

Butter a 9- by 5- by 3-inch loaf pan.

In a bowl, whisk together the flour, baking powder, baking soda, mustard, and salt. Mix in the cheese.

In a bowl, beat the buttermilk, oil, and eggs. Stir into the flour mixture until the ingredients are moistened. Turn into the prepared pan.

Bake 45 to 50 minutes, or until done. Let cool in the pan for 10 minutes, then unmold.

*Yield: 1 loaf*

*Note:* If buttermilk is not available, you can make soured milk by combining 1 tablespoon vinegar with 1 cup milk. Let it stand about 2 minutes.

*Flavoring Variations*

*Parmesan:* Substitute 1/4-cup grated Parmesan cheese for cheddar. If desired, stir in 1 teaspoon crumbled oregano.

*Salami:* Stir in diced cubes of salami, or any other favorite hard sausage.

*Herbed:* Add 1 tablespoon minced fresh dill or marjoram. Omit the cheese or substitute a cheese of your choice.

*Chevre and savory:* Add 1 cup crumbled chevre cheese and 1 teaspoon crumbled dried savory in place of the cheddar cheese.

## Salami Loaf

| | |
|---|---|
| 3 cups flour | 11 ounces cream cheese, softened |
| 2 tablespoons sugar | 1 cup milk |
| 1-1/2 tablespoons baking powder | 2 eggs, lightly beaten |
| 1-1/2 teaspoons salt | 1/4 cup salad oil |
| 1/2 teaspoon baking soda | 1 cup diced Genoa salami |
| 1 teaspoon fennel seeds | |
| 3 tablespoons grated Parmesan cheese | |

Preheat oven to 375°F.

Butter a 9- by 5- by 3-inch loaf pan.

In a bowl, whisk together the flour, sugar, baking powder, salt, baking soda, fennel seeds, and Parmesan.

Beat the cream cheese until smooth and beat in the milk, eggs, oil, and salami. Stir into the dry ingredients until moistened. Turn into prepared pan.

Bake 1 hour, or until done. Cool in the pan for 10 minutes, then unmold onto a cooling rack.

*Yield: 1 loaf*

## BISCUITS

Biscuits are a delicious accompaniment to soups and they are even quicker to make than quick breads. A well-organized cook can have everything ready to assemble and bake these biscuits so they are always served piping hot. This is a necessity because as biscuits cool they lose their wonderful fresh quality and seem "old," no matter how recently they were made. If you are preparing them for a crowd, freeze them as soon as they are cool.

Leftover biscuits are delicious when split, toasted, and served hot as a breakfast treat, or even to accompany soup. If they are allowed to cool, they will be very hard.

Biscuits can be difficult to prepare because they require delicate handling. The butter or fat is worked into the flour to create a mixture that resembles coarse meal. The milk or other liquid is added and the ingredients stirred just to moisten. Then the mixture is turned out onto a board and "kneaded" until smooth. This is the crucial point. Too much handling will result in "rock-like" biscuits. Instead of kneading like a yeast bread, literally press the ingredients together and pat them into a flat cake, about 1/2-inch-thick. Although recipes often suggest rolling the dough to this thickness, our experience has shown that gentle patting produces a more tender product.

---

## Baking Powder Biscuits

2 cups flour
2 teaspoons baking powder
1/2 teaspoon salt

1/4 cup butter
3/4 cups milk

Preheat oven to 450°F.

In a bowl, whisk together the flour, baking powder, and salt. Cut in the butter to make a mixture the consistency of coarse meal. Stir in the milk to make a medium-soft dough.

Turn out onto a lightly floured surface and knead about 30 seconds. Pat into a circle or rectangle, about 1/2-inch-thick. Cut into 2- or 3-inch circles, squares, or diamonds. Place on a baking sheet.

Gather any scraps and gently press together into a flat cake. Cut additional biscuits.

Bake 15 minutes, or until risen and golden.

*Yield: 18 biscuits*

*Note:* Before baking, the biscuits can be brushed lightly with beaten egg white, milk, or egg yolk. The tops can be sprinkled with poppy seeds, sesame seeds, or caraway seeds.

## Cheese Biscuits

Add 1 cup Parmesan cheese to the dry ingredients.

## Mustard Cheese Biscuits

Add 1 tablespoon dry mustard and 1 cup grated cheddar cheese to the dough after working in the butter.

## Rye Biscuits

Substitute 1 cup rye flour for 1 cup white flour.

## Caraway Rye Biscuits

Add 1 tablespoon caraway seeds to the recipe for rye biscuits.

# 4
# *Basic Recipes and Procedures*

Every cookbook contains certain recipes that are used more than once. They are basic to fine cooking, and many cooks know how to prepare them without reference to a recipe. Others of us, however, rely on recipes for correct quantities so that we can produce consistent results. This chapter provides the necessary recipes for this book. For the experienced cook, the section may serve as a reminder; for the new cook, all the needed information is here.

Several of the recipes are for foods that are readily available in markets, such as mayonnaise. We strongly believe that there is no substitute for homemade mayonnaise. No commercial brand has the fresh, unsweetened taste that you can achieve quickly and easily at home. This also applies to tartar sauce and Russian dressing. A vinaigrette made with a fresh, fruity olive oil and a quality vinegar is far superior to the tired flavors of bottled dressings. These recipes are worth the few minutes required to prepare them. Generally, they are also less expensive than the prepared versions.

This chapter also provides directions for some cooking tasks that are not fully explained in the text. Although many people know how to peel peppers or to prepare Chinese mushrooms, the directions are here for those who do not.

## HERB BUTTERS

Many of the sandwich recipes suggest herb butters. The following butters and those in the actual recipes should be considered only suggestions. Select a favorite flavor as a substitute, if you desire.

---

*Anchovy Butter*

---

6 tablespoons butter             2 anchovy fillets

In a food processor, cream the butter and anchovy fillets into a smooth paste.
Can be kept refrigerated for 1 week. Can be frozen.
*Yield: about 6 tablespoons*

## Garlic Butter

6 tablespoons butter                    salt and pepper
1 to 3 garlic cloves, crushed

In a processor, cream the butter until smooth. Work in the garlic for a smoother finish and force through a sieve. Correct the seasoning with salt and pepper.
Can be refrigerated for about 1 week. Can be frozen.
*Yield: about 6 tablespoons*

## Mustard Butter

6 tablespoons butter                    salt and pepper
1 to 2 tablespoons Dijon
  mustard

Cream the butter and mustard in a processor. Correct the seasoning with salt and pepper.
Can be refrigerated for 1 week. Can be frozen.
*Yield: about 6 tablespoons*

## Rosemary Butter

6 tablespoons butter                    salt and pepper
1 to 2 tablespoons fresh
  rosemary leaves, minced

Cream the butter and rosemary together. Season to taste with salt and pepper.
Can be refrigerated for up to 1 week. Can be frozen.

*Yield: about 6 tablespoons*

*Note:* Other herbs can be used in place of the rosemary, such as marjoram, chives, sage, and savory. Because fresh herbs vary in intensity of flavor, you may need to adjust the amount used. Dried herbs can be substituted using about 1/3 the fresh amount.

## DRESSINGS, SAUCES, AND SEASONINGS

### Vinaigrette Dressing

2 tablespoons vinegar, or
  lemon juice
2 teaspoons Dijon mustard

1/4 teaspoon salt
pinch of pepper
6 tablespoons olive oil

In a bowl, mix the vinegar, mustard, salt, and pepper. Whisk in the oil until the mixture thickens and emulsifies.

Keeps 1 week in the refrigerator.

*Yield: about 1 cup*

### Mayonnaise

2 egg yolks
1/2 teaspoon salt
pinch of white pepper
1/2 teaspoon dry mustard

2 tablespoons vinegar,
  approximately
1 cup olive and peanut oil
  (see note)

In a warm mixing bowl, mix the egg yolks, salt, pepper, and mustard with 1 teaspoon vinegar, using a wire whisk or hand mixer. Beat until the mixture starts to thicken.

Beat in the oil, drop by drop, until about 1/4 cup has been added and the mixture has thickened. Beat in 1 teaspoon vinegar and continue adding oil in a steady stream until about half the oil has been added.

Adjust the seasoning with vinegar and slowly beat in remaining oil. Correct seasoning with salt, pepper, mustard, and vinegar.

Keeps up to 2 weeks in the refrigerator.

*Yield: about 1-1/2 cups*

*Note:* For the best flavor, use a mixture of half peanut and half olive oil.

Vinegars vary greatly in the amount of acidity. This recipe is based on a relatively acidic vinegar. You may need a full 2 tablespoons of vinegar or lemon juice.

## Processor Mayonnaise

| | |
|---|---|
| 1 whole egg | 2 tablespoons vinegar, |
| 1/2 teaspoon salt | approximately |
| pinch of white pepper | 1 cup of oil (see note in |
| 1/2 teaspoon dry mustard | preceding recipe) |

In the beaker of a processor or blender, combine the egg, salt, pepper, mustard, and about 1 teaspoon vinegar.

With the machine running, add the oil in a thin, steady stream. When it is fully incorporated, correct the seasoning with vinegar, salt, pepper, and mustard.

Keeps up to 2 weeks in the refrigerator.

*Yield: about 1-1/2 cups*

## Sauce Tartare

| | |
|---|---|
| 1-1/2 cups mayonnaise | 1 tablespoon capers, minced |
| 1 dill pickle, minced | 2 teaspoons Dijon mustard |
| 2 scallions, minced | 1 tablespoon heavy cream |
| 1 anchovy, minced | 1/2 teaspoon lemon juice |
| 1 teaspoon minced parsley | salt and pepper |

In a bowl, mix the mayonnaise, pickle, scallions, anchovy, parsley, capers, mustard, cream, lemon juice, and salt and pepper to taste. Mix well. Cover, refrigerate, and let the flavors meld for at least 2 hours before serving.

Keeps 1 week in the refrigerator.

*Yield: about 2 cups*

## Sauce Remoulade

2 teaspoons dry mustard
2 teaspoons lemon juice
1 teaspoon capers
2 tablespoons minced dill
1 tablespoon minced parsley

1/2 teaspoon minced garlic
1 hard-cooked egg, minced
2 cups mayonnaise
salt and pepper

In a bowl, mix the mustard and lemon juice to a paste. Stir in the capers, dill, parsley, garlic, and egg. Fold in the mayonnaise and correct the seasoning with salt and pepper.
Keeps 3 to 4 days in the refrigerator.
*Yield: about 2 cups*

## Sauce Russe (Russian Dressing)

3 tablespoons chili sauce
1 teaspoon minced pimiento

1 teaspoon minced chives
1 cup mayonnaise

In a bowl, mix the chili sauce, pimiento, chives, and mayonnaise.
Keeps about 1 week in the refrigerator.
*Yield: about 1-1/2 cups*

## Béchamel Sauce

2 tablespoons butter
1 tablespoon minced onion
4 tablespoons flour
3 cups milk

1/4 teaspoon salt
3 white peppercorns
parsley sprig
pinch of grated nutmeg

In a saucepan, melt the butter and sauté the onion until soft, but not brown. Stir in the flour and cook the roux until bubbly and just beginning to turn golden.
With a wire whisk, beat in the milk. Cook, stirring constantly, until thickened and smooth. Add the salt, peppercorns, parsley, and nutmeg. Simmer gently 30 minutes, or until reduced to 2/3 of the original quantity. Strain.

Can be refrigerated for 3 to 4 days. Can be frozen.
*Yield: about 2 cups*

## Sauce Mornay (Cheese Sauce)

3 egg yolks
1/2 cup heavy cream
2 cups hot béchamel sauce

2 tablespoons butter
2 tablespoons grated Gruyère
  or Parmesan cheese

In a bowl, mix the egg yolks and cream. Add 1/4 cup hot béchamel to the egg mixture and stir. Turn the egg mixture into the remaining béchamel and cook, stirring, until almost to the boiling point. Do not boil.

Remove from the heat and stir in the butter and cheese.

*Yield: about 2-3/4 cups*

*Note:* Because of the possibility of overheating the sauce, it is best to add the egg liaison shortly before using. The béchamel can be made ahead.

## Tomato Coulis

3 pounds tomatoes, peeled,
  seeded, and chopped

2 tablespoons butter
salt and pepper

In a large skillet, sauté the tomatoes in the butter over high heat until most of the liquid has evaporated and it is a thick, pulpy mass. Correct the seasoning with salt and pepper.

Can be refrigerated for 2 to 3 days.

*Yield: about 2 cups*

*Note:* This mixture should have a fresh, clean taste similar to chopped, fresh tomatoes. The mixture should cook only a few minutes, 5 to 10 minutes at the most. If the tomatoes are very juicy, sprinkle them with salt and let drain in a colander before cooking.

## Bouquet Garni

There are two methods of adding seasonings that eventually will be removed from a liquid, such as soup or stew. One is a bouquet garni and the other is a faggot. They can be used interchangeably. A bouquet garni is wrapped in cheesecloth bags.

| | |
|---|---|
| 2 sprigs parsley | pinch of thyme |
| 1 bay leaf | 1/4 teaspoon peppercorns |

In a 3-inch square of cheesecloth, place the parsley, bay leaf, thyme, and peppercorns. Pick up the corners of the cloth and tie securely with kitchen twine.

I have successfully used a self-locking, stainless steel tea ball. It saves the time of cutting and tying the cheesecloth.

## Faggot

The reference is to a bundle of twigs.

| | |
|---|---|
| 1 celery stalk | pinch of thyme |
| 1 bay leaf | parsley sprigs |

Cut the celery in half across the center. In the inside of the larger section, place the bay leaf, thyme, and parsley sprigs. Place the round side of the other celery section on top and tie together firmly.

*Note:* If you grow your own herbs, you can dry them in branches. Tie the branches together, securely wrapping in the bay leaf, and omit the celery. If desired, these can be made in quantity and kept in an airtight container to be used as needed.

## CROUTONS AND CROÛTES

Many of the soups in this book call for croûtes or croutons, and so do several of the sandwiches. The common concept of a crouton is a small cube of toast, sometimes flavored with herbs, about 1/2-inch in size. For certain soups, these are suitable as long as they are unflavored. For others, the larger croûtes are more suitable.

## Small Croutons

3 slices firm white bread

Preheat oven to 350°F.

Cut the crusts from the bread and cut the slices into 1/2-inch cubes. Place on a baking sheet and bake, turning often, until golden brown on all sides. Cool.

Keeps several weeks in an airtight container.

*Yield: about 2 cups*

## Sautéed Croutons

Sautéing the croutons gives a different flavor that is often preferred to that of baked croutons.

3 slices firm white bread      3 tablespoons butter or olive oil

Remove the crusts from the bread and cut the slices into 1/2-inch cubes.

In a large skillet, heat the butter or oil and sauté the bread cubes until golden on all sides. Drain on paper toweling.

Can be kept 2 to 3 days at room temperature. Can be frozen.

*Yield: about 2 cups*

## Croûtes

For many sandwiches and soups, croûtes are used instead of croutons. Croûtes are larger slices of bread, between 1/4- and 1/2-inch-thick, cut from loaves of French bread, or cut from slices of white bread with a cutter.

Although they can be toasted in the oven, they are usually sautéed in butter or oil until golden on both sides.

1 loaf French bread, sliced      1/2 cup butter or olive oil

Sauté the slices in the butter or oil until golden brown on both sides. Add more oil as needed. The bread slices should just barely float in the butter or oil. Drain on paper towels.

Can be kept at room temperature about 3 days. Can be frozen. If frozen, reheat before using.

*Yield: about 36 slices*

## Garlic Croutons

The easiest way to impart a wonderful garlic flavor to croutons is to rub the crust of an unsliced loaf of French or Italian bread. Then slice the bread and sauté as for croûtes.

# MISCELLANEOUS PREPARATIONS

## Cracklings

Some of the soups, breads, and sandwiches call for cracklings. In some markets they are sold already prepared, but in most areas you must prepare them yourself.

2 to 3 pounds pork fat                  1/2 cup water

Cut the pork fat into 1/2- to 1/4-inch dice. Place the pork in a saucepan with the water and heat over low heat until the water has evaporated and the fat has become crisp and golden brown. Remove the cracklings and drain on paper towels. The rendered fat can be used as lard.

Keeps in the refrigerator 4 to 5 days. Can be frozen.

*Yield: about 1 cup*

*Note:* If fresh pork fat is not available, salt pork can be used. Blanch the diced salt pork in boiling water for 10 minutes, drain, and cook as for fresh pork fat.

## Chinese Mushrooms

Chinese mushrooms are available in many markets other than oriental markets. They are dried and quite stiff when purchased.

To use the mushrooms, place them in a bowl and pour on boiling water just to cover. Let stand at room temperature for 20 to 30 minutes, or until the caps are soft. The stems are always hard and should be cut out with a small knife and discarded. The mushroom caps can be used whole, sliced, or minced. The soaking liquid can be used for flavoring.

## Peeling Peppers

Fresh peppers often need to be peeled to get rid of the tough skin. There are several ways to peel them.

### Open Flame

Hold a pepper on the end of a kitchen fork over a gas flame and cook, turning, until the exterior is blackened. Place the pepper in a paper bag to steam for 5 minutes. Cut the pepper in half, remove and discard the seeds, and scrape away the charred skin with the back of a knife.

### Broiling

Broil the peppers on a baking sheet, turning often, until charred on all sides. Proceed with the previous instructions.

### Boiling

The peppers can be put into boiling water and simmered for about 30 minutes. Remove, let cool until you can handle, and peel.

## Chinese Steamer

Oriental food shops sell beautiful bamboo steamers for steaming foods. If they are not available, or you do not wish to spend the money on a bulky piece of equipment that is used on a limited basis, you can improvise a steamer that will be suitable for the recipes in this book.

Cut both ends from a tunafish can, or a can of similar size. Place the can in the bottom of a kettle and add enough water to come about halfway up the side of the can. On top of the can, place a plate about 1 inch smaller in diameter than the kettle. Place the food to be steamed on the plate and cover the pot securely.

# Index